DARK SALVATION

DARK SALVATION

The Story of Methodism as It Developed Among Blacks in America

HARRY V. RICHARDSON

C. Eric Lincoln Series on Black Religion
ANCHOR-PRESS / DOUBLEDAY
GARDEN CITY, NEW YORK 1976

Library of Congress Cataloging in Publication Data

Richardson, Harry Van Buren.
   Dark salvation.

   (C. Eric Lincoln series on Black religion)
   Includes bibliographical references and index.
   1. Afro-American Methodists.   2. Methodist Church
in the United States.   I. Title.   II. Series.
BX8435.R5   287'.8'09
ISBN: 0-385-00245-9
Library of Congress Catalog Card Number 76–3009

Grateful acknowledgment is made for permission to use excerpts from the following material:

The Abingdon Press: Excerpts from *The Life, Experience and Gospel Labors of the Rt. Rev. Richard Allen*, edited by George A. Singleton, 1960. Reprinted by permission.

A.M.E. Sunday School Union: Excerpts from *The Pilgrimage of Harriett Ransom's Son* by Reverdy C. Ransom. Published by A.M.E. Sunday School Union, 1950.

The Arno Press, Inc.: Excerpts from *Recollections of Seventy Years* by Daniel A. Payne. Reprinted by Arno Press, Inc., 1968.

The Associated Publishers, Inc.: Excerpts from *Richard Allen: An Apostle of Freedom*, by Charles H. Wesley, 1955. Reprinted by permission.

The Board of Higher Education and Ministry: Excerpts from *Two Centuries of Methodist Concern* by James P. Brawley. Published by Vantage Press, 1974.

David Henry Bradley: Excerpts from Volumes I and II of *The History of the A.M.E. Zion Church*. Published by Parthenon Press, 1956, 1970. Reprinted by permission of the author.

James P. Brawley: Excerpts from "Methodist Church from 1939," Octo-

ACKNOWLEDGMENTS

In the preparation of this volume many persons have assisted in many ways. I am especially indebted to Mr. Wilson Flemister, Librarian of the Interdenominational Theological Center, for his generous aid in locating documents and resources; and to the I.T.C. Library staff for constant help, particularly Mrs. Cassandra Norman, Miss Honor Jean Davenport, Mrs. Edith Jonathan, and Mr. Charles Freeney. Dr. Channing Jeschke of the Pitts Theology Library of Candler School of Theology, Emory University, and Dr. Kenneth Rowe of Rose Memorial Library, Drew University, helped greatly in making early documents and papers available.

I owe deep gratitude to Professors J. R. Coan, Thomas Hoyt, W. Thomas Smith and Henry J. Young of the I.T.C. faculty, and Vice-President Charles B. Copher for reading the manuscript and giving invaluable suggestions and corrections. Many church leaders provided information, some of which is not yet recorded. I am indebted to my brother, the Reverend Ben A. Richardson, for suggestions and documents on the early phases of the work, especially the slave era.

Lastly, but not least, I am indebted to my wife, Selma, for her enduring faith and encouragement through the years of this study.

The errors are mine.

HARRY V. RICHARDSON

CONTENTS

PART I
Background

   I   *The Beginnings of Methodism*   *3*

  II   *The Slave and His Religion: Faith in Chains*   *14*

PART II
Before the Civil War

  III   *Methodism Comes to America*   *35*

  IV   *Methodism and Slavery*   *50*

   V   *The Beginnings of Separation*   *62*

  VI   *The First Great Separate: The African Methodist Episcopal Church*   *76*

 VII   *The Second Great Separate: The African Methodist Episcopal Zion Church*   *117*

VIII   *Continuing Methodism*   *148*

  IX   *The Mission to the Slaves*   *157*

   X   *Early Black Methodist Preachers*   *167*

PART III
Reconstruction and Expansion

XI   *The A.M.E. Church*   *191*

XII   *The A.M.E. Zion Church*   *204*

XIII *The Christian Methodist Episcopal Church*   *224*

XIV   *Methodism in Mission*   *240*

PART IV
Today and Tomorrow

XV   *Current Developments*   *253*

XVI   *The Black Man in United Methodism*   *269*

XVII *Summary and Prospect*   *284*

NOTES   *292*

INDEX   *311*

FOREWORD

When all of the believers have said and sung their faith, and all of the nonbelievers have declared their doubts, religion will still stand as man's main effort to do something with the wicked side of himself. Man knows and has known that it is the goodness in his nature that helps him to survive, and it is the evil in his nature that wrecks him as a person, and, if not checked, will wipe him as a species from the face of the earth.

Religion, therefore, as man's conscious effort to make the goodness in himself dominant and the evil in himself recessive is the most essential enterprise to which the human mind can address itself.

Everything depends upon our understanding of religion and the faithfulness with which we apply it.

This book looks at one great religious movement as it touched the lives of a struggling people at a crucial time in their history. The movement was Wesleyan Methodism, and the people were the Negroes or blacks of America.

A WORD ON TERMINOLOGY

In this discussion the terms "Negro," "black," "colored," and "Afro-American" are used interchangeably without any imputation of difference in status being implied by any term. The vari-colored group of people of Afro-American heritage in America have been known by many names in their history. They doubtless will be known by more as each generation comes face to face with the fact of slavery in its ancestry, and tries to decide for itself whether this is a stigma from which to seek escape, or whether it was simply a painful burden, victoriously borne, in a marvelous march from slavery to freedom in this nation that the ancestors helped to build.

The battle of names is an old one. Perhaps we might do well in our day to heed the word of Henry Highland Garnett, a great militant, spoken over a century ago:

> Let there be no strife between us, for we are brethren, and we must rise or fall together. How unprofitable it is for us to spend our golden moments in long and solemn debate upon questions whether we shall be called "Africans," "Colored Americans," or "Blacks." The question should be, my friends, shall we arise and act like men, and cast off this terrible yoke?*

* Henry Highland Garnett, *The Past and Present Condition of the Colored Race,* Troy, N.Y., 1848, p. 19.

Also see Penelope L. Bullock, *The Negro Periodical Press in the United States, 1838–1909,* unpublished Ph.D. dissertation, University of Michigan, 1971, pp. 21–22.

PART I

Background

CHAPTER I

The Beginnings of Methodism

JOHN BENJAMIN WESLEY was the founder of the Methodist Church.[1] Closely associated with him was his younger brother, Charles.

John was born in 1703, Charles in 1708, in the little town of Epworth, England. Both were born into a large, devout family. Their father, the Reverend Samuel Wesley, was a priest in the Anglican Church. Being a man of strong convictions, he suffered a number of setbacks in his career because of his religious zeal and his uncompromising stands on social and political issues.

John and Charles, like all of the nineteen children, were reared according to strict religious precepts. Their mother, Susanna Wesley, was a wise and gifted woman who played the major role in the rearing of the family.

John entered Christ Church College in Oxford University in 1720. He was an excellent student. In 1726 he was elected a Fellow of Lincoln College in Oxford, and in 1727 he received his Master of Arts degree. In 1725 he took his Holy Orders and became, like his father, a priest in the Church of England. In 1725 he read also three books that greatly influenced the course of his life. One was Thomas à Kempis' *Imitation of Christ*. This book moved him toward strict, almost ascetic religious living. The other books were Jeremy Taylor's *Holy Living* and *Holy Dying*.

From these books "he adopted the plan of a detailed hour by hour schedule for every day in the week . . . which he slavishly followed to the year of his death. In 1725 he began to keep a *Diary* in which he recorded details of his daily program from four o'clock in the morning—his accustomed hour of rising—to retirement at eight, nine or ten at night. His custom was to spend some minutes of every waking hour, no matter where he might be or however occupied, in prayer, singing or other form of devotion. With the utmost energy of which he was capable he studied, worked and prayed."[2]

From 1727 to 1729 John served as curate of the church in the little town of Wroote. It was part of his father's parish. In 1729 he returned to Lincoln College to work as a Fellow. Meanwhile, in 1726, Charles Wesley, John's younger brother, had entered Christ Church College. Charles was much disturbed with the low moral level of life in the University as John before him had been. With fifteen other students they organized a "Holy Club," for mutual help and inspiration in their own personal living as well as for reforming the life of the University. When John returned in 1729 he was at once chosen leader of the group. They met three or four evenings a week for reading classics and books on divinity; but they also visited prisons, gathered children into classes for instruction in the Scriptures, carried food and medicine to the sick and needy, and secured clothing and funds for the poor. They gave heavily of their own possessions, often going without food. They also gave much time to communion and prayer. "They were called in derision the Sacramentarians, Bible-bigots, the Holy or the Godly Club. One person . . . observed, in reference to their methodical manner of life, that a new sect of Methodists was sprung up, alluding to the ancient school of physicians known by that name . . . [It] has become the appropriate designation of the sect of which Wesley is the founder."[3]

In 1732 the Wesleys were joined at Oxford by George Whitefield, the son of an innkeeper in Gloucester. He at once fell under the influence of the "Holy Club" and was deeply stirred religiously. At times "he spent whole days and weeks prostrate on the ground in prayer." He almost ruined his health in these "exercises." Eventually he came to feel that he was saved by "laying hold on the Cross by a living faith," thereby "receiving an abiding sense of the love of God, and a full assurance of faith."[4] In 1735, when John Wesley left for America, Whitefield became leader of the Club. He was ordained a priest in the Church of England in 1736. He had no idea at that time that he was destined to play an important part in the beginning of Methodism.

In 1735 both John and Charles Wesley came to the colony of Georgia in America, John to serve as missionary to the Indians and chaplain to the settlement at Savannah, and Charles to serve as secretary to General Oglethorpe and chaplain to the settlers at Frederica. However, for both of the Wesleys the trip to America was a failure. Charles soon became so deeply involved in personal conflicts with his parishioners that he was unacceptable as chaplain and in disfavor with Oglethorpe. He left America after only five months.

John's case was somewhat similar. As minister at Savannah at first he was successful and well liked. He of course worked tirelessly. He preached, taught school, and served as an interpreter for some of the European groups settled in and around Savannah. He wanted to work among the Indians, but at the time General Oglethorpe felt that this would be too dangerous.

After a few months, however, Wesley's austere, rigid pattern of living began to create problems. His requirements of his parishioners were so strict and burdensome, his interpretation of church rules and rites was so intolerant that the members came to resent his leadership. His sermons were regarded by many as caustic, personal attacks on members. Attendance at the services dwindled severely.[5]

In addition, his unfortunate love affair with Sophia Hopkey served to heighten his unpopularity. Miss Hopkey was the niece of the Chief Magistrate at Savannah. It was expected that they would marry, but Wesley, after being advised against it, ceased his attentions to her. When she saw that she was being jilted, she immediately married another man. The matter might have ended there, but Wesley's "austere notions led him wrong in every thing." Shortly after her marriage Wesley noticed some things in her conduct which he felt were objectionable. He spoke to her about them. She of course resented this. On the next Sunday Wesley refused to administer the Sacrament to her. Her husband regarded this as an effort to defame his wife in public. He had a warrant issued for Wesley, and he asked damages of £1,000. The case was a widespread scandal. Wesley lost many friends and most of his influence in the colony. The case dragged on for months. Wesley went to court several times but the case against him was weak, and some of the jurors protested that the case was largely an effort to blacken Mr. Wesley's character.

This series of troubles eventually convinced Wesley that he could no longer serve effectively, and that it was time for him to return to England: "I saw clearly the hour was come for leaving this place; and soon as evening prayers were over, about eight o'clock, the tide then serving, I shook off the dust of my feet, and left Georgia, after having preached the gospel there (not as I ought, but as I was able) one year and nearly nine months."[6]

Perhaps it should be said here that while John and Charles Wesley were in America they had very little contact with Negroes. The main reason is that Georgia, where they spent nearly all their time, was a free colony. In the founding of the colony slavery was forbidden. In Wesley's time the few Negroes who were in Georgia were mostly runaway slaves from other colonies.

John Wesley also had little direct contact with Indians. He was not able to work with them as a missionary as he had planned to do in coming to America. But such contacts as he did have completely reversed his opinion of them. Just before leaving England, in a letter dated October 10, 1735, he wrote: "I hope to learn the true sense of the gospel of Christ by preaching it to the heathen. They have no comments to construe away the text; no vain philosophy to corrupt it; no luxurious, sensual, covetous, ambitious expounders to soften its unpleasing truths. They have no party, no interest to serve, and are therefore fit to receive the gospel in its simplicity. They are as little children, humble, willing to learn, and eager to do the will of God.[7]

Before he left America two years later he wrote:

> Of the Georgian Indians in general it may be observed that they are not so properly nations as tribes or clans, who have wandered thither at different times—perhaps expelled their native countries by stronger tribes—but how or when they cannot tell, being none of them able to give any rational account of themselves. They are inured to hardships of all kinds, and surprisingly patient of pain. But as they have no letters, so they have no religion, no laws, no civil government. Nor have they any kings or princes, properly speaking; their meikos, or headmen, having no power either to command or punish, no man obeying them any further than he pleases. So that every one doeth what is right in his own eyes; and if it appears wrong to his neighbour, the person aggrieved usually steals on the other unawares, and shoots him, scalps him, or cuts off his ears, having only two short rules of proceeding—to do what he will, and what he can.
>
> They are likewise all, except perhaps the Choctaws, gluttons, drunkards, thieves, dissemblers, liars. They are implacable, unmerciful; murderers of fathers, murderers of mothers, murderers of their own children—it being a common thing for a son to shoot his father or mother because they are old and past labour, and for a woman either to procure abortion, or to throw her child into the next river, because she will go with her husband to the war. Indeed, husbands, strictly speaking, they have none; for any man leaves his wife (so called) at pleasure, who frequently, in return, cuts the throats of all the children she has had by him. Whoredom they account no crime, and few instances appear of a young Indian woman's refusing any one. Nor have they any fixed punishment for adultery; only, if the husband take his wife with another man, he will do what he can to both, unless speedily pacified by the present of a gun or a blanket.[8]

In sharp contrast, Wesley's opinion of Negroes was much higher. In his antislavery pamphlet, *Thoughts Upon Slavery*, he wrote:

> Upon the whole, therefore, the Negroes who inhabit the coast of Africa, from the river Senegal to the Southern bounds of Angola, are so far from being the stupid, senseless, brutish, lazy barbarians,

the fierce, cruel, perfidious savages they have been described, that, on the contrary, they are represented, by them who have no motive to flatter them, as remarkably sensible, considering the few advantages they have for improving their understanding; as industrious to the highest degree, perhaps more so than other natives of so warm a climate; as fair, just and honest in all their dealings, unless where white men have taught them to be otherwise; and as far more mild, friendly, and kind to strangers than any of our forefathers were. *Our forefathers!* Where shall we find at this day, among the fair-faced natives of Europe, a nation generally practicing the justice, mercy, and truth, which are found among these poor Africans? . . . We may [have to] leave England and France, to seek genuine honesty in Benin, Congo, or Angola.[9]

Two years after the Wesleys, Whitefield came to America. His experience was exactly the opposite of theirs. Whitefield at once became the most powerful and popular preacher in America. He was a highly gifted orator of marvelous persuasive power. He traveled up and down the colonies from Georgia to New England speaking to great masses which numbered at times, it is said, as many as sixty thousand. He is often held to be the most eloquent and attractive preacher in American history. Whitefield played a large part in starting the "Great Awakening" that flourished in the colonies in the early eighteenth century.[10]

Whitefield often preached to blacks. They would attend his larger meetings when permitted, and often he spoke to them in separate gatherings. Many were moved and converted under his preaching. He influenced Phillis Wheatley in her earlier poems and also Jupiter Hammond.[11]

On May 11, 1740, when he was about to leave Philadelphia, Whitefield wrote in his Journal:

> Many Negroes, near 50, came to say farewell, and to give me thanks for what God had done to their souls: How heartily did these poor creatures throw in their mites for my poor orphans. Some of them have been effectually wrought upon, and in an uncommon manner. Many of them have begun to learn to read. One, who was free, said she would give me her two children whenever I settle my school. I believe masters and mistresses will shortly see Christianity will not make their Negroes worse slaves.

I intended, had time permitted, to have settled a society for Negro men and women; but that must be deferred till it shall please God to bring me to Philadelphia again. I have been much drawn out in prayer for them, and have seen them exceedingly wrought upon under the preached word.[12]

Whitefield approved of Negro slavery and he kept slaves himself. He felt that slavery was good for the African. It gave the African, Whitefield believed, a chance for a much higher life than he could have had in his native, "savage," state. Some slaves were able to get educations. But above all, the African, though a slave, got the chance to hear the Gospel and to be saved, and thus to attain eternal life. This great good, eternal life and blessedness, transcended all earthly conditions and sufferings in Whitefield's view.

Whitefield in 1748 was one of the persons who urged the Trustees of Georgia to introduce slavery into that colony. He contended that the colony would never be prosperous until Negro slavery was permitted.[13] But while he approved slavery, he was deeply offended at the cruel manner in which masters treated their slaves. In 1740 he circulated a sharply critical open letter to slavemasters in which he charged that they drove their Negroes as hard as horses, and punished them like beasts. "Your dogs," he wrote, "are caressed and fondled at your tables, but your slaves . . . have not equal privilege." He also condemned masters who prevented their slaves from receiving religious instruction.[14]

In 1739 Whitefield and the Wesleys split over the issue of Calvinism, particularly the doctrine of predestination. Whitefield believed in the doctrine and preached it. Wesley abhorred the doctrine and preached against it. Wesley believed in the free and universal grace of God. He stated his belief in a sermon on "Free Grace" which he published and circulated in England and America. Whitefield replied in a sermon that he delivered and in which he attacked Wesley personally. The issue was much more than a theological disagreement. It was a personal, bitter feud. In 1741 Wesley called on Whitefield to see if agreement could not be reached. The effort was a failure. Wesley wrote in his Journal: "He told me he and I preached two different gospels, and therefore he not only would not join with, or give me the right hand of fellowship, but was resolved publicly to preach against me and my brother, wheresoever he preached at all."[15]

Despite Whitefield's personal popularity as a preacher, his theological views did not endure in Methodism. His separation from the Wesleys meant that he played little if any part in the subsequent development of Methodism, especially in America. It was the Wesleyan brand of Methodism that survived and played such a significant part in the life and development of American Negroes. Whitefield was a great preacher, but he left little or nothing in the way of an organized movement.

For John Wesley the failure of his American mission was deeply disillusioning. It caused him to doubt the genuineness of his religious experience and his nearness to God. He felt that he had not had the experience of personal fellowship with God or Christ as the Moravians had, and until one had this conscious personal experience he had no assurance that he was forgiven or saved or loved by God. On the voyage back to England, which lasted nine weeks, he underwent protracted periods of depression followed by earnest soul-searching. Upon arrival in London he sought the company of the Moravians or United Brethren, some of whom he had met on shipboard on the way to America and with whose spiritual life he was so deeply impressed. Indeed, it was the Moravians who on two occasions advised him not to marry Sophia Hopkey.

Wesley greatly admired the spiritual pattern of the Moravians. He felt that their living indicated that they had the true religion. In his quest for spiritual direction he regularly attended their meetings. In his Journal for May 24, 1738, he writes:

> In the evening I went very unwillingly to a society in Aldersgate Street, where one was reading Luther's preface to the *Epistle to the Romans*. About a quarter before nine, while he was describing the change which God works in the heart through faith in Christ, I felt my heart strangely warmed. I felt I did trust in Christ, Christ alone for salvation; and an assurance was given me that He had taken away my sins, even *mine*, and saved *me* from the law of sin and death.[16]

To Wesley, as the result of his long-continued, intensive seeking, [this personal experience of fellowship with God] not only became the center and soul of religion, but the rock on which his personal faith was founded. The dynamic of his religious life was his consciousness of intimate, personal union with God. In the climactic hour of his religious experience, God came alive in the totality of his being, and from that day the dynamic, wholly absorbing purpose of his life was to bring God into the consciousness, the conduct, and the character of individual men and women.[17]

Wesley's "conversion" or religious experience became the pattern, the archetype for the Methodist movement. It characterized Methodism not as a perfunctory, ritualistic faith, but rather as an experiential or "experimental" faith through which the member was brought into a redeeming conscious fellowship with God. To awaken this godly experience in others, and to proclaim the message of salvation to suffering and "dying" humanity caught in sin under the righteous wrath of God was the noblest and most urgent task for anyone, especially the preacher. It became the flaming impulse for Methodist preachers in succeeding generations, sending them out with unquenchable zeal to proclaim the word of salvation to every creature of whatever station, in spite of persecution, privation, and death. It was a clarion call to righteousness in this world in order to escape eternal damnation in the world to come.

Charles Wesley had had a conversion experience similar to John's three days earlier. Shortly after John's conversion, the Wesleys, for a while with the collaboration of Whitefield, began to preach the new pattern of faith and its message of salvation. They preached with such vigor, and aroused such "excessive" emotional response in the hearers, that they were soon excluded from the churches. Undaunted, they took to the open fields, and to the streets, anywhere a crowd could come together. Great numbers flocked to hear them, expressing their feelings with cries, tears, prostrations, and "fits." Many were converted.

To care for the converts Wesley organized them into "Societies," and these were divided into "classes" with a "leader" over each class. Eventually he appointed "lay preachers" to keep the members of the Societies instructed and inspired. As the Societies were organized in different towns, they needed "traveling preachers" to go from town to town. Here arose the itinerant ministry of Methodism. Wesley was committed to the itinerant preacher. In a letter to Francis Asbury of September 30, 1785, he said: "Were I to preach three years together in one place, both the people and myself would grow as dead as stones.[18]

It should be said that John Wesley had no desire to organize a new or separate church. Methodism under Wesley was a drive for holiness within the long-established Church of England. Wesley himself lived and died a priest in the Anglican Church.

The people to whom the Methodists preached were largely the poor and neglected masses in the declining rural districts, the new towns, and the mining areas of England, people who were suffering the adverse effects of the industrial revolution. Though they became members of the Methodist Societies, they still remained members of the Anglican Church. For the sacraments of the Church, Baptism and the Lord's Supper, they looked to the Anglican Church. This, however, soon became a problem. Through jealousy or honest disagreement, many Anglican priests refused to give Communion to Methodists. Since Wesley's lay preachers were unordained, they could not administer the sacraments. Wesley appealed repeatedly to Anglican bishops for the ordination of his preachers, but they steadfastly refused. Having no other recourse, and working out Biblical ground for his action, Wesley began to ordain his preachers, first for America, in 1784.

The Methodist movement grew rapidly in spite of opposition from the Church and from the public. Many people were not in sympathy with Methodist doctrines or patterns of life. Wesley himself and his preachers, too, faced persecution, violence, and even death in their evangelistic efforts.

> Wesley and his preachers [were able] to stand unperturbed and immovable against the onslaught of abuse, slander, and persecution endured year after year, and decade after decade. The bitterness of the vilification and the violence of the attacks of the mobs are today almost beyond belief. Wesley's *Journal* describes no less than sixty riots . . . Again and again Wesley was in danger of his life, but always he was calm, undaunted, patient. At Walsall in

Staffordshire, for example, he found the street full of "fierce Ephesian beasts," who "roared and shouted and threw stones incessantly," beating him down three times. Never for a moment did he consider ceasing to preach, even temporarily, or confining his efforts to the places of least danger.[19]

But the persecution only spurred them on to greater effort. Gradually "meeting houses" were built, the preachers became an established clergy with rules and regulations for its orders, and Methodism became an established organization in the land. Forms of worship were developed, with Charles Wesley providing much of the hymnody, becoming, as he has been called, "the sweet singer of Methodism."

On June 25, 1744, in London, Wesley held a Conference with some of his preachers. Ten persons were present: John and Charles Wesley, four ministers from the Anglican Church who had been friendly to the Methodists, and four of Wesley's lay preachers. The conference lasted six days. They discussed the Methodist form of faith and the General Rules for the Societies. This was the beginning of the Annual Conference which is generally regarded as Methodism's most unique contribution to ecclesiastical polity.[20]

Such in barest outline was the beginning of the Wesleyan brand of Methodism which developed in England, and which in 1760 was brought to America from Ireland by two Wesleyan converts.

Note: "The term 'annual conference' has three meanings as it is used within Methodism. In the first sense it refers to the administrative body which has jurisdiction over two or more district conferences. In the second sense it refers to the geographical territory administered by an annual conference. In the third sense, the term is used to refer to the meeting itself which is held once a year by this body for the purpose of regulating the affairs of all the churches located within its territory."

From an unplublished manuscript by Yorke S. Allen, Jr.

CHAPTER II

The Slave and His Religion: Faith in Chains

MOST OF THE NEGROES who were brought into the Western Hemisphere came from the west coastal regions of central or sub-Saharan Africa, roughly the section that extends from Senegal (Dakar) in the north to Angola in the south. The city of Accra in what is now the nation of Ghana was one of the focal points of the trade.

Some of the Africans who were sold into slavery were captives in intertribal wars. Others were the hapless victims of slave raiders. These raiders, both white and black, were utterly ruthless. Their typical method was to descend upon an unsuspecting village, kill off all who resisted the attack, and then march the remainder of the population, men, women, and children, in chains to the sea, where they were kept in pens or compounds in coastal ports until sold to slave traders with their waiting ships. In this, the first step of the slave trade, black Africans, Arabs, Europeans, and Americans all had an ignominious part.

The people of West Africa had well-developed religions. Religion played a large and fervent part in their lives. Unfortunately we do not know enough about African religion as it was in the days of the slave trade. There are several reasons. First, the serious and unbiased study of African culture is a recent, twentieth-century development. Prior to this the main reporters on things African were travelers, traders, soldiers, adventurers, slave traders, and highly biased missionaries, persons hardly capable of accurate religious observations. Also, since most African languages had not been reduced to writing, there were no written records. For much of our understanding we are forced to assume that African religion as we find it today is about the same as it was two or three centuries ago.

Yet our understanding of African culture and history is much more accurate now than it has ever been because of the work of competent scholars, such as Melville Herskovitz in America, Geoffrey Parrinder in England, and Roger Bastide in France. The most fortunate development to date, however, is the rise of indigenous black African scholars. These men, competently trained, with their better knowledge of native languages and their more intimate understanding of the meanings of words and practices, have given us a far better comprehension and appreciation of the nature and quality of the African's religion. They have clearly shown, as Professor Gayraud Wilmore says, "that the African religions are not mere crude and unenlightened superstitions," but they are mature, enlightened beliefs and practices common to many religions and similar in many ways to contemporary Christian faith.[1]

Two further cautions must be kept in mind in considering things African. First, Africa is not a single nation of homogeneous people. It is a continent comprising many nations and a multiplicity of tribes large and small, each with its own language or dialect, its own culture and its own history. This diversity of peoples, languages, and cultures has been black Africa's main handicap in intra- and inter-group communication and in organized resistance to exploitation from outside. Even today in the city of Accra, a five-minute radio news broadcast takes thirty minutes. It must be given in five tribal languages in addition to English. Only in the broadest sense can one speak of anything as commonly or uniformly "African."

Secondly, we have the warning of Professor Bastide that care must be taken not to write ideas and phenomena of our own time into the history of three centuries ago, and not to arrange such knowledge as we do have to suit contemporary interests and biases.[2] With these cautions in mind, a trustworthy understanding can be derived of the religion that obtained in many tribes at the time of the slave trade.

First, the Africans believed in spirits, good spirits and evil spirits, and among them were the spirits of their ancestors. These spirits were associated with or controlled natural forces that affected human life, such as light, heat, air, water, fertility, and health. Thus the spirits had much to do with the daily lives and destinies of men. They could help or hurt as they were appeased or angered. The spirits dwelt in or were associated with certain locations such as mountains, lakes, and rivers. Communing with the spirits was formerly regarded as "animism," and when the spirits of ancestors were involved, as "ancestor worship." But we know now that the African practice was much like that of the ancient Hebrews, who believed that Jehovah dwelt in Mt. Sinai; or like the modern Catholic belief in saints whose spirits may be met at certain shrines for healing and other blessings.[3]

Over all of the lesser spirits was one Supreme Spirit who was Creator and Father of all. In many ways this Supreme Spirit corresponded to the Christian concept of God. He was known by different names in different tribes; the very name often indicated eternal or metaphysical attributes of God. Some examples are: among the Akamba of Kenya God is called Mulunga or Mumbi, meaning "Creator, Maker, Fashioner"; among the Amkore of Uganda, God is named Mukameiguru, "He who rules or reigns in the sky"; among the Ashanti of the Ivory Coast, God's name is Nyame, which means "Alone, the Great One"; among the Duala, Cameroon, His name is Loba or Ehasi, "Omnipotent Father"; among the Suknma-Nyamwesi of Tanzania God is called Mulungu or Kube, "the One Who embraces all."[4]

The tribes also had many beliefs about God's dealings with men, some of which are surprisingly like beliefs in the Judaeo-Christian tradition.

> The Bambuti tell in another myth, that after creating the first man (Baatsi), God gave him and his children one rule. He said to them, "From all the trees of the forest you may eat, except the tahu tree."

The man had many children, he taught them God's command, and eventually he "returned to God in the heavens." One day a pregnant woman developed an irresistible desire to eat the fruit of the tahu tree, and she asked her husband to fetch it for her. At first he refused, but she persisted until "her husband crept into the forest secretly, plucked the fruit of the tahu, peeled it quickly, and hid the peel carefully in the foliage, so that his act should not be discovered. But all the precaution was in vain. The Moon had already seen him and had told what she had seen to God: 'The people which thou hast created have disobeyed thy command, and have eaten of the fruit of the tahu tree!' God was so angry at the disobedience of his people, that he sent death among them as punishment."[5]

Secondly, in African religion there is not the sharp distinction between sacred and secular such as we profess in Western culture. The Africans saw life as a whole; it was a unity. Thus for the African the priest could also be the medicine man. There was no conflict. His medicinal function did not imply the unwholesome practice of magic as was previously supposed.[6] Indeed, the priest-healer duality is much like that which obtains in the Christian faith. Jesus proclaimed the "good news" of the Gospel, but He also healed. In St. Luke's Gospel His healing is both the sign and the vindication of His Messiahship.[7] John Wesley published a book on *Primitive Physick*, or medical treatment.[8] Contemporary examples of priestly or ministerial healers are Leslie Weatherhead in England, and Oral Roberts of current television popularity in America.[9] There is evidence that the compartmentalization of life into mutually exclusive sectors such as "sacred" and "secular" is being recognized as unnatural and abortive. There is now a definite tendency to recapture the working union between science and religion or between belief and life such as the Africans and other peoples have known. An example of this tendency is the employment of religion in psychosomatic therapy.

It was formerly thought that Africans practiced nature worship, worshiping, for example, the sun. But here again, thanks to African scholarship, we know that it was not so much nature worship as nature appreciation, looking upon the sun as an evidence of the power, majesty, and omnipresence of the Supreme Creator Spirit. To quote M'biti:

> Among many societies, the sun is considered to be a manifestation of God himself . . . There is no concrete indication that the sun is considered to be God, or God considered to be the sun, however closely these may be associated. At best, the sun symbolizes aspects of God, such as His omniscience, His power, His everlasting endurance, and even His nature.[10]

Christian parallels for this kind of thinking may be seen in Joseph Addison's majestic hymn of cosmic praise, "The Spacious Firmament on High"; or in the currently popular Swedish hymn, "How Great Thou Art."

The African religions had elaborate moral and ethical systems. As M'biti points out:

> There exist, therefore, many laws, customs, set forms of behaviour, regulations, rules, observances and taboos, constituting the moral code and ethics of a given community or society. Some of these are held sacred, and are believed to have been instituted by God or national leaders. They originate in the Zamani where the forefathers are. This gives sanctity to the customs and regulations of the community. Any breach of this code of behaviour is considered evil, wrong or bad, for it is an injury or destruction to the accepted social order and peace. It must be punished by the corporate community of both the living and the departed, and God may also inflict punishment and bring about justice.[11]

But the Africans knew as we know that religious beliefs are one thing and human behavior is another. In their religions they had their full share of sinners. They saw at firsthand the impotence of religion as an effective social corrective. To quote M'biti again:

> Within this intensely corporate type of society, there are endless manifestations of evil. These include murders, robberies, rape, adultery, lies, stealing, cruelty especially towards women, quarrels, bad words, disrespect to persons of a higher status, accusations of sorcery, magic and witchcraft, disobedience of children and the like. In this atmosphere, all is neither grim nor bright. It is hard to describe these things: one needs to participate or grow up in village

life, to get an idea of the depth of evil and its consequences upon individuals and society. A visitor to the village will immediately be struck by African readiness to externalize the spontaneous feelings of joy, love, friendship and generosity. But this must be balanced by the fact that Africans are men, and there are many occasions when their feelings of hatred, strain, fear, jealousy and suspicion also become readily externalized. This makes them just as brutal, cruel, destructive and unkind as any other human beings in the world. By nature, Africans are neither angels nor demons; they possess and exercise the potentialities of both angels and demons. They can be as kind as the Germans, but they can be as murderous as the Germans; Africans can be as generous as the Americans, but they can be as greedy as the Americans; they can be as friendly as the Russians, but they can be as cruel as the Russians; They can be as honest as the English, but they can also be as equally hypocritical. In their human nature Africans are Germans, Swiss, Chinese, Indians or English—they are men.[12]

In addition to their purely religious beliefs, Africans, like the ancient Greeks and Romans, also had their folk myths and legends, some of which were vivid and beautiful, symbolizing the ways of nature and of men. J. G. Frazier in *The Golden Bough* relates this one:

A West African story from southern Nigeria relates how a king kept his soul in a little brown bird which perched on a tall tree beside the gate of the palace. The King's life was so bound up with the life of the bird that whoever should kill the bird would simultaneously kill the King and succeed to the throne. The secret was betrayed by the Queen to her lover, who shot the bird with an arrow and thereby slew the King and succeeded to the throne.[13]

Such in outline are some of the salient features of the religion of the people who came to America as slaves. It was an enlightened, sophisticated body of belief and practices based in part on theistic speculation, but also based on the accumulated experiential wisdom of centuries of observant living.

It was this African native with his well-developed religion and cultural pattern who was caught and bound and sold into chattel slavery under foreign masters in a foreign world. It was a traumatic experience of the severest kind, both psychologically and physically. To be taken from his native soil, his family, friends, possessions, and his gods was bad enough. But worst of all was the trip across the Atlantic, the indescribably horrible "Middle Passage." Packed almost on top of each other and forced to lie in such position for weeks on end in the stinking holds of filthy, tossing slave ships, it is no wonder that many died from disease, from heartbreak and from the brutality of captors. Some when brought up on deck for a few moments of exercise would break away and leap overboard, thus ending forever their unbearable plight. It is said that schools of sharks would follow slave ships for days for the bodies that would be constantly coming over. It has been conservatively estimated that for every thousand natives taken from African villages, three hundred or more would die en route. U. B. Phillips estimates that in the years of the slave trade more than five million natives were transported to America from Africa.[14] A more likely figure is ten million. This heartless, systematic brutality, almost without parallel in human history, led John Wesley to write that slave traders, some of whom were wealthy, powerful, and respected people, were lower than brutes. He said:

> It is impossible that it should ever be necessary for any reasonable creature to violate all the laws of justice, mercy and truth. No circumstances can make it necessary for a man to burst in sunder all the ties of humanity. It can never be necessary for a rational being to sink himself below a brute . . .[15]

In his Journal entry for February 12, 1772, Wesley describes slavery and the slave trade as "the execrable sum of all villainies"; and later in a letter to Wilberforce, probably the last he ever wrote, February 24, 1791, he refers to American slavery as "the vilest that ever saw the sun."[16]

It was in this state of frustration, subjection, and unimaginable pain that the Africans, now slaves, arrived in the Western world. They arrived devoid of everything but life, and even life would hardly seem worth holding. For people caught in such hopeless misery there is always the open option to curse the gods who had failed them and die, either in futile rebellion or in suicidal despair. The fact that most did not die, but were able to live on and even to hope for a better day is silent witness to their spiritual strength as well as to their physical hardihood.

The first slaves brought into the Western Hemisphere were sold to planters in the West Indies islands for work on the sugar and other plantations. Here in the islands the pattern of slavery under the Spanish, French, and British was based on the ancient Roman model, with the master having absolute dominion over the slave.

Negro slavery was not introduced into the continental colonies until 1619, when the first Negroes were landed at Jamestown, Virginia. These first importees were more like indentured servants. They were not good workers, however. They were intractable, and they were unaccustomed to Western ways. As a result, slave labor was not popular at first with colonial farmers. Neither was it popular or profitable with the farmers in the colonies north of Delaware. Slave labor was best suited to the tobacco farms of Maryland and Virginia, and it was best of all suited to the rice plantations of South Carolina. Thus in 1760 slavery existed in all the colonies, but slaves constituted only 10 per cent of the colonial population north of Maryland, while they were 41 per cent of the other colonies. In Virginia they were 47 per cent, and in South Carolina, 70 per cent.[17]

The American system of slavery was one of gradual development. In early colonial times it was "a kind of continuous indentured service with the master being required to provide proper food and care for his slaves. From this the system developed or descended until, in the nineteenth century, the owner was complete master and the slave was bound for life with few legal rights or protections.[18]

In the colonial period in the North, and in the cities both North and South, the slaves worked as household servants, farm hands, and as laborers in commerce and industry. Some became skilled craftsmen even in the South. Their work may still be seen in elegant homes, public buildings, and other structures still standing. To the south of Maryland, the slaves were plantation hands. They also did much of the work in clearing forests and building roads as the nation spread steadily south and westward.

In the colonial period, except for the plantation areas, slavery, as far as restrictions and punishments of slaves were concerned, was milder than it became in the nineteenth century, particularly after 1830. Under the equalitarian feelings of the Revolutionary period, there was strong opposition to slavery of any kind, even in the South. Both Thomas Jefferson and George Washington owned slaves, but they disliked slavery and wanted it abolished. They were at a loss, however, as to what to do with the freed Negroes. By 1790 all states north of Delaware either prohibited slavery or provided for its gradual eradication.[19] Many slaves during this period were able to attain "free" status, some by manumission, some by self-purchase through heroic labor and sacrifice, and some by dangerous escape. There were, for example, 59,557 free Negroes in the United States in 1790. The number had grown to 108,435 by 1800.

It was the coming of cotton, however, around the beginning of the nineteenth century that sealed the Negro's fate as a slave. A series of remarkable inventions, starting with the application of steam power to the spinning and weaving machines in England and culminating with the invention of Whitney's cotton gin in America, greatly increased the production of cotton goods for which there was a rapidly rising world demand. The soil of the Southern states was admirably suited to grow the necessary cotton if an adequate supply of labor could be obtained. That labor was found in African slaves who first were legally imported, then later illegally smuggled, and all the while bred to meet the great demand. In 1790 there were about seven hundred thousand slaves in the United States. In 1860 there were four million. Over three million were in twelve Southern states, engaged for the most part in producing the cotton, sugar cane, rice, tobacco, and other crops that were rapidly building up the fortunes of the wealthier group among Southern planters.[20]

Cotton and sugar cane required the plantation type of agriculture, and the plantations developed a pattern of slavery that was severest and worst of all. With hundreds and sometimes a thousand or more slaves kept on a single plantation, these large numbers required the severest restrictions and suppressions on the life and movements of the slaves if they were to be held in subjection. They were kept almost like cattle in slave quarters, given minimum requirements for life and health such as food and clothing, and deliberately deprived of all opportunities for cultural development such as education or the arts. Learning to read and write was punishable by whipping, fine, and imprisonment. Admission to skilled crafts or trades was permitted only when and as far as was necessary for the masters' purpose. On many plantations slaves seldom saw their masters. They worked at forced labor under "overseers," who often were brutal taskmasters. Below the overseer was the Negro "driver," who also could be a brutal boss.[21]

To enforce these repressions and to keep this pattern of life intact, a rigid system of police controls was maintained. Passes were required for leaving the plantation or for travel of any kind. "Patrols" or special officers policed the movements and activities of the slaves. Marriages could be made only with the consent of masters, and families could be broken up at any time for the sale of parents or children. A slave had few if any legal rights or protections. No matter what the offense, a slave could not testify in court against a master.

Such in outline was the slave system which developed in the South with the coming of cotton and which also prevailed in the rice fields and sugar cane lands. The system spread in many of its aspects into other states of the nation.

It was into this system that the captive Africans were brought and others later were born. It was within this system that they fashioned a life for themselves, a life hard and restricted, but not wholly without sunshine or success. Some few, about 13.5 per cent according to the U.S. Census of 1810, often with the aid of kindly whites, attained freedom, that is, the limited freedom possible for a black person at the time. The great majority, however, began and ended their lives in the toil and tribulation of the slave system. It was in this system that black people, some originally from Africa, but many more born in America, tried to find meaning and purpose in existence. It was in this system that some slaves tried to find God.

Upon arrival on the American continent the slaves became widely scattered. This dispersal made it difficult for African culture to survive. Cut off from his fellow Africans who spoke his tribal language and shared his culture, the slave was forced as quickly as possible to acquire the language and culture of his new environment. The language, of course, was English, and the culture was that of his white masters. This was one of the reasons for the rapidity with which the African mastered American culture. This rapid cultural assimilation evinced the Negro's natural social adaptability, a quality highly valuable in minority adjustment to a dominant majority situation, and consequently, in the human world, to minority survival. The decline of African elements, more and more with each succeeding generation, meant that the Negro culture in America was a new culture, with some residual African features, to be sure, but a culture growing out of and suited to the African's American situation.[22]

SLAVE RELIGION

It is the opinion of scholars that prior to the American Revolution, comparatively few Negroes were converted to Christianity. The reasons are:

1. Interest in religion was low in colonial times. Masters were not concerned for the spiritual welfare of their slaves.

2. The sparsely settled country and the difficulties of travel made it hard for the few ministers to serve their own members, to say nothing of evangelizing the unchurched.

3. Many slaves, especially new importees, could not understand the religious teachings.

4. The churches were few, mostly of the Church of England. The ministers were not evangelistic-minded and were not much concerned for the spiritual welfare of Negroes and Indians.[23]

The Society for the Propagation of the Gospel had been set up in England in 1701 for the purpose of "the conversion of the Indian savages, and the conversion of the Negroes," but its actual results were meager. Quakers, Presbyterians, and Moravian Brethren were opposed to slavery and interested in Negro conversion, but the number of Negroes actually touched again was small.

In the colonial period, therefore, lacking widespread evangelization, and with few Negroes converted, it is likely that cults tinged with African as well as Christian elements existed where there were slaves in sufficient numbers to constitute such groups. On the other hand, where the slaves had intimate contact with whites, such as the household servants, they learned of the Christian faith, joined churches where permitted, and were good Christians. They doubtless held, where they could, meetings among themselves for prayer and for expressing their sorrows and their hopes.[24]

The picture changed, however, with the coming of the Methodists, Baptists, and Presbyterians. These groups, aspiring to preach the Gospel to every creature, actively sought the slave's soul, but they were concerned for his body as well. They openly condemned slavery and called for its immediate eradication from American life. Most active among the evangelical bodies that began around the time of the Revolution were the Methodists. Their work among the slaves is told in a later chapter.

The vigorous evangelistic drives conducted by the Methodists, Baptists, and others following the Revolution converted thousands of Negroes. Among Methodists, for instance, there were 42,304 black members in 1816; in 1844 there were 145,409.

The religious response of the black converts was typical. They expressed the excessive emotionalism that was characteristic of the evangelistic meetings. To quote just one instance, during the revival that swept over parts of eastern Virginia in 1776, Thomas Rankin, the Methodist preacher, "had to pause in the midst of his sermon on the prophetic vision of the valley of dry bones, to beg his hearers to compose themselves. 'But they could not,' he says; 'some on their knees, some on their faces crying mightily to God all the time I was preaching. Hundreds of Negroes were among them with tears streaming down their faces.' "[25]

Upon conversion the blacks were taken into the white churches. Segregation soon developed in the churches, however, with the Negroes seated in balconies or in the back, and having to commune after the whites. This led some Negroes, especially in the North, to withdraw and form their own congregations, and later their own denominations.[26] But for the blacks who remained in the white churches and for those who formed churches of their own, there seem to have been no unique or distinctive features about their religion, certainly in theology and church polity. There were, of course, limitations of understanding and interpretations due to the fact that most Negroes could not read. But the resultant differences were minor. Also, any distinctive African elements in the religion of the converts are hard to find.

It was on the plantations of the Southern states where the concentrations of slaves were greatest and where the slaves were most sharply cut off from contacts with whites that African culture could best have survived and that a distinctive type of religion could have developed. Yet here again, the finding of African elements is not to the degree one would expect.

In 1860 there were three million slaves in the twelve Southern states. At no time was even a fifth of this number effectively touched by Christian evangelists or teachers. The Reverend J. O. Andrew, later Bishop, delivered a great address before the anniversary meeting of the Methodist Missionary Society in 1832. He called attention to the lack of religion among the slaves and the lack of concern by both masters and churchmen. To be sure, Methodists, Baptists, and Presbyterians all conducted missions to the slaves, but the numbers actually reached were small in proportion to the total population. The Methodist mission, which was largest of all, had 21,063 members and as many catechumens (children) in 1844. This is a small proportion of three million.[27]

Besides, the instruction in the missions was inadequate and ineffective.[28] Since the slaves were not permitted to read even the Bible, the instruction was entirely oral. The missionaries had to use "catechisms," which taught some elements of Christian doctrine, but the teaching was definitely slanted toward submission on the slave's part and toward making the slave satisfied with his earthly servile status. This some slaves resented.

While the missions were aimed at the great masses on the sugar, rice, and cotton plantations, the churches in Southern cities were steadily taking in black members who sat in separated sections or met in separate services. In 1860 there were 207,000 Negro members in the Methodist Episcopal Church, South. This is an impressive number in itself, but very small in proportion to the total slave population.

Since the great mass of slaves were not directly touched with Christian teaching, what kind of religion, if any, did they have? It is certain that most slaves had a "smattering" of Christianity. They got this in several ways. First, if they were members of the liturgical churches, such as the Lutheran or Episcopalian, they doubtless received systematic instruction. If they were members of the evangelical churches or missions, such as the Methodist, Baptist, or Presbyterian, their instruction was less systematic, but it did give fairly well-organized knowledge of the basic elements of Christian faith. But the number of such slaves was small. By far the great majority of slaves got their knowledge of the Christian faith from fellow slaves, including volunteer or self-appointed religious leaders.

Quite naturally this knowledge was imprecise and filled with their own imaginings; and, since the slaves could not read, it became distorted in transmission. This was especially true of the detailed theological, moral, and ethical elements of Christianity. This conclusion is derived from statements of missionaries and others who for various reasons commented on the spiritual life of the slave. For instance, Charles Colcock Jones, the most outstanding Presbyterian missionary, wrote:

> Their notions of the Supreme Being; of the character and offices of Christ and the Holy Ghost; of a future state; and of what constitutes holiness of life, are indefinite and confused. Some brought up in a Christian land, and in the vicinity of the house of God, have heard of Jesus Christ; but who he is, and what he has done for a ruined world, they cannot tell. The Mohammedan Africans remaining of the old stock of importations, although accustomed to hear the Gospel preached, have been known to accommodate Christianity to Mohammedanism. God," they say "is *Allah*, and Jesus Christ is *Mohammed*—the religion is the same, but different countries have different *names*."
>
> They believe in second sight, in apparitions, charms, witchcraft, and in a kind of irresistible Satanic influence. The superstitions brought from Africa have not been wholly laid aside.[29]

In addition to statements of missionaries and other observers, much can be learned about what the slaves believed from their songs and other forms of expression. They believed in God, a

god of love, who cared for each one of His children, even the
suffering slave. But this God was also a god of justice and venge-
ance who hated evil and oppression, and who in time would destroy oppression, slavery, and evildoers. It was this faith in the ultimate righteousness of God that enabled the slave to bridge the
contradiction between the good god as taught by the missionaries
and the god who would let His black children suffer.

They believed in heaven and hell. Heaven let them look to a
good end to this painful life, if not here, then at least hereafter.
Hell let them believe in the ultimate righting of wrong.

The slaves loved the Bible. They especially treasured the stories of the creation, of the Egyptian bondage with the miraculous
deliverance at the Red Sea. They loved the New Testament
teachings on the power, death, and resurrection of Jesus. They
were especially fond of the apocalyptic stories in the New Testament on the end of the world and the coming of a new heaven
and a new earth. They could not read the Bible, but they heard
these stories from missionaries, preachers, and fellow slaves, and
they remembered them.

But the main features were clear. They believed in a God who
was both good and just, who would reward righteousness and
punish evil, and who, in his own good time, would destroy
slavery and elevate the slaves. Here was the religious expression
of the unquenchable passion of these bound, black people to be
free.

This faith not only served to give the slaves hope in the midst
of their burdened lives, but it also served to meet their psychological and spiritual needs for daily living. It is not to be forgotten that all of the sins common to human beings were to be
found in the slave communities too, such as robberies, adultery,
lies, stealing, domination by stronger persons, and treacherous
talebearing to masters. All of this, in addition to the crushing
effect of slave cruelties, made life far heavier than for ordinary
men. The slave needed forgiveness if he were the sinner, and he
needed strength if he were sinned against. To maintain personal
dignity, moral integrity, and self-respect in such a morally tan-
gled environment required a sustaining faith. The slave found

this sustaining power in his own adaptation of the Christian Gospel.

There were many slaves, however, who did not have this faith. Many could not accept the white man's God as taught by the missionaries and converted blacks. Charles Colcock Jones mentions a graphic example:

> I was preaching [he writes] to a large congregation on the Epistle to Philemon; and when I insisted on fidelity and obedience as Christian virtues in servants, and, upon the authority of Paul, condemned the practice of running away, one-half of my audience deliberately rose up and walked off with themselves; and those who remained looked anything but satisfied with the preacher or his doctrine. After dismission, there was no small stir among them; some solemnly declared that there was no such Epistle in the Bible; others, that it was not the Gospel; others that I preached to please the masters; others, that they did not care if they never heard me preach again.[30]

These resistant slaves, if they had a religion, must have belonged to the secret cults that practiced Voodoo and Obeah worship, and which were led by African priests or medicine men, especially among the recent importees from Africa and the West Indies. In the Caribbean Islands these cults are a mixture of African beliefs and Christianity, especially Catholicism. The Catholic belief in saints is an easy substitution for the African belief in spirits. Little is known about these cults since they represented resistance to white religion, white culture, and white domination. Membership was highly dangerous and severely punishable. Very likely their membership was small.[31]

From the figures before us the conclusion is inevitable that many slaves, maybe most, had little if any formal religion. Comparatively few were touched by the churches and the missions. We do not know how many were touched by volunteer slave religious teachers and leaders. Fewer still were members of the clandestine African-oriented cults. Also, African elements in slave culture tended to be more and more recessive with each succeeding American-born generation. They looked upon African practices as superstition and magic. The great mass of slaves, therefore, were religiously untouched, and like most Americans of their time were religiously indifferent. In 1860 only 12 per cent of Americans were church members. The rest lived without a formal faith.

This explodes the stereotype of "the slave in religion." Every slave was not a suffering, sorrowing, helpless person patiently awaiting the "sweet chariot" of death to swing low and bear him away to home in heaven. Neither was every slave a deeply religious seeker anxiously awaiting the chance to be converted. The slaves were human. Some were religiously inclined; some were not. Those who were religious joined a church and sought to fashion a faith that could sustain them in their painful, burdened lives. Those who were not religious found their life satisfactions in nonreligious ways. As early as 1749 a Reverend Thomas Bacon in Maryland, at the request of masters, preached a widely circulated sermon to slaves in which he commented on slave behavior. He urged the slaves to be patient with their lot. To be sure, they had it hard here, but after this life, if they were good and faithful, they would find happiness in heaven. But, he said, he was afraid that many would not get to heaven because of their sinful behavior here. For instance, on Sundays instead of resting and worshiping as they should, they spend the day drinking, fighting, rambling, whoring, using the best of days to the worst of purposes. Moreover, at nights, when they should be resting in preparation for the next day's work, they take their master's horse or anyone else's and ride the poor beast nearly to death, so that the next day neither they nor the horse are ready for labor.[32]

With many masters reluctantly permitting religion on their plantations; with religious meetings rigidly restricted and scrupulously watched; and with any expression, even a prayer, for freedom being regarded as resistance or rebellion, subjecting both preacher and members to severe punishment, the wonder is that there was any religion on the plantations at all.

Yet many slaves were religious, hundreds of thousands, and to them religion was the power that enabled them to retain their dignity, their moral integrity, their sense of personal worth, their faith in the goodness of life, and their indomitable conviction that someday they would be free. These ones were able to come out of the degradation of human slavery with their spirits radiant, their sense of human decency intact, and their passion for progress burning like a flame in their hearts. They formed the vanguard in the black man's march toward self-fulfillment and freedom.

EXTRACTS FROM THE SERMON OF THE
REVEREND THOMAS BACON
(*It is typical of the preaching to slaves
prior to the early Methodist preachers.*)

A second reason why you ought to serve God, is—*Because you have souls to be saved.* If you have nothing in this world but hard labor, with your coarse food and clothing, you have a place provided for you in Heaven, when you die and go into the next world, if you will but be at the pains of seeking it while you stay here.

It gives me great satisfaction, and I bless God for it, that I see so many of you come here on Sunday . . . But I cannot help saying, that many more might come if they would, who spend their Sundays in idling and visiting, drinking, hunting, and fishing, and spending the best of days to the worst of purposes.

When you were last here, I endeavored to show you,—that God made you and all the world, and that he made you and all mankind to serve him;—That it is he who places every man in the station or rank which he holds in this world, making some kings, some masters and mistresses, some tradesmen and working people, and others servants and slaves. That every one of us is obliged to do the business he hath set us about, in that station in life to which he hath been pleased to call us.

Do not think that I am against your meeting together at proper times and seasons, or that I would find fault with any of your innocent diversions—But, from what I have seen myself, and what I have been told by others,—you meet and make merry together, much oftener than most white people do; that many idle, scandalous, and wicked things are done among you at such times, without any shame or concern; and that your Saturday nights are very often spent in rioting and drunkenness.

You well know, that there are many among you so fond of rambling, that unless there be some revelling at home, they are seldom or never to be found at nights in their own masters' houses or quarters; but as soon as it is dark, take the first horse they can get, either their master's or a neighbor's, and after spending the whole night in revelling and drunkenness, and riding the poor creatures almost to death, come home by day-dawn, heavy and drowsy, unfit to do any business as it ought to be done, and often bringing upon themselves dangerous disorders, to the great hazard of their own souls, and the great expense and damage of their owners.

Chastity and modesty are things which some of you know little of as yet, though well enough acquainted with the opposite vices of whoring, and filthy discourse and behaviour. These two great sins of drinking and whoring bring many of you into the most wretched circumstances.[33]

PART II

Before
the Civil War

CHAPTER III

Methodism Comes to America

IN 1760 A GROUP of persons from Ireland arrived in New York City. They were of German descent, their ancestors having fled Germany a century before to escape religious persecution. John Wesley had preached in their German-Irish settlements and had won many converts. In the group that arrived in New York in 1760 were two persons who were to play a large part in planting Methodism in America. One was Philip Embury, who had been a Methodist class leader and local preacher in Ireland, and the other was Barbara Heck, Embury's cousin.

In 1766 Barbara Heck visited a home of the Irish emigrants. She found a card game in progress. Angered at the sight, she threw the cards into the fire, and went to Embury's house to urge him to start preaching and to hold Methodist services. Embury finally agreed, and Mrs. Heck rounded up five persons for the first service.

Among those present for the service was a Negro servant woman named "Betty," who worked in a nearby home. This is the first recorded instance of black participation in Methodism in America.

Nothing except her name is known about "Betty." She must have been a person of good character with a genuine interest in religion and its promotion.

Embury's home soon became too small for the numbers that

attended. A room was rented, but after a year they undertook to build a "meeting house." Contributions were solicited. In the list of contributors there are the names of several Negro slaves. Here again is further indication of the interest of blacks in religion and in Methodism. They were converts to the new faith and they were taken into membership in the Society.[1]

The Society started in Embury's house eventually became the John Street Church in New York City, known as the mother church of Methodism.

The membership of blacks in the Society grew rapidly. By 1795 there were 155 black members. Interestingly enough, it was from this group of blacks that some members withdrew in 1801 to organize the African Chapel which eventually became the African Methodist Episcopal Zion denomination.

Philip Embury began preaching to the little Society in New York City in 1766. He was soon joined by Captain Thomas Webb, a retired British army officer who was an attractive, powerful preacher. He insisted on preaching in his army uniform with his sword by his side or on the pulpit. He preached not only in the city, but also in the surrounding regions, such as Long Island, New Jersey, and even as far south as Philadelphia. In that city he founded the Society that eventually became the historic St. George's Church.

The field was ripe for harvest. The potential for great growth was seen. Appeal was made to John Wesley in England for additional preachers. In 1769 at the Conference in Leeds, two preachers were sent as missionaries to America. They were Richard Boardman and Joseph Pilmoor. In true Methodist fashion a collection was raised for sending them, out of which " £50 were allotted toward the payment of their debt, and about £20 given to our brethren for their passage."[2]

Meanwhile other preachers were active on the American scene. Robert Strawbridge, an Irish Methodist preacher, had come to America on his own in the mid-sixties of the eighteenth century. He settled in the back country of Maryland on Sam's Creek, and used his home as a center for Methodist services. He traveled into Pennsylvania, Delaware, and Virginia, preaching, founding

Societies, and raising up Methodist preachers. Richard Owen, the first native American preacher, was a convert of Strawbridge.[3]

Robert Williams and John King were two other Englishmen who came to America on their own to join the Methodist cause. Both became highly effective preachers. Of John King it was said that when he preached in St. Paul's Church in Baltimore he preached so loudly that "he made the dust fly from the old velvet cushion." It was he to whom Wesley wrote:

> My dear brother, always take advice or reproof as a favor . . . Scream no more at the peril of your soul . . . Speak as earnestly as you can, but do not scream . . . Herein be a follower of me as I am of Christ, I often speak loud, often vehemently, but I never scream . . .[4]

The work in America continued to grow so rapidly that appeals for still more preachers were made to Wesley. In 1771 he sent five additional preachers, among them a young man who was destined to play the leading part in founding and establishing the Methodist Episcopal Church in America. That young man was Francis Asbury, just twenty-six years old when he arrived at Philadelphia in 1771.

At the time Asbury arrived there were about 600 Methodists in the Colonies. Two years later there were 1,160. Three years after this in 1776, at the outbreak of the American Revolution, there were 4,921; in 1786, 20,689; and in 1800 there were 63,958. In 1771 there were ten traveling preachers; in 1800 there were nearly two hundred.[5] The growth was neither automatic nor easy. It was due to tireless, sacrificial labors of the preachers. The list of them includes Embury, Webb, Williams, King, Strawbridge, Owen, Pilmoor, Boardman, Asbury, Coke, Rankin, Shadford, Gatch, Abbott, Lee, Cooper, Garrettson, Harry Hosier, Henry Evans, Richard Allen, James Varick, Abraham Thompson, O'Kelly, George, McKendree, and many others like them who are among the most hallowed names in Methodism.

These men at first were ordinary laymen, some of them poorly educated, but they take their places among the great apostles of Christian history. Indeed, in their lives and labors they are strikingly like the Apostles of the early Church. At the cost of severe sacrifice and personal suffering they carried their form of the faith to the people wherever they were. They preached in homes and churches, "meeting houses" or open fields. They preached on crowded city streets or by country lanes; on jailhouse steps or, as in the case of Asbury, from a hangman's gallows after a public hanging. They preached to receptive crowds or in spite of attacks by brutal, violent mobs. They did this with little thought of personal safety or reward. Robert Strawbridge, for example, often left his family without food, saying as he departed, "Meat will be sent here today."[6] "Who will keep the wolf from my own door while I am abroad seeking after lost sheep?" he asked. His neighbors supplied both the answer and the food.

A French author writing on the life of Wesley accurately said: "Methodist preachers did not take a vow of poverty on entering the itinerancy, but they practiced a voluntary course of self-renunciation that was never excelled by the followers of St. Francis."[7]

Somewhat more detailed is the tribute of Abel Stevens:

> What clerical men since the apostolic age ever traveled and labored like these? What public men ever sacrificed equally with them the ordinary comforts of life? Their salaries or "allowance" (for they disclaimed the word salary) scarcely provided them with clothes. Asbury's allowance was sixty-four dollars a year. His horses and carriages were given by his friends, all donations of money from friends he assigned to his fellow-sufferers, his fellow-laborers. At one of the early Western Conferences, where the assembled itinerants presented painful evidences of want, he parted with his watch, his coat, and his shirts for them. He was asked by a friend to lend him fifty pounds. "He might as well have asked me for Peru," wrote the bishop; "I showed him all the money I had in the world, about twelve dollars, and gave him five." Most of the early itinerants had to locate, at last, on account of their broken health, or the sufferings of their families. Of six hundred and fifty whose names appear in the Minutes, by the close of the century, about five hundred died located, and many of the remainder were, for a longer or shorter interval, in the local ranks, but were again to enter the itinerancy. Nearly half of those whose deaths are recorded died before they were thirty years old; about two thirds died before they had spent twelve years in the laborious service. They fell martyrs to their work.[8]

The early preachers were aflame with a burning zeal to save their brethren from "the wrath to come." They all were products of Wesley's type of religious experience. It included, first, a conviction of sin and a sense of guilt; secondly, faith in the possibility of divine forgiveness through the merits and death of Jesus Christ, who died that men might be saved; and thirdly, a feeling of justification or divine pardon for previous sins and failings. This feeling of forgiveness always came in a joyous, releasing, transporting experience that confirmed to the repentant sinner that he was forgiven, and therefore was an heir to life eternal.

This was the "experimental" or experiential form of faith characteristic of Methodism. It was simple, personal, and direct. It required no mediation on the part of priests, and very little liturgical or sacramental accompaniment. It was well suited to the unlettered and rough masses of the colonies, and it was especially suited to the illiterate and oppressed slaves.

This was the religious experience of all of the early Methodist preachers. Their biographies are replete with examples. It was John Wesley's experience in Aldersgate Street in 1738 when he felt his heart "strangely warmed" and he at last "knew" that Christ was his personal savior and that his sins were forgiven.

It was the experience of Philip Gatch, one of the first native American Methodist preachers. He was reared in a devout Anglican family, and he tried to live in keeping with the teachings of his Church. He felt, however, a disturbing sense of insufficiency about his spiritual life. In January 1772 he heard for the first time Methodist preaching by Nathan Perigau. "His prayer alarmed me much. I never had witnessed such energy nor heard such expressions in prayer before," he says in his biography. "The sermon was accompanied to my understanding by the Holy Spirit. I was stripped of all my self-righteousness. It was to me as filthy rags when the Lord made known to me my condition. I saw myself altogether sinful and helpless, while the dread of hell seized my guilty conscience." He heard Perigau again and was "confounded under the word." He continued in this state of anguished depression until April 26, when in a prayer meeting,

[I] bowed myself before the Lord, and said in my heart, "If thou wilt give me power to call on thy name how thankful will I be." Immediately I felt the power of God to affect me, body and soul. I felt like crying aloud. God said, by his Spirit, to my soul, "My power is present to heal thy soul, if thou wilt but believe." I instantly submitted to the operation of the Spirit of God, and my poor soul was set at liberty. I felt as if I had got into a new world. I was certainly brought from hell's dark door, and made nigh unto God by the blood of Jesus.[9]

Basically similar and yet in some respects quite different was the experience of Benjamin Abbott, one of the most effective of all the early preachers. He was not converted until he was forty. His early years were spent "in sin and open rebellion against God, in drinking, fighting, swearing, gambling, etc.; yet I worked hard and got a comfortable living for my family." In a vision, to which he was frequently subject, he saw all of his sins before him. "I awoke with amazement at what I had seen," he writes in his biography, "and concluded that I should shortly die, which brought all my sins before me, and caused me to make many promises to God to repent, which lasted for some time; but this wore off again, and I went to my old practices."

Like Gatch, Abbott went to hear a Methodist preacher. "All my sins that I ever had committed were brought to my view; I saw it was the mercy of God that I was out of hell, and I promised to amend my life in future." This, however, brought further suffering, for as he said, "I knew not the way to Christ for refuge . . ." Under more Methodist preaching, he says, "the word reached my heart in such a manner that it shook every joint in my body; tears flowed in abundance, and I cried out for mercy . . ." These alternate states of hope and despair continued until he actually contemplated suicide, and would have killed himself had he not reflected that the pains of hell where he would go were much worse than those he was suffering here. He drove home from the suicidal attempt "under the greatest anxiety imaginable with his hair rising on his head," and the Devil in hot pursuit. Eventually one night, October 11, 1772, after a bad dream, he awoke to see the Lord Jesus with extended arms, saying, "I died for you." "At that moment," he says, "the Scriptures were wonderfully opened to my understanding. My heart felt as light as a bird, being relieved of that guilt which before had bowed down my spirits, and my body felt as active as when I was eight-

een, so that the outward and inward man were both animated."[10]
He moved in the power of his experience to be the means of conversion to vast numbers.

The Methodist meetings were characterized by rapturous
bursts of thanks and praises on the one hand, and cries, groans,
and pleas for pardon on the other. Many were seized with spells
of jerking and weeping; some fell prostrate on the floor, lasting
at times for hours. The masses of the colonies had received very
little religious service. They were spiritually hungry. It was natural and inevitable that pent-up spiritual yearnings now given
freedom of expression should burst forth in these reactions.

Benjamin Abbott, who was most effective in arousing these expressions, gives this description of some of his meetings:

> Sometimes we used to assemble in the woods and under the trees,
> there not being room in the house for the people that attended.
> Often some of them would be struck to the ground in bitter lam-
> entations. The Lord wrought great wonders among us . . . The
> first time I preached [in New Mills, Pemberton] God worked
> powerfully; we had a weeping time, and one fell to the floor; this
> alarmed the people, for they had never seen the like before; when
> the meeting was over, we took him to a friend's house, and prayer
> was made for him till he rejoiced in the love of God. Next day I
> preached again, and the Lord poured out his spirit among us, so
> that there was weeping in abundance, and one fell to the floor;
> many prayers being offered for him, he found peace before he
> arose. Next day I travelled some miles, and preached in a Presby-
> terian meeting-house. I had a large congregation and spoke from
> these words, "Ye must be born again." God attended the word
> with power; some wept, some groaned, others cried aloud. I believe
> there were twenty Indians present, and when I came out of the
> pulpit they got all round me, asking what they should do to be
> saved, and tears ran in abundance; many of the white people also
> wept. This was a day of God's power . . .[11]

In carrying the Gospel to the people the early evangelists were
highly successful, but it was a hard, costly labor in which they
paid a dear price. In the first place, there were the hardships and
hazards of travel in colonial times, all on foot or horseback, over
trails mostly for there were few roads; streams and rivers had to

be forded or swum; widely scattered towns or settlements with few stopping places between; the constant danger of attack by Indians or robbers; open exposure to the elements, heat and rain in summer, cold and snow in winter, these made travel difficult and dangerous, but a tribute to the courage and hardihood of the early preachers.

A second source of suffering was the rough and immoral tenor of much of colonial life. The people resented the denunciations of the preachers and their challenges to their immoral practices. It must be remembered that the early Methodist preachers were *lay* preachers, unordained and bearing the authority of no church, their only authority being the will of God as they had known it in a central experience. Consequently they were often attacked by mobs or rowdies, sometimes beaten, frequently jailed, barred from churches and constantly denounced. Perhaps the sufferings of the preachers is never better described than by Freeborn Garrettson one of the greatest of the preachers and most influential:

> My lot has mostly been cast in new places, to form circuits, which much exposed me to persecution. Once I was imprisoned; twice beaten; left on the highway speechless and senseless (I would have gone into the world of spirits, had not God in mercy sent a good Samaritan, that bled and took me to a friend's house); once shot at; guns and pistols presented at my breast; once delivered from an armed mob, in the dead time of night, on the highway, by a surprising flash of lightning; surrounded frequently by mobs; stoned frequently; I have had to escape for my life at dead of night.[12]

A third source of trouble for the preachers was the anti-British feeling which was strong and growing at the time. Embury began preaching in 1766. This was just ten years before the outbreak of hostilities at Bunker Hill. The revolutionary-minded colonists were hostile to all things British, and Methodism was very British. Wesley was an Englishman and lived in England. The first preachers were all English. Some of them quite naturally were in sympathy with and loyal to their mother country. To heighten the problem, in 1775 John Wesley wrote a pamphlet in which he criticized the colonies and denounced the Revolution.[13] Copies of the work were circulated in America. This made the Methodists appear as "Tories," and it made the Methodist movement unpopular and under suspicion. Preachers were attacked and banned. Even Asbury had to go into seclusion, if not hiding, at the home of a friend, Judge White, near Baltimore.[14]

A fourth cause of trouble for the preachers was the Methodist stand on slavery. This issue and all of the problems it entailed will be discussed in later pages.

Thus it can be seen that even though the early preachers were highly successful in their evangelistic efforts, winning converts and setting up societies at a remarkable pace, it was a success bought at a very high price, a price that could be paid only by strong, devoted men, the kind of men who have carried the faith even to the ends of the earth.

BLACK RESPONSE

There is abundant evidence that from the very beginning Negroes responded to the Methodist appeal and shared in its promotion as much as they were able. It has already been stated that one of the five persons who were present in the first Methodist service under Embury was a Negro servant woman named Betty. Among the list of contributors to the fund for building the first Methodist "meeting house" in New York City are the names of several slaves who gave of their meager means to this good work.

In a letter to John Wesley written in 1768 by "T. T.," evidently Thomas Taylor, appealing for more preachers, it is stated:

> About this period Mr. Webb, whose wife's relations lived at Jamaica, Long Island, took a house in that neighborhood, and began to preach in his own house, and several other places on Long Island. Within six months, about twenty-four persons received justifying grace, nearly half of them white, the rest negroes . . .

Asbury soon saw and was deeply impressed with the response of Negroes to Methodism. On his way to New York after landing in Philadelphia, he writes: "I feel a regard for the people, and I think the Americans are more ready to receive the word than the English; and to see the poor Negroes so affected is pleasing; to see their sable countenances in our solemn assemblies, and to hear them sing with cheerful melody their Redeemer's praise affected me much, and made me ready to say, 'Of a truth, I perceive God is no respecter of persons.' "[15]

Thomas Rankin writes in 1774:

> We concluded the evenings with a general love feast, in which the Lord's presence was powerfully felt by many persons. Many declared with great freedom what God had done for their souls. Some of the poor black people spoke with power and pungency of the loving-kindness of the Lord. If the rich in this society were as much devoted to God as the poor are, we should see wonders done in the city. Holy Jesus, there is nothing impossible with thee.[16]

Again, Thomas Rankin gives this experience on the Baltimore Circuit:

> We rode to Henry Watters's, near Deer Creek, where we intended holding our Quarterly Meeting for Baltimore and Kent Circuit, on the Eastern Shore. After an early breakfast, we spent about two hours in the affairs of the circuits. At ten our general love feast began. There was such a number of *whites and blacks* as had never attended on such an occasion before. After we had sung and prayed the cloud burst from my mind and the power of the Lord descended in such an extraordinary manner as I had never seen since my landing in Philadelphia. All the preachers were so overcome with the Divine presence that they could scarce address the people, but only in broken accents say, "This is none other than the house of God, and the gate of heaven!" When any of the people stood up to declare the loving-kindness of God, they were so overwhelmed with the Divine presence that they were obliged to sit down and let silence speak his praise. Near the close of the meeting I stood up and called upon the people to look toward that part of the chapel where all the blacks were. I then said, "See the number of Africans who have stretched out their hands unto God!" While I was addressing the people thus, it seemed as if the very house shook with the mighty power and glory of Sinai's God. Many of the people were so overcome that they were ready to faint and die under his Almighty hand. For about three hours the gale of the Spirit thus continued to breathe upon the dry bones; and they did live the life of glorious love! As for myself, I scarce knew whether I was in the body or not; and so it was with all my brethren . . . Surely the fruits of this season will remain to all eternity.[17]

Perhaps the sincerity and depth of the Negroes' Christian commitment can be seen in this incident related by Abel Stevens, the Methodist historian:

> Henry D. Gough, wealthy planter, heard Asbury preach. He was deeply impressed and burdened. He could no longer enjoy his accustomed pleasures.
>
> He became deeply serious and, at last melancholy, and was near destroying himself under the awakened sense of his misspent life; but God mercifully preserved him. Riding to one of his plantations, he heard the voice of prayer and praise in a cabin, and, listening, discovered that a negro from a neighboring estate was leading the devotions of his own slaves, and offering fervent thanksgivings for the blessings of their depressed lot. His heart was touched, and with emotion he exclaimed, "Alas, O Lord, I have my thousands and tens of thousands, and yet, ungrateful wretch that I am, I never thanked thee, as this poor slave does, who has scarcely clothes to put on or food to satisfy his hunger. The luxurious master was taught a lesson, on the nature of true contentment and happiness, which he could never forget. His work-worn servants in their lowly cabins knew a blessedness which he had never found in his sumptuous mansion.[18]

On November 4, 1769, Richard Boardman wrote to John Wesley:

> Our house contains about seven hundred people. About a third part of those who attend get in, the rest are glad to hear without. There appears such a willingness in the Americans to hear the word as I never saw before. They have no preaching in some parts of the back settlements. I doubt not but an effectual door will be opened among them. O! May the Most High give his Son the heathen for his inheritance. The number of blacks that attend the preaching affects me much.[19]

Again, in April 1771, he wrote to Wesley:

> It pleases God to carry on his work among us. Within the month we have had a great awakening . . . I have lately been comforted by the death of some poor negroes who have gone off the stage rejoicing in the God of their salvation. I asked one on the point of death, "Are you afraid to die? O no, said she; I have my blessed savior in my heart; I should be glad to die; I want to be

gone, that I may be with him forever. I know that he loves me, and I feel that I love him with all my heart." She continued to declare the great things that God had done for her soul, to the astonishment of many, till the Lord took her to himself. Several more seem just ready to be gone; longing for the happy time when mortality shall be swallowed up of life. I bless God. I find, in general, my soul happy, though much tried and tempted.[20]

Perhaps Negro participation is never more touchingly described than in this statement by Freeborn Garrettson:

"In September I went to North Carolina, to travel Roanoak circuit, and was sweetly drawn out in the glorious work, though my exercises were very great particularly respecting the slavery, and hard usage of the poor afflicted negroes. Many times did my heart ache on their account, and many tears run down my cheeks, both in Virginia and Carolina, while exhibiting a crucified Jesus to their view; and I bless God that my labors were not in vain among them. I endeavored frequently to inculcate the doctrine of freedom in a private way, and this procured me the ill will of some, who were in that unmerciful practice. I would often set apart times to preach to the blacks, and adapt my discourse to them alone; and precious moments have I had. While many of their sable faces were bedewed with tears, their withered hands of faith were stretched out, and their precious souls made white in the blood of the Lamb. The suffering of those poor out-casts of men, through the blessing of God, drove them near to the Lord, and many of them were amazingly happy."[21]

The above statements taken from contemporary biographical writings give a clear picture both of the nature and the extent of Negro participation in early Methodist activities. It can be seen that the religious experience of the blacks was sincere and profound. Like all human beings they had sins and failings and from these they needed to be saved. But above all, the Christian faith gave hope to people caught in a cruel, bitterly hopeless plight. To be a slave for life with no hope of relief can easily become a living death. But Christianity with its belief in the love of a great, good God who knew the sufferings of each of His children, even His black ones, at once gave the slave hope for a good ending to his life, if not to be attained in this world, then to be enjoyed forever in the world to come. This belief in an ultimate good end to his existence was like a bright ray of sunshine in a dark day. It enabled the slave to live in his painful status with both hope and serenity. Thus Henry Gough heard a slave leading devotions in a cabin and "offering fervent thanksgivings for the blessings of their depressed lot." The fact that Jesus was a *suffering* savior was especially appropriate for the slave. It gave him an identity and oneness with Christ that transcended any theological unity. Thus the dying slave woman could say, "I would be glad to die. I want to be gone, to be with him forever. I know that he loves me, and I feel that I love him with all my heart."

Secondly, in the Christian faith, God was not only merciful and sympathetic, but also righteous and just. He hated evil and He would eventually destroy it, and punish the evildoers. In the light of Christian teachings, slavery was wrong. Christianity taught brotherly love. The brutal oppressions of the slave system had to be an offense to God. If God lived, slavery someday would surely be destroyed. Here was the ground, as has been previously said, for the spirit of endurance which the slaves developed and which was sociologically so remarkable. Slaves were enabled to endure slavery with all its pains without ever accepting it. It also enabled many to strive as hard as they could to preserve their sense of dignity, to seek to attain at least some measure of self-fulfillment even in slave quarters, and to look for any chance to secure their freedom by self-purchase, by manumission, or by flight.

For the slave, therefore, becoming a Christian represented a complex of aims and hopes in which his soul's salvation was only one. It accounts for the readiness and earnestness with which many slaves took to the faith, and for its rapid growth among the blacks.

The first preachers preached openly and freely to blacks apparently with little or no distinction. With them the Gospel was meant for every creature. The slaves had souls that needed to be saved. Therefore they preached alike to white and black, bond and free. The result was that Negroes responded in large numbers, in some cases equaling or exceeding the whites. In Thomas

Webb's converts on Long Island, over half were black. In 1776, ten years later, Thomas Rankin writes:

> At four in the afternoon I preached again . . . I had gone through about two-thirds of my discourse, and was bringing the words home to the present *now*, when such power descended that hundreds fell to the ground, and the house seemed to shake with the presence of God. The chapel was full of white and black, and many were without that could not get in. Look wherever we would, we saw nothing but streaming eyes and faces bathed in tears; and heard nothing but groans and strong cries after God and the Lord Jesus Christ.
>
> Sunday 7. I preached at W's chapel, about twenty miles from Mr. J's. I intended to preach near the house, under the shade of some large trees. But the rain made it impracticable. The house was greatly crowded, and four or five hundred stood at the windows, and listened with unabated attention. I preached from Ezekiel's vision of dry bones: "And there was a great shaking." I was obliged to stop again and again, and beg of the people to compose themselves. But they could not; some on their knees, and some on their faces, were crying mightily to God all the time I was preaching. *Hundreds of Negroes* were among them, with the tears streaming down their faces.[22]

The heavy participation of blacks in the early Methodist meetings is truly remarkable when one considers the relatively small proportion of Negroes, both slave and free, in the colonial population, and also considering the limitations on movements of slaves, that is, their lack of freedom to attend religious or any other kinds of meetings. In many cases slaves could only attend with the master's consent, and many masters were opposed to religion for their slaves.[23]

Yet despite the difficulties, Negroes came in large numbers to the meetings. Perhaps one attractive aspect was that at first Negroes could attend these services without many of the humiliations and discriminations usually imposed on slaves and free Negroes.

It is also seen that Negroes shared fully in the services. Asbury mentions their singing "in cheerful melody." Rankin mentions their testifying to what God had done for their souls; Boardman mentions their being moved and being overcome as were the whites. Certainly in its beginning, Methodism welcomed the slave and the free black into its fold with very little distinction.

It must be remembered, however, that Methodism began not as a church or as a separate religious movement, but rather as a holiness movement within a church, the long-established Church of England. Wesley lived and died a priest in the Anglican Church. His aim was a drive for piety within that church. The early Methodist meetings were simply revival meetings such as are conducted today by modern nondenominational evangelists. The purpose of the meetings was to call men to repentance and to conversion. The converts were expected to continue as members in their own churches and there to receive the sacraments of Baptism and Holy Communion. For their spiritual nurture the converts were organized into "Societies," and these were subdivided into "Classes" with a leader over each class. But until 1784 the Societies were not to be taken as a new church.

In such an elementary organization, slaves could be taken into full participation more easily than in a settled and established church. This doubtless accounts for their acceptance and participation in such full measure.

Yet in the early and elementary stages of Methodism there were evidences of separations and distinctions which eventually led to problems of the most serious nature and even to withdrawals. Boardman says that in a service he pointed to the section of the chapel where "the blacks usually sat." Freeborn Garrettson, one of the most liberal of the early preachers, says he often held separate services for blacks.

In light of the fact that the blacks were slaves and that already the slave occupied a severely degraded cultural level, distinctions in status and association were almost to be expected. The wonder is that they were not more stringent, and that the slaves were as welcome as they were. The invitation to and the acceptance of blacks were largely due to the early preachers who had the determined purpose of preaching the Gospel to every creature. All souls needed to be saved.

CHAPTER IV

Methodism and Slavery

WHEN WESLEYAN METHODISM came to America, 1766, African Negro slavery had long been well established both as a social pattern and as an economic system. There were laws in all of the colonies making the slave a chattel for life with few legal rights and protections. There were laws also making it difficult to free or manumit slaves; and there were laws severely defining the status and restricting the movement of the comparatively few Negroes who were free.[1]

Slave labor was usually profitable and had come to be essential in almost every phase of life, such as domestic service, clerical and commercial work,[2] in trades and industry, in farming both small and large scale, in clearing new land and building roads as the nation spread steadily south and westward. After 1793, with the invention of the cotton gin, slavery was especially necessary in the South to grow cotton, which had become the world's chief source of fiber for making cloth and thread.

There is little wonder, then, that many American families, including some of the leading ones, owned and traded slaves, among them George Washington, Thomas Jefferson, William Penn, and even Patrick Henry.

The slave trade, too, despite its horrible brutality, was world-wide and growing. It was hazardous, to be sure, but fortunes were made in building and operating slave ships, and in the actual buying and selling of slaves. Many American family fortunes were founded on the slave trade.

But even though in the colonies slavery was entrenched and growing, there had always been protest against it. The protests at first were against the more brutal aspects of slavery, and pleaded for amelioration in the slave's lot, such as having respect for slave marriages and providing opportunities for slaves to buy their freedom.

In the mid-eighteenth century as the spirit of revolt against England grew and as the colonists were demanding more and more their own freedom from British oppression, the protests against slavery became more intense. Eventually the call was not only for amelioration but also for abolition of the slave system altogether. Many saw the inconsistency of resisting oppression of themselves while at the same time keeping near half a million souls in bondage. The Reverend Samuel Webster, a minister of Salisbury, Massachusetts, in 1796 said in a published sermon, "For God's sake, break every yoke and let these oppressed ones [Negroes] *go free without delay*—let them taste the sweets of that liberty, which we so highly prize, and are so earnestly supplicating God and man to grant us; nay, which we claim as the natural right of every man."[3]

The Quakers as a group were the leaders in the call for abolition. They had made owning or trading in slaves a cause for expulsion from the Societies. There were also the pamphleteers such as Thomas Paine and Anthony Benezet who vigorously denounced slavery and called for freedom for the slaves.[4]

But while these voices were strong and clear, they did not represent the majority opinion of the colonies. Slavery was a fixed institution and continued to grow even through the years of the American Revolution. It thus made the new young nation the symbol of incongruity in the eyes of much of the world.

Wesleyan Methodism began in America with a strong antislavery impulse, which was received from John Wesley. Whitefield did not oppose slavery, but Wesley did. He fought it all his life. In 1743 Wesley wrote into the General Rules governing the Societies a rule against slave trading, "buying the bodies and souls of men, women and children with the intention to enslave them."[5] In 1772, just six years after American Methodism began, he wrote his celebrated pamphlet, *"Thoughts Upon Slavery."*[6] He wrote this after reading Anthony Benezet's pamphlet on Negro life in Guinea.[7] Wesley drew heavily on Benezet's work in attacking arguments that justified the slave trade. To the claim that in their native state Negroes were barbarous savages, Wesley showed that Africans had highly developed cultures which in some ways were superior to white. But even after being enslaved, instead of becoming the brutes that slavery normally would have made them, many Negroes showed highest moral qualities even under cruel oppression. But above all, he said, there could never be any justification for the heartless brutality of the slave trade. Nothing can justify "severing every human tie."

Near the end of his life Wesley wrote to William Wilberforce a letter encouraging the English reformer to continue his fight against the slave trade until American Negro slavery, "the vilest that ever saw the sun," is completely abolished.[8]

In addition to the impulse from Wesley, there were other reasons for Methodism's opposition to slavery. The first preachers from England were offended at the pitiful plight of the slaves. They uniformly refer to them as the "poor blacks" or the "poor sons of Ham." The fact that despite their enslaved condition the blacks came in large numbers to attend the meetings, hear the Gospel, and seek conversion made all the more poignant the inhumanity of slavery and the sin of it. Asbury upon his first contact with slaves in religious meetings saw that "of a truth God is no respecter of persons." He also wrote in his Journal, 1778, "I find the most pious part of the people called Quakers, are exerting themselves for the liberation of the slaves. This is a very laudable design; and what the Methodists must come to, or, I fear the Lord will depart from them."[9]

Convinced of the sin of slavery, the early preachers called for its abolition. They wanted slavery abolished, and as a step to this end, they wanted all Methodists to free their slaves immediately. No Methodist if truly converted could ever be a slaveholder or a slave trader. This was especially true for Methodist preachers, both local and traveling. Thus Freeborn Garrettson upon his conversion in 1777 immediately freed his slaves, declaring: "It was God, not man, who showed me the impropriety of holding slaves."[10] Also Philip Gatch freed his slaves.

The Methodist opposition to slavery was given formal expression in Conferences held between 1780 and 1784. In the Baltimore Conference of 1780, slavery was condemned and Methodist laymen were advised to liberate their slaves.[11] In the conference in the spring of 1784, it was voted to expel from a Society any member who bought a slave or sold one; to grant a year of grace to local preachers in Virginia for freeing their slaves, but to suspend all local preachers in Maryland, Delaware, Pennsylvania, and New Jersey who did not free them; and discontinue the employment of all traveling preachers who did not free their slaves.[12]

The high point of Methodism's organized opposition to slavery came in the famous Christmas Conference of 1784. It was in this Conference made up of representatives from the entire connection that the Societies were organized into the Methodist Episcopal Church. It was in this Conference also that Francis Asbury was first ordained an elder in the new church on one day and on the next was consecrated a Superintendent to serve jointly with Dr. Coke in supervising and promoting the work in America.[13]

Thomas Coke was bitterly opposed to slavery, exceeding even Asbury. It is not surprising, therefore, that the General Conference of 1784 declared, "It is our bounden duty to extirpate this abomination," and took the following actions:

1. To expel all slaveholding members of Methodist societies who would not in twelve months manumit their slaves after they had reached certain ages. (Methodists in Virginia "because of peculiar circumstances" were given two years of grace.)

2. To expel immediately all members who bought or sold slaves, except for the purpose of liberation.[14]

These rules are the strongest passed by the Methodist Church. They express the Church's abhorrence of slavery and its desire to see it eradicated. Yet despite the severity of the language, there were ambiguities and grounds for interpretations that provided opportunities for escape. For example, the "peculiar circumstances" of Virginia Methodists were not defined, and it is still not known what the "circumstances" were, unless it was the large number of slaves in Virginia. In 1790, the first U.S. census, Virginia had 292,627 slaves, more than twice as many as any other state.

Also, the rules of 1784 were so rigid that they were unacceptable to many laymen, especially in the South. They never were strictly enforced. They also aroused the opposition of many persons who were moderate in their attitudes on slavery. Thus Dr. Coke, the new Superintendent or Bishop, barely escaped physical violence at the hands of a mob when he spoke against slavery at a meeting in Virginia. Coke wrote: "A high-headed lady also went out and told the rioters (as I was afterwards informed) that she would give fifty pounds, if they would give that little Doctor one hundred lashes."[15] The Reverend Devereaux Jarratt, an Anglican priest who had been a loyal friend and supporter of the Methodist movement, openly differed with Coke on the slave issue. In fact, Jarratt kept slaves himself. A group of laymen in Virginia came to Coke in a body to protest against the rules and to state that they had no intention of keeping them.[16]

There was some slight favorable response to Coke's and Asbury's efforts, but for the most part the rules of 1784 were unacceptable and were openly resisted. Thus in June of 1785, within six months after the rules were passed, Coke and Asbury decided to "suspend the minute regarding slavery, for the church was in too infantile a state to push things to extremity." They added a note, however, that they still "deeply abhorred slavery and would not cease to seek its destruction by all wise and prudent means."[17]

The year 1784 marked the high point of Methodist opposition. From 1784 on, the rules against slavery indicated a steady retreat. For ten years the slave issue was not revived in the General Conferences of the Church, and the rules against slavery were not enforced. The Methodist Church grew in membership from 18,000 in 1785 to 56,664 in 1796. Many of the new members were slaveholders.

But while the Church as a whole retreated in its stand against slavery, there were a number of individuals who did not give ground and who called for abolition more strongly than ever.

One of the most outspoken of these was the Reverend James O'Kelly, pastor of a Methodist church in Virginia. Convinced of the evil of slavery, in 1785 he freed his own slaves and vigorously wrote and preached against slavery. In a published statement he said: "Be well assured that slavery is a work of the flesh, assisted by the devil; a mystery of iniquity that works like witchcraft, to darken your understanding, and harden your hearts against conviction." To the statement that God had ordained slavery, he replied: "If there be such a being in existence as may be called God, who was the author of this tragedy, it must be one of those gods that ascend from the bottomless pit. Such a god I defy in the name and strength of Jesus, and declare eternal war against him!"[18]

Another most effective voice against slavery was Ezekiel Cooper, the young preacher who had saved the Methodist Book Concern. In a widely read pamphlet he declared:

> I blush at the conduct of many who are free men in principle, have declared for, and supported the cause of liberty and still persist in holding their fellow creatures in bondage . . . The same that wounds and pains us wounds and pains them . . . O compassion awake in the breasts of men!"[19]

But despite the strong and advanced positions of individual Methodists, the Church as a whole continued to retreat in its struggle with slavery. The General Conference of 1796 said we are "more than ever convinced of the great evil of slavery," yet it ruled that a member should be expelled only if he *sold* a slave. The Conference of 1784 had called for expulsion if a member *bought* or *sold* a slave. The 1796 ruling meant that members were free to buy slaves if they would agree to free them after a number of years to be determined by the Quarterly Conference.[20]

The Conference of 1784 said no future slaveholders could be members of the Church. The Conference of 1796 said a slaveholder could unite with the Methodist Church if a preacher spoke with him "freely and faithfully on the subject of slavery." The General Conference of 1800 defeated a motion to refuse admission to slaveholders. It also passed a rule that itinerant slaveholding preachers "shall forfeit their ministerial character in the Methodist Episcopal Church, unless they execute, if it be practicable, a legal emancipation of such slave, agreeably to the laws of the state wherein they reside." Here, again, was a rule so full of contingencies and ambiguities that it was virtually worthless or unenforceable. Also, there is recognized here, as in other cases before, the superior authority of the civil government.

Each General Conference for the next sixteen years continued this retreat. In 1804 the Conference exempted members in North Carolina, South Carolina, and Georgia from observing the rule with respect to buying and selling Negroes. The Conference also requested preachers to admonish slaves to render due respect and obedience to their masters' commands and interests. In 1808, upon motion of Bishop Asbury, the Conference authorized the printing of 1,000 Disciplines without the section and rule on slavery for circulation in the South Carolina Conference, which included Georgia and part of North Carolina. It also permitted annual conferences to set their own rules with respect to buying and selling slaves.

The Conference of 1812 tabled a motion to inquire into the moral nature of slavery.

The General Conference of 1816 appointed a nine-member committee to examine the slavery question and recommend action. The committee was only able to report that a slaveholder could not hold an official position in the Church if the state in which he resides permits manumission. It was obvious that the Church could do and would do little to attack the question of slavery which was so clearly morally wrong.

What were the reasons for this constant, deliberate retreat of the Church on an issue which was obviously a moral one and a sin?

There were several. The first and main reason was the growth and power of the slave system, really the "slaveocracy," which completely dominated the life and thought of the South, and especially of the Southern Church. By 1837 the Church in the slave states was so dominated that the Georgia Annual Conference of that year declared: "*Resolved*, that we view *slavery* as a civil and domestic institution, and one with which, as ministers of Christ, we have nothing to do, further than to ameliorate the condition of the slave by endeavoring to impart to him and his master the benign influence of the religion of Christ, and aiding both on their way to heaven."[21] Thus the Southern Church capitulated completely on the moral issue of slavery and followed from then on a policy of noninterference except for reproofs and scoldings on the more brutal aspects of slavery and failure of slaveowners to provide for the religious instruction of their slaves. In the national meetings of Methodists the Southern churchmen defended slavery and their own position, saying that this was the only way the Church could survive in the South, and that this was the only basis on which the slaves could be served religiously.

A second reason was the upsurge of anti-Negro feeling that occurred in the 1830s. The liberal feelings during and following the Revolutionary War had subsided. Cotton growing was in the South, but the manufacture of cotton products was in the North. Thus many Northerners were indirectly involved in the cotton economy, which in turn was largely based on slave labor. There was a growing tolerance toward slavery in the North in the first half of the nineteenth century. Many of the new members taken into the Church were moderates on slavery, and less favorable to Negroes.

There was a widespread resentment of Negro labor in the North. The large number of European immigrants to America were competitors for the lower level jobs which otherwise would be held by free Negroes. The bitter feelings resulted in 1834 in riots in New York City, Philadelphia, Rochester, Trenton, Lancaster, Pennsylvania, and other cities.[22]

A third reason for the moderation of the Church was the desire to preserve unity within the Church. Southerners were becoming more and more aggressive in their defense of slavery and in the effort to get their position accepted in church life and legislation. The leaders of the Church in the hope of keeping peace mildly held on to the action that slavery was a moral evil, but at the same time they refrained from taking any direct action against the Southerners. The Church strongly denounced abolitionist activity and urged members and preachers to have nothing

to do with that disturbing subject.[23] The Church was more interested in growth than in a moral crusade.

But at the same time that the Church was acting conservatively, a new force was arising in the nation, and in the
Church. This was the new abolition movement with its demand
for the immediate abolition of slavery. The antislavery interest in
the Northern Church had never been completely silenced. Although a small minority, there were a number of publications
and preachers who were opposed to slavery.[24] About 1819 there
began a sharp increase in this group. Among Methodists the leading antislavery periodicals were *The Wesleyan Journal, The
American Wesleyan Observer, The New England Christian Advocate,* all of New England, and *Zion's Watchman* of New York
City. Among the leading editors and advocates of abolitionism
were Orange Scott, LaRoy Sunderland, and George Storrs.[25]

The leading spirit in the national abolition movement, of
course, was William Lloyd Garrison. Through his writings in his
paper, *The Liberator,* and through his tireless, courageous speaking and organizing, he soon began to reach the national conscience and to get the attention of religious leaders. "His forth-
rightness and determination: 'I am in earnest—I will not
equivocate—I will not excuse—I will not retreat a single inch;
and I will be heard' recalled to their Wesleyan heritage many
Methodist preachers who had become lethargic concerning the
sinfulness of human bondage."[26]

The abolitionists saw the moral wrong of slavery. They said it
was a sin; that it was economically ruinous; it perverted the
morals of masters as well as slaves, and that it should be removed
from the nation's life immediately and completely. As is well
known, Frederick Douglass, an escaped slave, self-educated, became associated with Garrison in the abolition movement, and
became one of the most effective workers in America and
abroad.

The conscience of the Church became aroused. Many felt that
the Church was too tolerant. Because of this weak attitude toward slavery, a large number of Methodists withdrew from the
M.E. Church in 1843 and formed the Wesleyan Methodist Connection. They seceded on account of slavery and church gov-

ernment.[27] They claimed a membership of 14,600 and 200 preachers.

The loss of so large a body of members was disturbing to Northern moderates. They saw that something must be done to curb slavery and the South if further secessions were to be avoided. As the General Conference of 1844 approached the Church was becoming more and more polarized into two determined sections, each convinced that its position must be maintained for the survival of the Church in its area.

When the General Conference opened on May 1, 1844, in New York City it was already seen that division might be inevitable. The Conference received national attention. Two cases determined the fate of the Conference, one the case of a preacher, the other the case of a bishop, and both were concerned with slavery. Francis A. Harding, a preacher in Baltimore, had been suspended by his Annual Conference because he owned a slave. The title to the slave actually inhered in his wife. He refused to accept the decision of the Annual Conference, and appealed to the General Conference of 1844. The General Conference sustained the action of the Annual Conference, and Harding remained suspended.[28] This was a blow to the Southern delegates.

The Bishop's case was that of James O. Andrew. He was charged with holding slaves. His defense is best stated in his own words:

"several years since an old lady, of Augusta, Georgia, bequeathed to me a mulatto girl, in trust that I should take care of her until she should be nineteen years of age; that with her consent I should then send her to Liberia; . . . When the time arrived, she refused to go . . . continuing to live in her own house on my lot; and has been, and still is at perfect liberty to go a free state at her pleasure; but the laws of the state will not permit her emancipation, nor admit such deed of emancipation to record, and she refused to leave the state. In her case, therefore, I have been made a slaveholder legally, but not with my own consent.

2dly. About five years since, the mother of my former wife left to her daughter, not to me, a negro boy; and as my wife died without a will more than two years since, by the laws of the state he becomes legally my property . . .

3dly. In the month of January last I married my present wife, she being at the time possessed of slaves, inherited from her former husband's estate, and belonging to her. Shortly after my marriage, being unwilling to become their owner, . . . I secured them to her by a deed of trust. "It will be obvious to you, . . . that I have neither bought nor sold a slave; that in the only circumstances in which I am legally a slaveholder, emancipation is impracticable . . . I have thus plainly stated all the facts in the case, and submit the statement for the consideration of the General Conference."[29]

Bishop Andrew was a Southerner and a slaveholder, but he was also a kind, sincere man. He played a leading part in setting up the Mission to the Slaves, and was outspoken in calling for more humane treatment of slaves. When he saw that his case was the focal point of contention in the Conference, he offered to resign, but the Southern delegates would not permit it. They made his case their *cause célèbre*, and they were determined to win or lose with it.

They contended first, that there was nothing wrong with slavery or slaveholding; that slavery was a political issue and not a moral one, and that it was beyond the province of the Church; that if some sections of the country objected to a Bishop who had slaves, he could be assigned to other sections that did not object.

The arguments on both sides were carefully drawn and brilliantly stated. It was agreed that the 180 delegates to this Conference contained the best minds in the Church. For ten days the debate continued amid parliamentary maneuverings to give one side or the other some advantage. Finally on June 1 the following resolution was introduced:

Whereas the Discipline of our church forbids the doing anything calculated to destroy our itinerant general superintendency; and whereas, Bishop Andrew has become connected with slavery by marriage and otherwise, and this act having drawn after it circumstances which, in the estimation of the General Conference, will greatly embarrass the exercise of his office as an itinerant general Superintendent, if not in some places entirely prevent it; therefore,

Resolved, That it is the sense of this General Conference that he desist from the exercise of his office so long as this impediment remains.[30]

The Resolution was adopted, 111 for, 69 against.

A few days after the decision in Bishop Andrew's case, the Southern delegates submitted a statement saying that "the decision must produce a state of things in the South which renders a continuance of the jurisdiction of the General Conference over these conferences inconsistent with the success of the ministry in the slaveholding states."[31]

A committee was appointed to "plan for a mutual and friendly division of the Church provided they could not devise a plan for an amicable adjustment of difficulties." The difficulties could not be adjusted. One year later, in Louisville, Kentucky, delegates from the Southern annual conferences met to form the Methodist Episcopal Church, South. "The Methodist Church was no longer a national institution."[32]

CHAPTER V

The Beginnings of Separation

FROM THE VERY BEGINNING Negroes responded readily to the Methodist movement. They attended the preaching services in large numbers and they reacted to the preaching with their full share of convictions and conversions.

There were many reasons for this bountiful response. In the first place, the early preachers actively sought the blacks. They felt that all men needed salvation whether bond or free, rich or poor, white or black. Therefore since it was their mission to preach the Gospel to every creature, they pursued their mission with vigorous determination.

In the second place, the Methodist message was understandable to the unlettered blacks. As has been previously stated, it consisted of three main elements, a conviction of sin, faith in Christ, and forgiveness by God which constituted salvation. This last element came in a joyful, transporting experience which was aroused by the preaching of the evangelists. Also, the preachers preached in language the blacks could understand. One leading Negro Methodist convert wrote: "I feel thankful that I ever heard a Methodist preacher. We are beholden to the Methodists, under God, for the light of the Gospel we enjoy; for all other denominations preached so high flown that we were not able to comprehend their doctrine."[1]

Thirdly, there was the Gospel message itself: the message of a just God who hated evil, and who would punish evildoers both here and hereafter, both master and slave. But this God of justice was also a loving God, who cared for each of His children, and who had given His son to die for their salvation. That salvation was open to everyone who would truly repent and accept Christ as personal savior. Here was a message of hope and comfort that oppressed blacks went anxiously to hear.

A fourth factor was the attitude of the preachers. The early preachers were both opposed to slavery and in sympathy with the suffering slaves. Over and over they speak of the "poor blacks." In some cases they complain against the cruelty with which masters treated their slaves, and they warned that this could bring down the wrath of a just God.[2]

For reasons such as these the slaves and free Negroes took to the Methodist cause in great numbers, in some cases exceeding the whites. The phrases "a large number of both whites and blacks," "people stood about the door both white and black," or in the case of separate meetings, "a large number of blacks attended" run through all contemporary accounts of early Methodism.

Upon conversion the Negroes were taken into the Societies, and into the classes. At first they were enrolled without regard to race or slave status. This was especially true in the Middle Atlantic colonies such as New York, New Jersey, Delaware, Pennsylvania, and Maryland. Thus we find on the membership rolls of the society that became John Street Church in New York City the names of several slaves. Also among the contributors to the first meeting house are a number of slave names.

But despite the Gospel fervor of the early evangelists and the drive for holiness among the members, religion then as later could do little to break down rigid social customs. A slave was still a slave, and a Negro though free was still a Negro. There were laws and customs, long before Methodism came, sharply drawing the distinction between slave and free, and black and white, and sharply limiting association between the two. It is not long, therefore, before there begin to appear in the Methodist writings of the period statements, sometimes unwitting statements, that indicate rankest discrimination in the holy Societies. For example, Benjamin Abbott writes:

> We soon fell into conversation on the things of God. At time of family worship, abundance of black people assembled in the kitchen, and the door was set open that they might hear without coming into the parlor. I gave out a hymn, brother Sterling went to prayer, and after him myself. The power of the Lord came down in a wonderful manner among the black people; some cried aloud, others fell to the floor, some praising God and some crying for mercy: after we had concluded, brother S. went among them, where he continued upward on one hour, exhorting them to fly to Jesus, the ark of safety.[3]

Another example is seen in a letter that Joseph Pilmoor wrote to John Wesley on August 12, 1792: "As the ground was wet they persuaded me to try to preach within and appointed men to stand at the door to keep all the Negroes out till the white persons were got in, but the house would not near hold them . . ."

The practice of segregation in worship intensified after 1784 when Methodism became a Church with church buildings, a resident, ordained ministry, a more diverse white membership, and a growing black membership. The segregation in worship was most rigid in the South, of course, where slavery was a fixed system and the subordinate status of the slave was rigidly enforced. Special balconies or extra rooms were provided for the slaves, or separate services and class meetings were conducted for them either before or after the regular services. On the larger plantations often there were special buildings or "meeting houses" where slave services were held. Under the "Mission to the Slaves" these separate services were conducted by the missionaries.

In the North it became the practice to seat the Negroes in special sections, sometimes in a balcony, if there was one, or on the side or in the back of the church. This was especially the case where the Negro membership was large and growing. These arrangements were often inconvenient, and when seated behind posts or partitions, it was difficult for Negroes to see and hear and to share fully in the services.

To the Negroes, especially to the free Negroes in the North, the practice of segregation in worship was disappointing and offensive. It seemed to them that the church of Jesus Christ, to whom all Christians, white and black, looked for their salvation, was the one place where Christians should meet as brothers and discriminations should not obtain. This feeling of resentment against distinctions in worship shows perhaps better than anything else how the Christian faith kept alive in the slave and in the black freedman the sense of his inherent dignity and equality as a person and as a child of God. It helped to show the wrong of slavery as a defiance of the will of God.

The resentment of Negroes against segregation in worship and in the other activities of Methodism is given almost classic expression by Richard Allen, a member of St. George's Church in Philadelphia who later became the first active bishop of the A.M.E. Church. In 1787 one Sunday morning a scuffle arose during the service when an overzealous sexton attempted to force Allen and two other Negro members to sit in a special section of the balcony of the church. They withdrew and held meetings in a storeroom. Later, when they undertook to build a separate house of worship, and when the elder of St. George's ordered them to desist, Allen writes:

> We told him we had no place of worship, and we did not mean to go to St. George's Church any more, as we were so scandalously treated in the presence of all the congregation present; "and if you deny us your name, you cannot seal up the Scriptures from us, and deny us a name in heaven. We believe heaven is free for all who worship in spirit and truth."[4]

Segregating practices such as these led some Negroes to seek their own worship services where they not only could worship without the humiliations imposed by whites but where they could have services suited to their needs. They wanted and they needed services that would express their hopes and hurts, their sorrows and aspirations, and even though in veiled and covert terms, their unspoken but undying hope for freedom.

The frustrating efforts of blacks to achieve unfettered worship on the one hand and specially adapted worship on the other led to the formation of a number of separate black congregations among Methodists, one in Philadelphia in 1794, named Bethel Church; another in New York City in 1796, named Zion Chapel; others in Baltimore, Long Island, Wilmington, Delaware, and Attleboro, Pennsylvania.[5]

For example, in Baltimore Negroes were members of both Lovely Lane and Centennial M.E. Churches. In 1786 and 1787 the Negro members were required to sit in the galleries and to wait for Communion until after the whites had communed. This aroused strong dissatisfaction, and the Negroes decided to withdraw from the Churches. They held separate prayer meetings in homes for ten years. In 1797 they purchased a building which became Bethel Church. They issued this statement:

> In view of the many inconveniences arising from the white and colored people assembling in public meeting, especially in public worship of Almighty God, we have thought it best to procure for ourselves a separate place in which to assemble, therefore, we invite all our Methodist brethren who think as we do, to worship with us."[6]

But the formation of separate congregations did not end problems for the Negro Methodists. It really created more. For instance, separate congregations required separate church buildings. But who should own the buildings? In Methodism, church buildings and properties are under the control of the Annual Conferences. However, since Negroes, being unordained, could not be voting members of Annual Conferences, it meant that they would have no final control over their properties.

In addition, there was the problem of ordained preachers. If the Negroes were to have separate services, they naturally wanted their own ministers. But the Methodist Church, prior to 1800, would only permit Negroes to be licensed exhorters and local preachers. These, however, were not able to perform the sacraments or other functions of the full ministry. This meant that even in their separate congregations Negroes had to have white preachers for full religious service. They were willing to accept the white preachers, but they had varying experiences with them. Some white preachers were understanding and responsible, and rendered faithful, efficient service. Others took the

Negro work with indifference or reluctance. Some others were antagonistic and domineering and seemed bent upon the subjection and humiliation of the black members.

This welter of feelings and forces, strivings and frustrations naturally led to actions that were contradictory and confused. Indeed, many of the racial problems that have plagued Methodism for two hundred years and Christianity for two thousand are to be found in Methodism's first fifty years. How these conflicting issues led to separation can be clearly seen in the histories of two separate black Methodist congregations, each of which became the focal unit in the formation of two separate black denominations.

At the time that Allen was mistreated in St. George's Church, he was a free Negro, but he had not always been. In his autobiography he states: "I was born in the year of our Lord 1760, on February 14, a slave to Benjamin Chew, of Philadelphia, Chief Justice of Pennsylvania."[7] When still a child his father, mother, and four children were sold into Delaware, near Dover. Fortunately for Allen the new master was a good master, kind and considerate of his slaves when compared with others. Allen says he was more like a father than a slave master. In fact, his treatment of his slaves was so considerate that he was criticized for it by his neighbors. Allen lived with his master until he was in his early twenties.[8]

Meanwhile, the master fell heavily in debt. He was not able to pay for the slaves he bought from Benjamin Chew, and he therefore had to sell Allen's mother and three children. (She had several other children after leaving Chew.) There is no further mention of his mother in Allen's writings. This was the second time that the family had been broken by sale. This separation of families was one of the most brutal aspects of slavery. Yet a sensitive person like Richard Allen had become so inured to such treatment that it is taken almost as a matter of course.[9]

In his autobiography Allen gives no indication of his education. It could have been that under the temperate conditions in which he lived, he learned the elementary aspects of the three "R's," reading, writing, and arithmetic.

At seventeen, Allen was converted. It was a typical Methodist conversion. He says:

> I was awakened and brought to see myself poor wretched and undone, and without the mercy of God, must be lost. Shortly after I obtained mercy through the blood of Christ, and was constrained to exhort my old companions to seek the Lord.

For a while after this, however, he doubted the genuineness of his conversion and

> went with my head bowed down for many days . . . I was tempted to believe there was no mercy for me : . . one night I thought hell would be my portion . . . I cried unto Him who delighted to hear the prayers of a poor sinner; and, all of a sudden, my dungeon shook, my chains flew off, and "Glory to God!" I cried. My soul was filled. I cried, "Enough! For me the Savior died!"[10]

After conversion Allen joined a Methodist class that met "in the forest." His master permitted him and his brother to go to meetings every other Thursday evening. In appreciation for this kindness on the master's part, the two brothers worked extra hours to see that the crops were kept up to and ahead of schedule. As has been said, the master was criticized for his kindly treatment of his slaves, therefore Richard and his brother agreed that they would do their work so well that they would show the neighbors that religion and kindness paid off in the treatment of slaves, and made the slaves better and not worse. Here is a direct indication of Allen's high integrity and self-sacrificial loyalty.

Richard not only attended Methodist preaching meetings, but he induced his master to have preaching in his, the master's, home. One preacher who held service in the home was Freeborn Garrettson, one of the greatest of the early evangelists and a strong opponent of slavery. Garrettson preached from the text "Thou art weighed in the balance and art found wanting," and he classed slaveholders among those who were "wanting." Allen's master was deeply touched. Shortly after this he gave Richard and his brother the option to buy their freedom for sixty pounds in gold and silver, or two thousand dollars Continental money.

If Richard Allen's account is correct, we have here a most remarkable incident. It is one of those unexpected, unpredictable happenings that occur in most unlikely circumstances. Allen's master permitted the two brothers to leave the farm and go where they would seeking work to pay him for their freedom. Here was implicit trust of a master in his slaves, and here was perfect integrity on the slaves' part to be faithful to their obligation and not seek escape. It indicates how highest virtue can be found sometimes in most unpromising conditions.

Richard left his master's house with regret. He had to work long and hard to earn the money with which to buy his freedom. He cut wood, worked in a brickyard, drove a wagon hauling salt in the Revolutionary War. Eventually he succeeded and the day of his freedom came. "It had often been impressed upon my mind," he says,

> that I should one day enjoy freedom, for slavery is a bitter pill, notwithstanding we had a good master. But when we would think our day's work is never done; we often thought that after our master's death we were liable to be sold to the highest bidder, as he was much in debt, and thus my troubles were much increased, and I was often brought to weep between the porch and the altar. But I have reason to bless my dear Lord that a door was opened unexpectedly, for me to buy time and enjoy my liberty.[11]

With his freedom attained, he was now able to travel, to work, and to preach. He was a licensed exhorter. This gave him authority to preach wherever hearers could be assembled. He preached in the state of Delaware (1783) and, following that, for several months in New Jersey. Here he met and worked with the mighty evangelist Benjamin Abbott. Allen was deeply impressed with Abbott and looked upon the evangelist as a "friend and father." In 1784 he made his way from New Jersey to Pennsylvania, preaching, getting conversions, and enjoying happy relationships with the people. In Radford Township, near Philadelphia, for example, he relates:

> They invited me to stay till Sabbath day and preach for them. I agreed to do so, and preached on Sabbath day to a large congregation, of different persuasions, and my dear Lord was with me, and I believe there were many souls cut to the heart, and were added to the ministry. They insisted on me to stay longer with

them. I was frequently called upon by many, inquiring what they should do to be saved. I pointed them to prayer and supplication at the throne of grace, and to make use of all manner of prayer, and pointed them to the invitation of the Lord and Savior Jesus Christ who had said, "Come unto me all ye that labor and are heavy laden, and I will give you rest." Glory to God! and now I know that he was a God at hand not far off. I preached my farewell sermon and left these dear people. It was a time of visitation from above. Many were the slain of the Lord. Seldom did I experience such a time of mourning and lamentation among the people. There were but few colored people in the neighborhood—the most of my congregation white. Some said, "This man must be a man of God. I never heard such preaching before."[12]

Allen's biographers agree that he was not a great orator and that his preaching was not noted for eloquence. But people were impressed with the sincerity and fervor of his messages and with his practicality. People followed him for his helpfulness and his Christian leadership. He was a leader more than a preacher.[13]

Richard Allen was solidly rooted in the Methodist tradition. He was aflame with the urgency to save "lost" mankind from the impending wrath of God. He preached for conversions, and was successful.

In 1784 the General Conference of Methodism met in Baltimore. This was the celebrated "Christmas Conference," in which the Methodist Episcopal Church was formed. Francis Asbury was consecrated there a Superintendent by Dr. Thomas Coke who previously had been consecrated by John Wesley. Both men later were called "Bishops," giving American Methodism its episcopal character. It was here that Methodism began to ordain its preachers, giving the preachers the right to serve the sacraments, and making the American church independent of England.

Richard Allen was aware of the Conference and its significance. Whether or not he attended as a spectator or visitor is not known. He did say that "many of the ministers were set apart in Holy Orders at this Conference, and were said to be entitled to the gown; and I have thought that religion has been declining in the Church ever since."[14]

In 1785 Allen traveled with evangelist Richard Whatcoat on

the Baltimore circuit. He also preached for a while in Baltimore. It was at this time that Bishop Asbury sent for him, and proposed that Allen travel with him, not only in the North, but also in the slave "countries" or states of the South. Allen did not go. In telling why he says:

> Rev. Bishop Asbury sent for me to meet him at Henry Gaff's. I did so. He told me he wished me to travel with him. He told me that in the slave countries, Carolina and other places, I must not intermix with the slaves, and I would frequently have to sleep in his carriage, and he would allow me my victuals and clothes. I told him that I would not travel with him on those conditions. He asked me my reasons. I told him if I was taken sick who was to support me? and that I thought my people ought to lay up something while they were able, to support themselves in time of sickness and old age. He said that was as much as he got, his victuals and clothes. I told him he could be taken care of, let his afflictions be as they were, or let him be taken sick where he would, he could be taken care of; but I doubted whether it would be the case with myself. He smiled, and told me he would give me from then until he returned from the eastward to make up my mind, which would be about three months. But I made up my mind that I would not accept his proposals.[15]

Here may be seen Allen's practical turn of mind as well as his ability to make decisions and hold to them.

Leaving Baltimore, 1785, Allen returned to Pennsylvania. He preached in Radnor, near Philadelphia, until February 1786, when the elder at St. George's Church called him to preach there. He says: "I strove to preach as well as I could, but it was a great cross for me . . ."[16]

Allen saw the need for religious development among his people in Philadelpha, and he felt this could best be achieved in a house of worship of their own. He had only three persons who were willing to join with him in erecting a place of worship. These were the Reverend Absalom Jones, William White, and Darius Jinnings, all members of St. George's.

They organized in 1787 the Free African Society, a benevolent association which, while having economic and social improvement objectives, also included religious activities, such as prayer meetings and preaching services. He adds, "the Lord blessed our endeavors, and many souls were awakened." The elders of St. George's strenuously opposed the separate building, one elder even using "very degrading and insulting language." But Allen's tenacity showed itself. He said, "We viewed the forlorn state of our colored brethren, and saw that they were destitute of a place of worship." At St. George's, with their increasing numbers, "they were considered a nuisance."[17]

A climax was reached one Sunday morning. In Allen's words:

A number of us usually sat on seats placed around the wall, and on Sabbath morning we went to church, and the sexton stood at the door and told us to go in the gallery. He told us to go and we would see where to sit. We expected to take the seats over the ones we formerly occupied below, not knowing any better. We took those seats. Meeting had begun, and they were nearly done singing, and just as we got to the seats the elder said, "Let us pray." We had not been long upon our knees before I heard considerable scuffling and loud talking. I raised my head up and saw one of the trustees, H_____ M_____, having hold of the Rev. Absalom Jones, pulling him off his knees, and saying, "You must get up; you must not kneel here." Mr. Jones replied, "Wait until prayer is over." Mr. H_____ M_____ said, "No, you must get up now, or I will call for aid and force you away." Mr. Jones said, "Wait until prayer is over, and I will get up and trouble you no more." With that he beckoned to one of the other trustees, Mr. L_____ S_____, to come to his assistance. He came and went to William White to pull him up. By this time prayer was over, and we all went out of the church in a body, and they were no more plagued by us in the church. This raised a great excitement and inquiry among the citizens, insomuch that I believe they were ashamed of their conduct.[18]

The members of the Society rented a storeroom, where they could worship by themselves. The elders continued to oppose their efforts, and even threatened them with expulsion if they did not desist. Allen and his group continued, however, and began a public solicitation for funds with which to build a house of worship. They were assisted in their efforts by two friendly whites, Dr. Benjamin Rush, a distinguished citizen, a Quaker and a strong abolitionist; and Mr. Robert Ralston, a merchant and philanthropist, who served as treasurer for the group. They had "great success," the first day raising $360.00.[19]

Yet, as Allen says, "the elder of the Methodist Church still pursued us." The black members replied in effect that they had not violated any Conference or Discipline rule in seeking a suitable place to worship, and that they would not return to St. George's since they "were treated so scandalously in the presence of all the congregation present. 'And if you deny us your name, you cannot seal up the Scripture from us, and deny us a name in heaven.'"

The effort for the church building was successful. A lot was purchased, and Richard Allen "put the first spade into the ground to dig the cellar." Their problems were not over, however. In 1794 the question arose as to what denomination the group should be affiliated with. Allen and his friend and co-worker, Absalom Jones, who also was a licensed preacher in the Methodist Church, wanted to remain with the Methodist denomination. Allen wanted this because, as he said:

> Notwithstanding we had been violently persecuted by the elder, we were in favor of being attached to the Methodist Connection, for I was confident there was no religious sect or denomination that would suit the capacity of the colored people as well as the Methodist, for the plain and simple Gospel suits best for any people, for the unlearned can understand, and the learned are sure to understand; and the reason that the Methodist is so successful in the awakening and conversion of the colored people is the plain doctrine and having a good discipline.[20]

But Allen and Jones were the only two. The majority favored going to the Episcopal Church. When this was apparent, Absalom Jones decided to go with the majority and to become their leader. Bishop William White took them in, ordained Jones a deacon, and in 1804 ordained him a priest. Absalom Jones thus became the first Negro ordained in the Protestant Episcopal Church.

Although Jones and Allen parted company in their denominational affiliation in 1794 they did not part in friendship. They remained firm friends. Jones was the older of the two by fourteen years. Jones was well known and established in Philadelphia when Allen came in 1787. In the terrible yellow fever epidemic of 1793 in Philadelphia, which killed hundreds, Jones and Allen worked together heroically to tend the sick, bury the dead, and render all possible service to the victims, most of whom were white. They were commended by the mayor of the city for their work.[21] Jones was more conciliatory than Allen and better educated. In their personalities they complemented each other and remained friends until Jones's death in 1818.

Of the group that joined the Episcopal Church in 1788 there were many who were dissatisfied with that type of worship. They wanted the Methodist service. Allen proposed building a place of worship for them on his own ground at his own expense. This would create a separate black Methodist church. When the elders of St. George's learned of this, "they opposed it with all their might, insisting that the house should be made over to the Conference," and if this were not done, then the elders would publish in the newspapers that Allen and his group in seeking funds for their building were "imposing on the public, as we were not Methodists." Allen however, went on with the building, and in 1794 it was completed. Bishop Asbury was invited "to open the house for Divine service; which invitation he accepted, and the house was named Bethel."[22]

Elder McClaskey of St. George's proposed that the church should be incorporated so that they might receive legacies and other donations. He offered to draw up the articles of incorporation for them. They agreed to this, but soon found that he had done so in a way that put them again under the Conference, and "we were brought under bondage to the white preachers." In this situation, Allen says, they "experienced grievances too numerous to mention."

Allen became local or assistant pastor of Bethel Church in 1794. The tug of war with white Methodist elders continued for nearly twenty years. During these years Negro Methodists in other cities were having the same problems. In Baltimore, for example, the Negroes had been forced to withdraw in 1786 and organize a church for themselves. There were similar churches in Wilmington, Delaware, Attleboro, Pennsylvania, and Salem, New Jersey.

Richard Allen traveled among these separate, disowned, and struggling groups. He counseled and inspired them, and kept them in the Methodist faith. He became without question the leader and the central personality around whom centered the struggle for unfettered worship on the one hand and a certain amount of special privilege on the other. To a large degree the story of the move toward separation in Methodism is the story of Richard Allen.

The attitude of the elders in St. George's and many white Methodist laymen besides is difficult to understand. Negroes had been part and parcel of the Methodist movement from its beginning. They had shared as fully as they could in its development and had contributed of their meager resources to its support. Allen says that slaves would work often until midnight in little gardens trying to earn a few extra pennies to give to Methodist preachers.[23] Methodists sought Negro members, and listed them proudly in the statistical reports. Yet they insisted upon segregating the Negro members in the worship services, and seemed to resent the effort to avoid segregation. When the Negroes attempted to set up Methodist churches of their own the white elders opposed the efforts, demanding that they return to the white church under segregated conditions. The claim that Negro property should be under the Conference is certainly legitimate, but in the light of actual conditions, it seems reasonable that an exception could have been allowed.

It was the overriding attitude of whites along with the determined if sometimes apologetic attitude of blacks that led Richard Allen, Daniel Coker, and James Champion to call a meeting of disaffected churches to meet in Philadelphia on April 9, 1816. "Delegates from Baltimore and other places met those from Philadelphia, and taking into consideration their grievances, and in order to secure their privileges, promote union and harmony among themselves, it was resolved, 'that the people of Philadelphia, Baltimore, etc., etc., should become one body, under the name of the African Methodist Episcopal Church.'"[24]

CHAPTER VI

The First Great Separate: The African Methodist Episcopal Church

BY THE YEAR 1816 there were at least seven black separate Methodist churches in the states of Pennsylvania, New York, New Jersey, Maryland, and Delaware. There may have been more. Some had been in existence, like Bethel Church in Baltimore, for twenty years or more. They all had one thing in common. They were trying to find a satisfactory situation for themselves within the Methodist movement.

The members of these churches were for the most part free Negroes. They had joined the Methodist Church in the conviction that here was a faith that could transcend sin and personal failings, and they had joined in the hope that this marvelous new faith could somehow transcend social barriers, even in a society that harbored human slavery, and somehow set up at least one area where all could be one in the body or fellowship of Jesus Christ.

For a time it seemed that their hopes might be realized, especially in Methodism's early days and in the years of the Revolutionary War. But now in the nineteenth century, when the War was over, slavery was becoming more and more entrenched, when the Church was lowering its voice of protest against slavery, and when caste patterns and racial segregation were becoming accepted and fixed in the Church just as in society, the black Methodists found themselves disillusioned, disappointed, and resentful. The separate black churches felt the need of getting together, talking over their particular situations, and deciding on what was best for them to do. It was in this spirit that Richard Allen, Daniel Coker, and James Champion wrote a letter of invitation to other churches to come together in Philadelphia for a meeting on April 9, 1816.

The step was taken reluctantly.[1] Black Methodists did not prefer to separate completely from the mother Church. Their love of the faith was deep and genuine, and they always were grateful for the spiritual awakening that Methodism had given them. They did want consideration for their special needs as a disadvantaged racial group, such as special rights in owning and controlling their church properties, their right to have ordained black preachers, and the opportunity to have from time to time services by themselves. But these privileges would not require separation. These conditions had already been met in some cases by specially drawn agreements or "supplements." The Negro members, however, were frankly humiliated by the discriminations and segregations imposed upon them in the worship services and other aspects of church life, and they were puzzled at the attitude of some Methodists who wanted them to continue in the Church under the humiliating conditions.

This conflict of hopes and feelings continued for almost three decades leading up to 1816. It was in 1787 that the group of black Methodists withdrew from St. George's Church in Philadelphia. From then to April 1816 covers about twenty-nine years. The impression is generally given that when Absalom Jones was pulled from his knees on a Sunday in November 1787, Richard Allen went out forthwith and started the A.M.E. Church. Nothing could be further from the facts.

Three men were involved in the pulling-up incident: Absalom Jones, Richard Allen, and William White. They did pull Jones, they started to pull White, but the prayer ended, and they all left before they got to Allen. The three went out and, as Allen says, "we all went out of the church in a body, and they were no more plagued with us in the church."[2]

These three men set about to secure a meeting house where black people could worship together without humiliation. The first church that resulted was an Episcopal Church, St. Thomas, of which Absalom Jones became rector. The second church was a Methodist church, all black, led by Richard Allen, but pastored by white elders from St. George's. St. Thomas Church was dedicated in 1794. Bethel Church was dedicated two weeks later in 1794 by Bishop Asbury. Thus, it was seven years, from 1787 to 1794, before a black Methodist church was organized. Bethel continued in the Methodist fold for twenty-two years. During those years the Bethelites tried in many ways to get along with the white elders of St. George's. Dispute after dispute would arise, however, sometimes over the rights of the elder, or over pay for the elder's services, or over personal problems of the members. On two occasions the Bethelites had to go to law over issues. But still the black members held on to their Methodist affiliation, still hoping for some kind of workable solution.

Bethel in Philadelphia was not alone. The black Methodists of Baltimore were having a very similar experience. In two Baltimore churches in 1786 and 1787 the blacks were required to sit in the gallery and were told to wait until after the white members had communed. This the blacks resented. They withdrew and began to hold prayer meetings by themselves in private homes. In 1797 they purchased a building and named the church "Bethel." They drew up a resolution which said: "In view of the many inconveniences arising from the white and colored people assembling in public-meeting, especially in public worship of Almighty God, we have thought it best to procure for ourselves a separate place in which to assemble, therefore, we invite all our Methodist brethren, who think as we do, to worship with us."[3]

Daniel Coker, an ordained Methodist preacher, joined the Bethel Society in 1801. He was born a slave in Maryland. He was of mixed parentage, his father was a slave of Edward Coker, and his mother an English woman who was an indentured servant to Coker. As a child Daniel Coker learned to read through his friendship with his master's son. While still young he ran away to New York State where he found freedom. There he was ordained deacon by Bishop Asbury. He later returned to Baltimore, purchased his freedom from his former master, and took over the leadership of Bethel Church. He also opened a school for black children in Baltimore which was the first such school in Baltimore, and which numbered at one time more than a hundred and fifty students.[4]

Coker was an outstanding leader in many ways. He published a pamphlet in 1810, probably the first by a black man in America, entitled *"A Dialogue Between a Virginian and an African Minister."* He soon became acquainted with Richard Allen, and worked with him in many ways. He maintained a close touch between Bethel Church in Baltimore and Bethel in Philadelphia. When Bethel in Philadelphia gained a favorable decision preventing the elder of St. George's from taking over Bethel's pulpit, Daniel Coker preached and published a sermon on January 21, 1816, celebrating the victory.[5]

With the close contact between Bethel in Baltimore and Bethel in Philadelphia, it is no wonder that Coker joined with Richard Allen in April 1816 in the call for the meeting in Philadelphia. He played a leading part in getting the independent African Methodist movement started in America.

Again, quite similar was the case in Wilmington, Delaware. Under the leadership of the Reverend Peter Spencer and William Anderson the Negro members of Asbury M.E. Church withdrew and formed an African church which later came to be known as the Union American Methodist Episcopal Church. Spencer wrote: "We thought that we might have more satisfaction of mind than we then had if we were to unite together and build a house for ourselves; which we did the same year. The Lord gave us the favor and good will of all religious denominations and they all freely did lend us help and by their good grace we got a house to worship in."[6]

This church was established in 1805. For several years after this there were troubles with the elders of Asbury Church. The church finally separated on September 18, 1813. They drew up articles of association for the "African Union Church in Wilmington, Delaware."[7]

Separate congregations had also been formed in Attleboro, Pennsylvania, and Salem, New Jersey. The reasons for their formation were similar to the others, the decision of the white churches to impose segregated arrangements on the Negro members, and the desire of these members to escape the humiliations. There were also two strong and growing separate churches in New York City. But since they pursued a separate course of development, their case is treated in detail in another chapter.

Here then in 1816 were several separate Methodist congregations, black to be sure, but loyal to the Methodist movement. All were reluctant to leave the Methodist Church, but all were frustrated and wearied from the constant struggle with the Methodist elders and congregations over their desire to enjoy the few special arrangements that their life situation demanded.

Through the years these churches had maintained contact with each other, especially through their preachers. For example, Daniel Coker had been closely associated with Richard Allen in his struggles for the independence of his congregation. Therefore, when the invitation to a meeting in Philadelphia was issued in 1816, it was natural for the five churches to respond.

The meeting opened on April 9, 1816. According to Bishop Daniel A. Payne, historiographer of the A.M.E. Church, sixteen persons were present: from Philadelphia, Richard Allen, Jacob Tapsico, Clayton Durham, James Champion, and Thomas Webster, all ministers; from Baltimore, Daniel Coker, Richard Williams, and Henry Harden, ministers, and Stephen Hill, Edward Williams, and Nicholas Gillard, laymen; the Reverend Peter Spencer from Wilmington, Delaware; Jacob March, William Anderson, and Edward Jackson, ministers, from Attleboro, Pennsylvania; and Reuben Cuff, layman, of Salem, New Jersey.

A full record of the meeting has not been preserved. Whether such a record ever existed is not known. We do have record of a few significant actions taken at this meeting. First, Richard Allen was chosen chairman, and Daniel Coker, vice-chairman. Stephen

Hill served as secretary, assisted by Richard Allen, Jr. Secondly, a resolution setting themselves apart as a separate Methodist denomination was adopted:

> Resolved, that the people of Philadelphia, Baltimore, and other places who may unite with them shall become one body under the name and style of the African Methodist Episcopal Church of the United States of America and that the book of Discipline of the Methodist Episcopal Church be adopted as our Discipline until further orders, except that portion relating to Presiding Elders.[8]

This resolution was offered by Stephen Hill, who, although a layman, made a large contribution to the work of the convention.

Thirdly, since they had set themselves up as a separate church, they needed a ministry. Several persons were ordained elders, including Richard Allen. They knew that the ordination of these elders was quite as valid as those of the Christmas Conference of 1784.

Fourth, an election was held for the office of bishop. When the meeting convened, three men were most prominent in the activities. They were Richard Allen, Daniel Coker, and Stephen Hill. Daniel Coker was the best educated and most brilliant. The election was held on the first day, April 9. Coker was elected. On the next day, the tenth, however, he declined the office. The reasons for this action are not known, and because of lack of records, may never be. Several explanations have been suggested. One was that Coker was too light-skinned to head an organization of blacks, and the blacks resented this.[9] Daniel Payne accepts this view in his *Recollections of Seventy Years*.[10] This is still questionable, however, for Coker had had no trouble in his leadership of the Baltimore church or in his collaboration with Richard Allen.

There is another account that Allen and Coker were both elected on the ninth. Allen was not present at the time. Upon returning the next day, he at once said that two bishops were not needed and declined the honor. His statement created much confusion; a second election was held, and since he was preferred by a majority of the members, he was elected.[11]

Although Coker did not retain the bishopric, he did play a great part in bringing the churches together and in completing the organization in Philadelphia. He takes his place as one of the founders of the A.M.E. Church.

After his election on the tenth, the next day, April 11, 1816, Richard Allen "was solemnly set apart for the Episcopal office by prayer, and the imposition of the hands of five regularly ordained ministers, at which time the general convention held in Philadelphia did unanimously receive the said Bishop Allen as their Bishop, being fully satisfied of the validity of his Episcopal ordination."[12] Absalom Jones was present at Allen's consecration.

The choice of Richard Allen to head the new organization was the most fortunate thing that could have happened. It at once gave the new church Allen's prestige and respectability, which were considerable.

In 1816 Richard Allen was one of the most substantial and respected black citizens in Philadelphia. While not rich, his personal estate was said to be about $40,000. This was a tremendous sum for a black man at that time. He was a successful businessman, operating at one time three thriving businesses in addition to being pastor of Bethel Church. But more than this, he was a public-spirited citizen who had shared generously in every cause affecting the welfare of the city. His service, along with Absalom Jones, in the yellow fever epidemic of 1793; his leadership, again with Jones, in recruiting black workers and soldiers when Philadelphia was threatened with attack in the War of 1812, all held him high in the public regard of the city. Any cause with which he was connected would at once enjoy public acceptance and public confidence.

Richard Allen was not a radical or a revolutionary. He was thoroughly progressive and completely dedicated to the progress of his people. Choosing him to head the new denomination relieved it of the charge of extremism, revolution or subversion, or attack on the established order. It spared the Church a great deal of opposition and harassment that it might have had, and which could have been disastrous in the early days of the Church. Allen's election went far to place the Church in a tradition of respectability. It saved the Church from the image of buffoonery which usually fell upon black efforts.

In another respect Allen's election was most fortunate. He was the undisputed leader of widest influence among blacks. On numerous occasions he had sacrificially led his people in constructive projects. His work in starting and building Bethel Church and his leadership of the church for twenty-two years is an example. On several occasions he helped the church financially, at one time putting up $11,700 of his own funds to save the building. He was widely known as "Father Allen" because of the high regard of his fellow blacks. If anyone would be able to guide the new church through the troubled times of its origin, that person would be Richard Allen.[13]

There is reason to believe that the sixteen men who met on April 9 were aware of the potential greatness of what they were doing. To be sure, five small, struggling churches with a total membership of 1,067 coming together to see what they could do to survive is not an impressive beginning for a denomination. Yet they thought large and planned large, thus making possible the tremendous later development of their Church. In doing this they established a number of "firsts" for black people in America. For example, they produced the first ordained black elders in the Methodist movement. They produced the first black Bishop in Protestantism. They made possible the first general church officers, such as a book steward, at a time when Negroes were forbidden to read. They set up the first interstate organization by blacks in America. This was an incredibly adventurous and progressive step, giving Negroes the opportunity to demonstrate that they had the capacity to carry on such an organization. They thus opened a new era of possibilities for Negroes. They did this at a time when interstate travel and communication among blacks was dangerous and difficult. The restrictions on travel by slaves and free blacks, and the possibility of capture by slave raiders made the thought of interstate activity a venture requiring high courage and dedication. Above all, they were demonstrating that Negroes could conduct a national church on a respectable level in the midst of slavery and the limitations of the freedman's status.[14] In a very real sense April 9, 1816, is a landmark in the cultural development of Negroes in America.

In the deepest sense what the delegates did in Philadelphia was what the members at home wanted. When the delegates returned to their churches they were cheered. Peter Spencer was not in accord with some of the actions in Philadelphia. He refused to join the A.M.E. Church. He returned to Wilmington and tried to make his Union American Methodist Episcopal Church into a denomination. It has grown very little.

THE FIRST DECADE

The new Church at once began to grow. Annual Conferences were held in Philadelphia and in Baltimore in the years between 1817 and 1820. The meetings were small, and they were held in private homes. The records for the Philadelphia meetings in these years are either missing or very fragmentary. The failure to preserve or make careful records may be due to several factors. For one, as has already been said, the new Church was small, and unimpressive in its beginning. It was little more at first than a fellowship of a few struggling churches. Secondly, most of the leaders were uneducated men. There were a few like Richard Allen and Stephen Hill who could read and write. There were very few, if any, like Daniel Coker, who could teach school. For the first year or two the minutes were taken by Richard Allen, Jr., a lad of fifteen, who was able to read and write well. The minutes greatly improved when Joseph M. Corr was made secretary in 1824. A third factor is that many movements in their origins are uncertain and faltering, and the accounts of their early histories are often not put into writing until a later time when the movements have become established. Even then the histories are written from the recollections of the early participants. White Methodism was fortunate to have faithful journalists like Wesley and Asbury who kept careful records of each day's happenings themselves, and also set this pattern for their colleagues. With the early black Methodists, however, because of lack of education, this kind of record keeping just was not possible.

The records of the Baltimore annual conference for 1818–20

are better than those of Philadelphia. From these we can better
see the young Church in action. Richard Allen, the Bishop,
presided at all conferences. He continued, however, as pastor of
Bethel Church in Philadelphia. In 1818 Daniel Coker was expelled
from the connection. His offense has never been made known. He
was, however, carefully tried, and the action against him was
taken with regret. He was fully restored to membership one year
later in 1819. Don Carlos Hall, a layman, was elected "Book
Steward." While reading for black people at the time, whether
slave or free, was at a low ebb, the creation of the Book Steward's office indicates the academic aspirations of the new Church.

In the Philadelphia Conference in 1818 five preachers were admitted on trial and six were taken into full connection. Morris
Brown, James Champion, and Jacob Tapsico were ordained
elders. The first of these, Morris Brown, played a large part in the
early development of the Church and became the second Bishop.

The growth of the Church in the two years from 1816 to 1818
is seen in the number of charges as well as the number of
members. They were:

Charges	Members
Philadelphia	3,311
Baltimore	1,066
Salem, N.J.	110
Trenton	73
Princeton	33
Snow Hill	56
Woodbury	29
Attleboro	41
New Hope	33
Frankfort	28
Westchester	46
Plemeth	8
Whitemarsh	29
Bridgeport	6
Brunswick	40
Charleston, S.C.	1,848
Total	6,757[15]

In 1816 the Church began with five churches and 1,067 members. In two years its membership had increased sixfold.

The Church was growing so rapidly that in 1822 at the Baltimore Conference it was felt that Bishop Allen should have an assistant. Three men were nominated for the post: Morris Brown, Henry Harden, and Jacob Matthews. Votes were taken in the Baltimore and in the Philadelphia Conferences. In both cases Jacob Matthews received the highest number of votes, but for some reason he was never consecrated and he did not serve.[16] Daniel Payne says: "In this instance we have an evidence that election to the episcopal office does not constitute any person a Bishop. 'The laying on of hands' must follow election in order that the individual may be a veritable Bishop."[17]

Growth of the Church continued steadily. By 1822 there were 43 charges with 7,257 members. Geographical expansion was as remarkable as the numerical. There were charges as far south as Washington, D.C., and as far west as Pittsburgh. The western work was under the direction of the Reverend William Paul Quinn, a courageous and tireless worker who led in establishing the Church in what was then known as "the Western Territories."

The Church was also expanding to the North. In 1819 Bishop Allen sent a young preacher, William Lambert, to New York City as a missionary to establish an A.M.E. church there. Lambert rented a schoolroom on Mott Street and soon had a church of twenty members organized. In 1820 Bishop Allen went to New York to dedicate the church.

The choice of Lambert for this work was unfortunate. He had formerly been a member of Zion Church in New York City. He left Zion and went to Asbury Church, another separate black Methodist church in New York. He decided that he wanted to preach. Asbury Church would not license him, but recommended that he apply to Bishop Allen in Philadelphia. Bishop Allen took him in, and after a year sent him back to New York with the commission to set up an A.M.E. church there. The members of Zion Church resented this. They felt that Allen was unfairly invading their territory and was using a former Zionite to do it. Up to this time there were many Zionites who felt kindly toward Allen and his movement. But when Lambert came promoting the new A.M.E. denomination in New York, they not only cooled in their attitude toward the Allen movement, but actually opposed it. They denied Lambert the use of the Zion and Asbury pulpits, and they forbade their ministers to sit with Bishop Allen in the dedicatory service of the Mott Street Church. It is possible that had Bishop Allen chosen a different person to promote the work in New York, relations between the A.M.E.'s and the New York Zionists (who later became the A.M.E. Zion Church) might have been different and might have prevented the formation of the black Methodist denomination.[18]

But in spite of this difficulty, the work continued to grow. The Reverend Henry Harden succeeded Lambert, and the membership increased. Two brothers, Benjamin and Peter Croger, organized a church in Brooklyn. They formerly had been in the Methodist Episcopal Church, but withdrew for the same reasons as Philadelphia and Baltimore. A Society was started in White Plains, New York, and a Society as far north as New Bedford, Massachusetts. In 1822 the Church had a membership of 9,888 members and 140 preachers, 14 of whom were elders.

Thus by the end of its first ten years, the A.M.E. Church had experienced truly remarkable geographical expansion: south to Washington, north to New Bedford, Massachusetts, and west to Pittsburgh. It had grown in numbers from 1,067 in 1816 to 7,637 in 1826. This was a decrease from the year 1822, which was due to the loss of the church in Charleston.

This expansion in members and preachers is all the more remarkable when it is realized that it was done by persons who had little or no formal education. In an organization stretching over many states, and embracing thousands of people, a lack of education, with the inability to read and write, makes communication difficult, following of procedures irregular, and transaction of business uncertain. Daniel Payne, the Church's first historian, states:

> In addition to the burdens imposed upon the youthful church by the outside world, she had to contend with dissension and turbulence within herself. Many of her ministers and elders were impatient under the rules of the Church, and frequent breaches of discipline took place. These ministers were unaccustomed to the laws governing the progress and purposes of the Church—unaccustomed

to command or to rule, and with a peculiar notion of the powers of their office, which were often exercised in a degree calculated to lead to complaint from the members of the Conference. As a result we find the time of that body occupied by listening to, and the rectification of complaints which should never have come before the Conference . . .

Perhaps the lack of literary improvement in the ministry might be considered the fault of the individual minister; but it must not be forgotten that the men appointed to the positions of elders and deacons were all full grown, and had reached manhood before they were so appointed. Many of them had had no opportunities to lay the foundation of an education, even of the most rudimentary kind in their youth, the time in which an education should be commenced. In manhood, and while acting in the various offices of the Church, their efforts had to be engrossed in the many practical cares of the world. Earning one's bread by the sweat of the brow is not conducive to any efforts in the way of improving literary attainments. Many of the ministers did improve, however, and showed that improvement in the course of their lives. Others did not advance far in the paths of literary acquirements.[19]

One of the most regrettable results of lack of education is that it results in poor records, so that much of history, the intimate, human side of history, is forever lost. But in spite of educational handicaps, the Church not only expanded but laid firmly its organizational foundation.

The expansion is more remarkable still because it required travel, and, as has been previously said, travel for blacks, whether slave or free, in the first years of the nineteenth century was difficult and hazardous. The common carriers, such as stagecoaches and boats, either refused to carry blacks or segregated them to inconvenient and uncomfortable accommodations. Or if one traveled with his own horse or team, there was always the danger of being seized by some outlaw slave-catcher who would take a free Negro and accuse him of being a runaway slave. If the Negro could not prove his freedom, which in a prejudiced judicial system was sometimes difficult, he could be taken South and sold into slavery. This once nearly happened to Richard Allen, and it was only through the interest of a friendly white sheriff that he was saved from such tragedy.[20]

In the first decade the Church grew, but it also suffered two serious setbacks. Failure to reach an accord with the members of Zion and Asbury churches in New York City denied the A.M.E. Church these bodies and their membership.

The most serious setback, however, was the loss of the church in Charleston, South Carolina. This church, with about 1,800 members, was founded by Morris Brown. Born in Charleston in 1770, of mixed parentage, he was converted at an early age and secured a license to preach in the Methodist Church. He at once started a movement for a church for Africans, and soon had a sizable membership. In 1816 he heard of the A.M.E. movement in Philadelphia. His church sent him to Philadelphia where he was warmly received by Bishop Allen. He was ordained a deacon in 1817 and an elder in the A.M.E. Church in 1818. He returned to Charleston, and took his church into the A.M.E. Connection. He soon had a membership of over 1,800.

In addition to preaching, Morris Brown was a prosperous boot- and shoemaker. But above all, he was a leader of wide influence. He was especially helpful to slaves, enabling a number of them to purchase their freedom.

In 1822 the Denmark Vesey plot of an insurrection was discovered. Vesey and others were caught and condemned for plotting a rebellion against the slave system. Morris Brown's church was suspected of being one of the meeting places for the conspirators, and he himself as abetting the plot. The charges against him were not proved and he was absolved of all complicity. But even though the insurrection did not occur—it was disclosed shortly before it was scheduled to happen—the recrimination against the conspirators and the colored people of Charleston generally was severe and cruel. Thirty-three men were hanged, a number were banished from the city; meetings among blacks were forbidden; the Methodist Episcopal Church, which was regarded as being friendly to blacks, came into public disfavor, and Methodist preachers were regarded with suspicion; education for both slaves and black freemen was prohibited, and Morris Brown's church was closed.

Because of threats and public disfavor Morris Brown left Charleston in 1822. White friends, among whom was General

James A. Hamilton, later governor of South Carolina, helped him to secure passage on a ship. He went to Philadelphia, and his family followed in 1823. Bishop Allen gave him work in the Church. Because of his zeal and outstanding abilities, he was made assistant to the pastor of Bethel in 1825, assistant to the Bishop in 1826, and he was elected the second Bishop of the A.M.E. Church in 1828.[21]

The closing of the Church in Charleston ended the A.M.E. Church in the Southeast until 1865. It reduced the membership by 1,800 members. But despite the loss, the Church had undergone remarkable growth in its first ten years.

Not the least of significant developments in the first ten years was the coming into the ministry of the Church of a number of men of exceptional abilities. In most cases they were not educated, but they were intelligent and gifted. They also possessed what was more important, great leadership ability. They showed this, of course, in the effective parts they played in the Church's growth and development. Two such men were Morris Brown and William P. Quinn. They were responsible for much of the early development of the Church.

If lack of education in the ministry led to problems in leadership and procedure, lack of education in the membership created problems too. Inability to understand and follow rules meant that preachers were often accused and tried for trivial or false offenses. In the Baltimore Conference of 1826, a preacher was charged with not paying his debts so that his horse had to be sold. After investigation the Conference replied that if the Church had paid the preacher his salary he could have paid his debts, and he consequently would not have lost his horse.[22]

But despite problems, at the end of its first ten years, black Methodism, like white, was soundly on its way with its eyes set firmly on heaven, but with its feet stumbling along the dusty roadway of human nature and weakness.

THE SECOND DECADE—FOREIGN MISSIONS

Very early in its history, the A.M.E. Church began its venture in foreign missions. President Boyer of Haiti invited free Negroes to come to Haiti and settle there. Several members of Bethel

Church, Philadelphia, responded and settled in Port-au-Prince. They met together for worship and set up a church. In 1826 they asked Richard Allen to send them a minister. At the Baltimore Conference of 1827, the Reverend Scipio Beanes volunteered to go. He was examined by a committee of three and was reported as a "fit person to be clothed as a missionary to Hayti." He was then ordained both a deacon and an elder within a week for the mission project. He left for Haiti, and at the next meeting of the Baltimore Conference in 1828 he reported 72 members in a church at Port-au-Prince. His health was not good, however, and he had to return to Baltimore in the next year.

Two years later, in the Baltimore Conference of 1830, two letters were received from the church at Santo Domingo. One letter asked that the A.M.E. Church receive the Reverend Isaac Miller into its ministry and ordain him for the leadership of the church at Semana. The other letter stated that at

> A Annual Conference Held in San daming [sic] by Brother Jacob Roberts, Preacher in charge, the Conference thought to devise Some Ways or means to remedy our deplorable Situation, then entered into a resolution to Send two of our Brothering on to the African Methodist Episcopal Church in North America, that are under the Control of the Affrican Methodist Bishops and conference, for the express perpose to know of them, to know whether they will acknowledge us to be a branch of the said conference, as we have unanimously agreed to submit ourselves to the Desipolin [sic] of the said conference that now is and may be devised hear or hearafter.[23]

After reading the letters the Conference at once voted "to receive Jacob Roberts and Isaac Miller in the African Connection," and that these brethren would return to Santo Domingo as soon as possible. Isaac Miller was to be ordained both deacon and elder, but Jacob Roberts was to be made only a deacon. Why this distinction is not known, especially since Jacob Roberts seems to have held a higher rank in the Santo Domingo church than Miller. The two men were not ordained at Baltimore. Isaac Miller applied later to the Philadelphia Conference, and was ordained both deacon and elder there. No more is known of Jacob Roberts. He evidently was offended at Miller's being made an elder ahead of him, and severed his connection with the A.M.E.

Church. A young man, Richard Robinson, was ordained both deacon and elder for the church at Port-au-Prince in Haiti to carry on the work of the Reverend Scipio Beanes.[24]

Reverend Beanes is a fine example of the devoted foreign missionary. He was born a slave in Maryland in 1793. His master, Dr. Beanes, permitted him to attend school, and in 1818 made him a present of his freedom. He was licensed to preach serving churches on the eastern shore of Maryland. The rigid conditions of his ministry, especially exposure to the extreme cold of winter, broke his health, and he was advised by his physician to seek a warmer climate. This was the reason why in 1827 he asked to be sent to Haiti.

By the end of his first year he had formed a church of 72 members as has been said. Less than a year later it had grown to 182. His health began to fail in Haiti, however, and he returned to Maryland, and took a church at Easton. With improvement in health he went back to Port-au-Prince in 1832 and took up the work again. He added largely to the membership. His illness, however, was fatal. He gradually grew weaker, and died in 1835. His wife had wanted to return to America, but he decided to end his life in Haiti, saying, "Heaven is as near to Port-au-Prince as to Washington." He died with the love and respect of his people. The first attempt at foreign service had been well planted by the young Church.[25]

THE DEATH OF RICHARD ALLEN

When Richard Allen was made Bishop of the new A.M.E. Church in 1816 he was fifty-seven years old. From then until his death in 1831, his years were filled with activity.

As Bishop of the new Church he not only had to plan for its development, but he had to direct it. He had to pass on the men who sought to join the ministry of the new Church. He had to make appointments and assignments, and supervise the pastors to keep them in line with Methodist rules and traditions. Since so many were uneducated, it was easy for them to deviate from rules that they could not read.

He had to oversee the organization of new churches, traveling constantly to serve at dedications and special services. Much of his time was taken in settling conflicts between pastors and people, and sometimes within individual churches. The separation of the Wesley African Methodist Church from Allen's own Bethel Church is a case in point. A dissident group of members led by Jonah Black withdrew from Bethel in 1820 and formed their own congregation. Relations between the two churches worsened and eventually led to a serious law suit in 1823 in which Allen and the Bethelites were the losers.[26] Bishop Allen, of course, had the responsibility of presiding at and conducting the annual Conferences and the quadrennial General Conferences.

At the same time that he was Bishop he was also the pastor of Bethel Church in Philadelphia. This was a large and growing congregation, in Allen's time numbering over five hundred. Following Methodist procedure, the church kept watch over the moral behavior of its members, imposing penalties for infractions. A "Trial" committee made up of church officers met regularly to hear cases. The proceedings were recorded in a "Minute and Trial Book" which is still preserved at the church. On August 19, 1823, for example, there was the case of Morris Dublin, who in the words of the record was "charged by his wife of selling the house holde goods, and some of their belongings to other people, and of taking his cloathes and marketting [them] elsewhere." Brother Dublin's defense was "that there rent was due and he told the landlord, that these was my goods, and to take them for the rent." Mrs. Dublin imposed her own penalty, for he said: "I was going to my work and was taking my wood. She struck me in the head with a brick bat, and cut my head." The decision: "We the Committee have taken the above case into consideration, and are of the opinion that Morris Dublin is guilty of imprudent conduct and he is to no longer hold an official office in the church. But he may remain on trial for 6 months."[27]

On April 15, 1829, the following case was recorded:

A charge brought Against Ann Golden of strikeing Ann Harris. A Harris say. that A. G. told the Nabourghers that she got Drunk & there could be no peace for her. I told her that it was not true. She called me a black infernall beach & said that I struck her child & she struck me in the mouth. A. Golden say. that A. H. struck her child About an old peace of carpet that thrown in the St. because my child tried to get it before her. I whent to talk with her about it. She denied & called me a black infurnall hornery Negor. I told her if she called me that againe I would strike her & [she] did it & I struck her.[28]

On July 22, 1829, there was "A charge brought against Isaac Cook by Samuel Valentin for imprudent conversation saying that the Trustees and Church might all go to hell, & 2ndly for drinking too much ardent spirits.

"The Committee entered into a due deliberation, and found him guilty of a violation of discipline in indulging in sinful words."[29]

Carol V. George in her biography of Allen mentions these and several other cases of trial, judgment, and penalties imposed by the church.[30] The pastor presided at many of the trials, and this necessarily took much of his time.

Because of Allen's wide influence, Bethel Church became a focal point for meetings and activities, both for the Philadelphia community and later for interstate or national activities. For example, in 1830 the "Free Produce Society," which Allen had been active in organizing, met at Bethel. Its purpose was to encourage the buying of goods made without slave labor. In 1830 also the First National Negro Convention, made up of leading free Negroes from many states, including Virginia, also met at Bethel. This was the first national meeting or convention attempted by Negroes in America. It was a daring venture and hardly seemed possible. It worked out well, however, and was largely the result of Richard Allen's effort and influence. It was almost natural for him to be elected President of the Convention. The purpose of the Convention was twofold: first to issue a positive statement against the American Colonization Society, that is, the movement that was started in 1816 to send Negroes, and especially free Negroes, back to Africa. Although Allen was sometimes represented as favoring the colonization scheme, he was strongly opposed to it, and he spoke and wrote against it vigorously. "America is our home," he said in a letter in the *Freedom Journal*.[31] The Convention opposed going back to Africa, but it favored location in Canada. The second purpose of the Convention was to plan means "for the speedy elevation of ourselves and brethren to the scale and standing of men." The Convention of 1830 issued a call for a second meeting in 1831. This all took work and planning, and it illustrates the pressure on Bishop Allen's time.

In addition to these public activities, Allen had the responsibility and care of his good-sized family—he had six children, four sons and two daughters. He saw that they were all educated. One of his sons, Richard, Jr., served as conference secretary in the early years of the Church. For his financial welfare and domestic needs Allen operated at least two businesses simultaneously: a hauling business and a boot and shoe business. Both were very successful. He also bought and sold property. Through his business acumen, as previously mentioned, he accumulated a fortune reputedly worth about $40,000. This was a tremendous sum for a man who had all the limitations of a "free" Negro.

Allen lived at a time when life for free Negroes was becoming more and more restricted. European immigrants in increasing numbers were flowing into the United States. In the ten years from 1790 to 1800 there were 50,000. From 1800 to 1810 there were 70,000, and from 1810 to 1820 there were 114,000, more than double the number of two decades before. These people for the most part were poor. They came seeking work and homes. They were in direct competition with free Negroes, and they generated much anti-Negro feeling. This resulted in restrictive and discriminatory laws against Negroes. They pushed many free Negroes out of work, thus increasing their poverty and idleness. This led to charges of crime and lawlessness against Negroes. Ohio, for instance, passed laws segregating its schools in 1827. Richard Allen and Absalom Jones in 1822 sought to curb the lawlessness in an appeal to the Negroes for a law-abiding community. But more than this, by Allen's persistent efforts to get Negroes organized on an interstate and even a national scale, and by his forthright efforts to bring Negro thought and concern to bear on central issues, he did much to save his people from the damage of false and defeatist propaganda on the one hand, and to maintain their sense of dignity and worth and to give them hope in the midst of degrading circumstances on the other. Above all, he gave the nation an impressive picture of the Negro's capacity for self-government and highest achievement in civic and religious affairs in spite of severest handicaps. His own life was the fullest proof.

Physically Richard Allen was not unusually impressive. He was of medium height and weight, rather plump, and with a "chestnut brown complexion." He was, however, a man of sound judgment, a kindly helpful disposition, and an extremely strong will once a decision was reached. While his strong determination sometimes led to difficulties, it was of inestimable value in the uncertainty and irregularities of an organization in formation. As he grew older his wisdom and benevolence proved themselves and he was highly regarded by his associates and the people of his time. He was often referred to as "the venerable Bishop Allen" or "Father Allen." He was constantly honored with tributes and activities showing appreciation.

Richard Allen was a deeply religious person. It is impossible to understand him without this. He owed his religious awakening to early Methodist preaching. In his religious experience God was a real, living person, as near as any parent or friend, upon whose love and help he could rely in any and all conditions. Jesus Christ, of course, was God incarnate who embodied God in human experience and mediated the love of God to man through his self-sacrificial suffering and death upon the Cross. In his statement of his faith he declared:

> I believe it is my greatest honor and happiness to be thy disciple [Christ's]; how miserable and blind are those that live without God in the World, who despise the light of Thy holy faith. Make me to part with all the enjoyments of life; nay, even life itself, rather than forfeit this jewel of great price! Blessed are the sufferings which are endured, happy is the death which is undergone for heavenly and immortal truth.[32]

In this faith Richard Allen moved. It was this faith that enabled a man born a slave, and later living as a black freeman, which in so many ways was little more than a half-life, to keep his dignity, his sense of equality with all men, and to reach heights of human achievement such as few are able to attain.

Charles H. Wesley, who has given a most balanced and scholarly evaluation of Allen, says:

> Allen's faith in an unseen power upon whom he could depend became a basis of relief and intuition, and upon this he could build anything else in his life. No actions by men, although they were more numerous and more powerful, could cause him to turn from his objective. He could thus meet all the crises of his life with fortitude and strength . . . it made possible in him not only the contemplative religious life, but also the practical one. He could therefore help all men wherever he found them, whether in the church, the school, the streets, or the prisons.[33]

Succeeding generations have grown in their veneration and appreciation of Bishop Allen and his work. Richard R. Wright has enumerated the monuments erected to him, the churches named for him, and the organizations that carry his name and embody his teachings. The tributes run into the hundreds.[34]

Richard Allen's wife, Sarah Allen, was a gracious, motherly person, an ideal companion for her busy, striving husband. She made their home a welcome retreat for distinguished white clergymen on the one hand, and runaway black slaves on the other.

The Church was fortunate in having chosen Morris Brown to assist Allen and then, after his death in 1831, to succeed him. With dedication and vigor he led the Church in its continued development. He traveled incessantly, crossing the mountains on horseback in true Methodist tradition.

GROWTH

The Church from 1826 on continued to grow, but not as evenly or as rapidly as in the first decade. For example, in 1826, the end of the first decade, the membership was 7,937, a sevenfold increase over the beginning membership of 1,067 in 1816. In 1836, at the end of the second decade, the membership was 7,594, a slight decrease. This was due mostly to the loss of the church at Charleston. There was a tremendous increase by 1846 to 16,190 members, and less rapid growth to 1856, when the membership was 19,914.

When all the factors are considered, the growth of a black organization to such proportions was remarkable. First, the Church was limited to the Northern states where the Negro population was smallest. Also, the Church worked mainly with free Negroes which made its constituency smaller still. Secondly, the Black Codes, the fugitive slave laws, and other restrictive measures were imposed in these years, and these made interstate movement difficult and dangerous for black evangelists and other church workers. In some cases it made travel impossible. Maryland, for instance, in 1832 passed a law forbidding free Negroes to come into the state.[35] In 1834 the Annual Conference had to be held in Washington so that the members could attend.

> The state of affairs at this date was such that our churches in certain quarters were quite seriously threatened, which led to the attendance at this Conference of a delegation of three members of the society at Elkton for the purpose of requesting that something might be done in behalf of the churches in Maryland belonging to the Smyrna Circuit, as the Black Code of that state forbade any colored minister, as well as any colored people belonging to another state, from entrance there, unless they came in the capacity of slaves, or servants of some white person. They also prayed the Conference to ordain Brother Aaron Wilson, a local preacher, and ordain him to take the oversight of the churches alluded to, he being a resident of the state of Maryland; the said brother, however, was to remain pastor only until some change might take place in the laws or the feelings of the community so as to tolerate the presence of a minister of the Lord Jesus whom He had been pleased to make a man of color! In view of their peculiar circumstances, the prayers of these churches were granted, and Brother Wilson was ordained a deacon . . .[36]

Also:

> Inasmuch as the laws of Delaware did not allow the ambassadors of the Cross, who were colored men, to itinerate in that state, the churches on Lewiston Circuit petitioned the Conference to ordain Moses Robinson and Pete Lewis a local elder, to minister for them in holy things, and their petition was granted.[37]

A fourth factor affecting growth was the manner of acquiring members. The A.M.E. evangelists did not and could not engage in the free and wide-ranging quest for converts as did the Methodist Episcopal preachers. Camp meetings, for example, were not used nearly as widely by black preachers as by white. Many of the persons who joined the A.M.E.'s had already been converted by M.E. preachers. They were dissatisfied in the M.E. Church, and joined the A.M.E.'s in protest or retaliation. This also applies to the black sections of congregations as well as to persons. At times whole groups would leave the white churches and come to the black. Thus, with the A.M.E. evangelists, the emphasis was as much on organizing new churches and societies as it was on preaching and trying to reach the unconverted. This led to much slower growth.

LITERATURE AND PUBLICATIONS

One indication that the men who founded the A.M.E. Church thought large and planned for permanence is seen in the provision that they made for books and literature. Although they were but sixteen in number representing five small and troubled churches, one of the major actions that they took in the organizing convention of 1816 was to provide for a "Publication Department." This department and its work was described in the first Discipline of 1817. The new Bishop was put in charge of the printing and sale of books. In 1817, with the collaboration of three other men, Jacob Tapsico, Daniel Coker, and James Champion, there was issued both a Discipline and a hymnal. The Discipline not only stated the rules of church government, but it also contained the "Articles of Faith" and the "General Rules" which John Wesley had provided for the Methodists in England and America. The new Church was fully in the Methodist tradition.

But despite the high aspirations of the early churchmen, the first results of the Book Concern were meager indeed. At the Philadelphia Conference of 1833 the Book Steward reported "that one thousand copies of the Discipline had been published at a cost of $70; and five hundred had been bound at a cost of $40. The amount of books sold was $20."[38] Payne says: "but for the times and under the circumstances, perhaps it may be looked upon as flourishing creditably."[39]

Don Carlos Hall, who succeded Bishop Allen as Book Steward in 1820, served until 1832. He was succeeded by Joseph M. Corr who served only four years until his death in 1836. He was, however, a vigorous, efficient manager, and under him the Book Concern made splendid progress. He reported a thousand each of Disciplines and hymnbooks printed and $300 worth of them sold.[40] Shortly after, at the General Conference of 1836 which met in Philadelphia, George Hogarth was elected general Book Steward of the Connection. The Conference gave him permission to publish "such religious books, tracts and pamphlets as may be deemed best for the good of the Connection, the profits arising therefrom always to flow into the general book treasury."[41]

Hogarth proved to be an excellent choice. He was a fluent writer, an energetic promoter, and active in the affairs of the Church. In 1837 the publication of a magazine was authorized, to be published quarterly "for the use and benefit of the Connection as another step toward the exercise of what literary talent might be found among the members."[42]

For three years Hogarth was busy generating interest in the magazine and making preparations for its publication. In 1840 it was decided to make it a monthly publication instead of quarterly. The first issue appeared in 1841. It was called *The African Methodist Episcopal Church Magazine*. Its purpose was to present

primitive Christianity as was understood to exist in the Methodist Church in Mr. Wesley's day: a vindication of the rights and privileges of our Church in all its bearings in this country as African Methodists . . . holding up to our Christian brethren, regardless of color, the importance of union among us, not only as Methodists, but as worshippers before the same Lamb in whose blood we are washed; the extension of the Redeemer's Kingdom among our brethren of color in this country, . . . the importance of turning the attention of our brethren to the land of our fathers . . . that the prayers of our brethren may ascend to the ear of the Lord, that he may in mercy raise up some of our young men and prepare them to carry to Africa's shore the glad tidings of Salvation . . .[43]

The first issues consisted mostly of conference reports and editorials on various subjects related to Church life. Once again, the Church's aspirations were larger than its achievements. For example, in the first year only three issues were published. This was due to lack of sales. In the words of the editor:

> . . . upon the cover of our last number we there issued a circular informing the public that as soon as nine hundred subscribers, at one dollar per annum, could be obtained . . . our next number would be issued forthwith, monthly. We have waited upon the friends of our cause with longing eyes for their patronage of this laudable enterprise . . . , but we are sorry to say, to our astonishment, we find but few . . . have lent their aid and influence in support of this important work . . .

Lack of education and poverty were the actual facts with which the publishers had to deal. "It is evident," writes Daniel Payne, ". . . that while a few of the ministry were manfully struggling to sustain this literary enterprise, the great mass, both of the ministry and the people, were perfectly unconcerned about its success."[44]

Yet the magazine continued a "struggling existence" for eight years. Its birth and life are a great credit to the Church, and its death was no cause for shame. It was well managed and creditably produced. But with an illiterate membership and ministry, and people who were poor, it simply was not possible to sustain a magazine.[45]

There was at least one advantage in the separate black Church. It could express and nurture the hopes and aspirations of its members, and it could take steps toward the fulfillment of these aspirations. This could hardly have been done in a mixed Church. This is clearly seen in the matter of education. Education of blacks was legally prohibited in the slave states, and it was disapproved in some of the Northern states. In such a situation, keeping the people conscious of the need for education and providing the means for getting it, limited though they were, was a service of inestimable importance to the progress of the people. This service was rendered by the young A.M.E. Church in the days of slavery.

Early in its history the Church began to express its concern for popular education. In 1833 the Ohio Conference passed two significant resolutions:

> Resolved, As the sense of this Conference that common schools, and temperance societies are of the highest importance to all people; but more especially to us as a people.
>
> Resolved, that it shall be the duty of every member of this Conference to do all in his power to promote and establish these useful institutions among our people.[46]

However, Daniel Payne complains:

> Seventeen years had passed away since the founding of the African Methodist Episcopal Church before a word was said in its Conferences on the important subject of education; and it remained for this, the youngest and least of the four Conferences, to give the first utterance on a subject so vital to the interests of the colored race in the United States . . .[47]

A little later, in 1834, the Philadelphia Conference in a similar spirit resolved:

> that as the subject of education is one of high importance to the colored population of the country, it shall be the duty of every minister who has charge of circuits or stations to make use of every effort to establish schools wherever convenient, and to insist upon the parents of children that they send them to school; and that a sermon should occasionally be preached expressly upon that subject; and that it should be the duty of every minister to make yearly returns of the number of schools, the number of scholars in each, the places where they are located, and the branches taught on their circuits and stations, and that every preacher who neglects to do so be subjected to the censure of the Conference.[48]

Here was not just a recommendation. Here was a detailed requirement, a directive with teeth. There is evidence that this Conference, the Philadelphia, and others took the directive seriously. In 1842, eight years later, Princeton, New Jersey, had one common school of thirty scholars and one teacher; and a Sunday School with forty scholars and fifteen teachers. Christian education was regarded as fully as important as academic education, and, as might be expected, many more teachers were available for the Christian work. Trenton, New Jersey had one school and thirty students; one Sunday School with forty scholars and twelve teachers. Bucks County Circuit in Pennsylvania had one school with thirty students, and twenty-seven in a Sunday School with one teacher. In Philadelphia, D. A. Payne had one school and forty students, one literary society with twenty members, and a Sunday School with sixty scholars and nine teachers.[49] In New York City at Bethel Church there was a school of 121 students.

The Church was coming to recognize, too, that if education was necessary for the members, it was much more necessary for the ministers who were leaders of the members. In 1841 it was complained that the brightest young people in the A.M.E. Church were leaving it for the Presbyterian and Episcopal churches because the A.M.E.'s "would admit men into the itinerancy who had neither talents, nor culture, nor taste, which could get them to become sufficiently interested in the Sabbath-school to become themselves instructors of the children and youths who were growing up daily under their eyes."[50]

In an effort to get training opportunities for ministers, the Baltimore Conference of 1837 adopted the following resolution:

> Resolved, That our Rt. Rev. Father and Bishop, with such person or persons as he may associate with him, be a committee to prepare . . . an appeal or statement of the condition and wants of the Church of Christ among the people of color in regard to the ministry, and the obstacles which embarrass candidates for that office in obtaining suitable preparations, and often hinder access even to the ordinary means of education.
>
> That the committee lay the same before the presidents and officers of colleges and theological seminaries in the free states, with a respectful entreaty that the advantages of education which their respective institutions afford may be extended to all persons alike, without distinction of color.
>
> And further, that the Bishop or committee, by correspondence with brethren throughout the United States, with Christian philanthropists, by appeals from the pulpit and press, and by all suitable means, endeavor to awaken a general interest amongst ourselves and friends on this important subject, viz: a suitable preparation for the pulpit or ministry.[51]

Here was not only an expression of interest, but an earnest appeal for help.

As an effort at ministerial improvement the Baltimore Conference of 1841 required that any person applying for license to exhort or preach "shall be examined before the Quarterly Meeting Conference touching his acquaintance with the Articles of Faith and Doctrines of the Christian Religion taught in our Discipline, and if he gives satisfaction thereon, he may have a trial. And the preacher in charge shall appoint a committee of three or four to judge his abilities and report to the ensuing Quarterly Meeting Conference." This was an effort to formalize and standardize the educational requirements for entering the ministry.[52]

THE COMING OF DANIEL PAYNE

The whole question of education in the Church, both for laymen and especially for ministers, was taken up, pushed, and made a central issue in the Church by one man, Daniel Alexander Payne. Indeed, the coming of this man into the ministry of the A.M.E. Church is one of the pivotal points in the Church's history.

Daniel Payne was born in 1811 in Charleston, South Carolina. His parents were both free. They were devout members of Cumberland Street M.E. Church, and his father was a class leader. His parents had some measure of education. From his father, Payne learned the alphabet and his "monosyllables." Both parents died in Payne's childhood, and he was reared by a grand aunt. She continued the devout, Christian influence of his parents.

Daniel Payne had about five years of schooling in which he "learned to spell, read, and write, and 'cipher' as far as the 'Rule of Three.'" He became an avid reader, and he instructed himself in numerous subjects, among them geography and English grammar.

Payne, like Richard Allen, was deeply religious, almost a mystic. It was his religious faith that not only moved him to challenge unwholesome conditions, but that also sustained him through severe mental and physical suffering and opposition. He was converted at eighteen in a period of revival at Cumberland Street Church. He says:

Here I too gave my *whole heart*, and instantly felt that peace which passeth all understanding, and that joy which is unspeakable and full of glory. Several weeks after this event between twelve and one o'clock one day, I was in my humble chamber, pouring out my prayers into the listening ears of the Saviour, when I felt as if the hands of a man were pressing my two shoulders and a voice speaking within my soul and saying: "*I have set thee apart to edu-cate thyself in order that thou mayest be an educator to thy peo-ple.*" The impression was *irresistible* and *divine;* it gave a new di-rection to my thoughts and efforts.[53]

In 1829, when Payne was just nineteen, he opened a school in Charleston. In the first year it consisted of three children in the daytime and three slaves at night. For these he received fifty cents per month per person. The second year the school began to grow, so that he had to seek larger quarters. It had an attendance of sixty students and became the leading school among five for black students in Charleston.

A number of friendly white people knew of Payne's work and helped him in many ways. But one unfriendly lawyer, a slaveholder, upon learning what Payne was doing, that is, in-structing blacks in mathematics and the sciences as well as in lit-erary subjects, soon introduced a bill in the Legislature of South Carolina making it a crime for anyone to teach either free blacks or slaves to read or write. If a white person were found guilty, the punishment was a fine of $100 and six months' imprisonment; if a free black were guilty, the offender was to be "whipped not exceeding fifty lashes and fined not exceeding fifty dollars"; if a slave were guilty, the penalty was fifty lashes. Any informer would receive half the fine.[54]

The law was to take effect on April 1, 1835. Payne had to close his school by that date. This was a heart-rending experience for the young teacher. He almost despaired of life. Only his faith that God somehow would correct things sustained him in these days. Several whites did what they could to comfort and encour-age him through this crushing experience.

In despair Payne left Charleston for the North. He first went to New York, where he met distinguished people white and black. He also learned of the antislavery movement and met some of its leaders. He eventually went to the Lutheran Seminary in Gettysburg, Pennsylvania, to get a professional theological education which would doubly prepare him to be an educator of his people. Being overzealous in his studies, he injured one of his eyes and was not able to complete the course of study. In seeking a field of usefulness he was advised to join the A.M.E. ministry. He did not do so, however, because he was discouraged by the advice of a friend of his father who told Payne that the preachers of the A.M.E. Church were opposed to educated ministers. He said that

> it was a common thing for the preachers of that Church to introduce their sermons by declaring that they had "not rubbed their heads against college walls," at which the people would cry, "Amen!" they had "never studied Latin or Greek," at which the people would exclaim, "Glory to God!" they had "never studied Hebrew," at which all would "shout."

Payne did join the Lutheran Church in 1837, but because of lack of work among Negroes in that church, he served as a Presbyterian pastor in East Troy, New York, for two years.[55] He lost his voice for a year, however, by preaching too long and too hard, and had to resign his pastorate.

Meanwhile, when he regained his voice he opened a school in Philadelphia. It soon became the leading school for Negro youth in the city. His teaching work brought him in contact with Bishop Morris Brown and other leading A.M.E. members in Philadelphia. They invited him to join the A.M.E. ministry. In the winter of 1841 he did, when he was thirty years of age. In 1843 he was received into full connection.

He immediately took up the fight for an educated ministry. He wrote five "Epistles on the Education of the Ministry" which were published in the A.M.E. magazine edited by George Hogarth. "These," says Payne, "gave much offense to many of the clergy, and produced much excitement among the laity. It was said by one that these 'Epistles' were 'full of absurdities,' 'infidels could do no more.'" Some called him a "devil." The editor of the magazine said: "Great fear is entertained by some that if the measures proposed be adopted by the General Conference discord and dissolution will necessarily take place in the Church between the ignorant and the intelligent portions of it."

Payne himself says: "While the enemies of Christian culture belched and howled forth all manner of vituperation against me, there were friends who defended my course in private circles and in public gatherings." One of these friends was Bishop Morris Brown.[56]

Payne's second thrust was at the Philadelphia Conference of 1842 when he put through "the first formulated effort toward a course of regular studies for preachers." It was in the form of two resolutions:

> Resolved, That the elders and deacons of the Connection make use of all the means in our power from henceforth to cultivate our minds and increase our store of knowledge.

Secondly,

> That we recommend to all our elders and deacons, licensed preachers and exhorters, the diligent and indefatigable study of the following branches of useful knowledge: English Grammar, Geography, Arithmetic, Rollin's Ancient History, Modern History, Ecclesiastical History, Natural and Revealed Theology.

In the words of Payne, "These resolutions . . . were the first strong, entering wedges to rive the mass of general ignorance and force the ministry of our Church to a higher plane of intellectual culture."[57]

It was at the General Conference of 1844 in Pittsburgh, Pennsylvania, that Payne met his greatest resistance but also his greatest victory. The Conference was in the act of revising the Discipline. When it came to the section on education of the ministry, Payne introduced a resolution to institute a course of studies for the education of the ministry. He thought that the majority of the Conference would favor the resolution, therefore he did not make any introductory statements in defense of it. "But in that," he writes,

> he calculated without his host, for as soon as the Bishop had put the question to the house, the effect was like unto that which follows when a fire-brand is cast into a magazine of powder. With the

greatest apparent indignation the resolution was voted down by a large and overwhelming majority, and the house adjourned amid great excitement. The next day, the fifth of the session, as soon as the house was opened, and first of all, Rev. A. D. Lewis, a brother of lofty stature, venerable appearance, dignified mien and delectable countenance, rose to his feet and called for a reconsideration of the rejected proposition. His motion was seconded and stated by the chair. The venerable man then advocated its claims and demonstrated its utility in a speech of uncommon eloquence and power. He addressed the understanding, the conscience, the passions of the audience till it was bathed in tears, and from many a voice was heard the impassioned cry, "Give us the resolution, give us the resolution!"

It was then put and carried without a dissenting vote. A committee was appointed of which Payne was chairman.[58] The list of studies was carried in the Discipline.

With this action of the General Conference, the Church became committed to an educated ministry. It was a victory for Payne and the Church. Payne saw clearly the place of education in the liberation of his people. His faith in the goodness of God led him to believe that physical freedom in time would come, but he also knew that his people would never be free unless they could master the elements of the culture in which they lived. There could be no real freedom in ignorance. He knew that the A.M.E. Church and its ministry could be great instruments of liberation, if the ministry were properly prepared, but an ignorant ministry would be ineffective and a handicap to the people.

With the results of the Conference of 1844, Payne became the recognized spokesman for education in the Church, literally the apostle of education, and this made his subsequent efforts much easier. His crowning achievement, of course, was setting up Wilberforce University in 1863 after he had become a Bishop of the Church.

ETHICAL AND CULTURAL STANDARDS

The A.M.E. Church was founded by a group of people who had very limited opportunity for ethical or cultural development. Most of them were "free" Negroes, to be sure, but the freedom was more a term than a fact. Many of those who were "free" had been slaves, and had secured their freedom at a dear price. "Both North and South," states Wade C. Barclay, "the social and economic plight of freed Negroes was little if any better than that of slaves. In certain localities it was even worse. McMaster describes the situation objectively and in detail. He says in part:

> . . . nowhere did the black man have all the rights of the white. He could not vote; he could not serve in the militia; nowhere was he summoned to be a juror. Race prejudice shut him out of a long line of trades and occupations, and condemned him to a state of gross ignorance. No carpenter, no blacksmith, no wheelwright, mason or shoemaker would take him as an apprentice; no shopkeeper would have him as a clerk. He was excluded from every hotel, inn, and tavern, and from every school save such as benevolent persons had established for the especial benefit of his race.[59]

The moral and physical depravity in which most Negroes were forced to live, both by law and by fact, made it all the more remarkable that they had ethical ideals at all. Yet the portion of the black population that gave birth to the A.M.E. and other churches had ethical standards of the highest kind. They had an intense desire, almost a passion, for the best in American Christian culture. Their standards, of course, were those of the times in which they lived.

First of all, since they were Methodists, they accepted and were governed by the almost ascetic rules of the Methodist movement. Those rules were stated in the "Articles of Faith" and the "General Rules" set forth by John Wesley.[60] The acceptance of these Articles and General Rules was one of the first actions of the organizing convention in 1816. The Articles defined the elements of Methodist theology or belief, such as belief in God, Jesus Christ, the Holy Ghost, the Resurrection of Christ, Original Sin, Free Will, Good Works, Purgatory, the Church, Speaking in Tongues, the Sacraments, A Christian Man's Oath, and Christian Men's Goods.

The "General Rules" of the United Societies set the pattern of behavior for the members. They were formulated in 1739 in response to certain persons who were "groaning for redemption." They wanted guidelines in the effort to live in keeping with their new religious experience. Black Methodist converts, like white, governed their lives by these regulations.

The A.M.E. Church, like other Methodist bodies, accepted responsibility for overseeing the Christian behavior of its members. They were required to follow the "Rules," or to forfeit membership in the Societies or the Church. Thus the black Methodists had set before them the strictest standards of moral and ethical behavior.

These standards were taken seriously by the blacks for the regulation of their own lives, and also as the basis of their appeal to the American conscience for the amelioration or abolition of slavery and for improvement in the treatment of free blacks. For instance, it was on the basis of the Rules and similar religious and moral injunctions that Americans were called upon to give up the economic gains of slavery. Again, the most basic and irrefutable demand of the antislavery movement was the Rule that prohibited "Doing to others as we would not they should do unto us," or "Doing what we know is not for the glory of God."[61]

Enforcing the Rules and holding the members up to the Standards naturally led to conflicts, trials, and penalties. Much of the Church's time was spent in dealing with infractions, charges, and countercharges of errant members. Several cases from the Journal of Bethel Church in Philadelphia have been mentioned previously. Such cases were customary in the Methodist churches of the time. The aim of it all was to make Methodism a truly Christian community.

One of the most urgent concerns was that of temperance. A resolution passed by the Ohio Conference of 1834 states the A.M.E. Church's feeling concisely:

> Resolved that the subject of temperance be strongly recommended to all our members, and that every preacher in this Conference come under the obligation to abstain from ardent spirits, and to cry against it wherever they go.[62]

There were also resolutions in all of the Conferences against gambling and lotteries.

There were regulations on dress and conduct. Gaudy dressing, of course, was mentioned in the Rules as evidence of worldliness and carnal indulgence. But the Church was also concerned with slovenly and unkempt dressing. This kind of appearance served to support the charge of carelessness and indecency which was commonly made against Negroes. Decorum in the pulpit and in worship services was also stressed. Preachers were urged not to use tobacco in the pulpit.

The press of cultural ideals was greatly intensified with the coming of Daniel A. Payne. He not only insisted upon education, but on the attainment of the highest aspects of American culture in all areas of life. For instance, he waged a vigorous battle against the use of "fugue tunes" or "cornfield ditties" in worship services. He called for singing the hymns that were found in the Methodist and other hymnals. Today we would regard the tunes Payne opposed as indigenous folk music, possibly as precursors of the now-accepted "spirituals." But Payne felt that they were neither good music nor good religion,[63] and he opposed their use. He encountered, of course, terrific opposition.

It should be said that in the aspiration for highest ethical and cultural standards Negroes were not simply trying to ape white patterns. They were convinced that the best in the society was as good for them as for the dominant whites. They wanted the best for themselves. But more than this, Negroes were determined to free themselves completely from the degrading aspects of human slavery, both physically and mentally. To this end they sought to attain the very highest elements in the dominant culture. Also Daniel Payne and those who thought like him were determined to keep their church out in the group of major Christian denominations. They did not want their Church to become a clandestine, hybrid sect or cult cut off from other Christian bodies by peculiar, vestigial beliefs and practices. They wanted it to be what it did become, a fully representative Christian body, equal in every way to its sister American churches.

CONTINUED EXPANSION

With the closing of the church in South Carolina under Morris Brown in 1822, the A.M.E. Church had little growth in the South. To be sure, a church was established in New Orleans,

Louisiana, in 1842, but this was done only through special permission of the Legislature of Louisiana and the city of New Orleans. It was severely restricted even in its worship services, and no evangelizing or expansion was permitted. A church at Louisville, Kentucky, was also established, but this too was so rigidly restricted that growth was practically impossible.

The Church did expand, however, steadily and extensively in the North and West. The Ohio Conference was added in 1840, the Indiana Conference in 1840, and the Missouri Conference in 1855. Meanwhile churches had been started in towns around the northern shore of Lake Ontario in Canada. A large number of Negroes had settled in this area. It was one of the terminal areas in the "Underground Railroad," the system through which fugitive slaves escaped or were assisted in their flight for freedom. The area also was a haven for free Negroes who wanted to escape the discrimination and handicaps of life in America, even in the North. As a matter of fact, Canada was approved as a desirable area for Negro migration in the Negro Convention of 1830. Emigration to Africa was opposed, but emigration to Canada was recommended. The A.M.E. Church sought to establish itself among the liberated former slaves in Canada.

The Church not only grew geographically, but it also grew steadily in membership. In 1826, for example, at the end of the first decade, there were 7,937 members. These were in three Districts or Conferences, the Philadelphia, Baltimore and New York. There were 17 pastors or itinerant preachers. In 1856, at the end of the fourth decade, there were 19,437 members, seven Conferences or Districts, 110 pastors or itinerant preachers, and 281 houses of worship. In 1826, there was one Bishop, Richard Allen. In 1856 there were three: Daniel A. Payne, William P. Quinn and Willis Nazrey. Three had died, Allen, 1816–1831; Morris Brown, 1828–1849; and Edward Waters, 1836–1844. One significant item of increase is that in 1826 the amount reported for 16 preachers' salaries was $1,062.50 In 1856 for 110 preachers it was $14,887.00, more than double the amount paid to the individual pastor.[64]

PIONEERS AND MISSIONARIES

The men who established the Church in the new areas were intrepid, committed, zealous pioneers, equal in all essential respects (with the exception of education in many cases) to early Christian evangelists or to the circuit-riding preachers of early Methodism. They had to be brave and adventurous because of the fugitive slave laws and the activity of outlaw slave hunters. They were always in danger of being seized and carried South where they could be sold into slavery with little hope of escape or release. They had to be strong because of the hardships of travel. In addition to the usual hazards in lawless frontier areas, they suffered the inconveniences of segregated accommodations. Sometimes common carriers refused to ride blacks at all. Having to live among black and poor members, their living conditions were often much worse than those of the Methodist Episcopal preachers. They received meager salaries for the service they rendered, sometimes no salary at all. For the great majority it was a sacrificial labor, undertaken first to carry the unfettered Gospel to a people who otherwise might not have received it; and secondly, to advance their people in the social and cultural scale of American life. We have few biographies that show these men at work. Occasionally there are obituaries and memorial statements at annual conferences that give us little glimpses.

THE EPISCOPACY

The growth of the Church both in members and in extent called for more leaders to keep the enlarging structure in order and growing. Despite its personalistic, experiential, and evangelical nature, the Methodist Church is a highly ritualistic and legalistic organization requiring close supervision for orderly and efficient functioning. Such an organization among a people who were largely illiterate required even more intensive supervision.

To meet the need for additional supervision, Jacob Matthews in 1822 was elected in separate votes by the Baltimore and Phila-

delphia Conferences as an Assistant Bishop to Richard Allen. For
some reason that we do not know, he was never consecrated and
never filled the office. Six years later in 1828 Morris Brown was
elected a Bishop, was consecrated, and served concurrently with
the aging Bishop Allen.

Richard Allen died in 1831. Morris Brown served alone until
1836, when it was clear that effective supervision of the Church
was too much work for one man. Edward Waters was elected in
1836, but he was not an effective supervisor.

> He never presided in an annual conference, only as a silent
> looker-on, assistant to Bishop Brown, and though he sat in the epis-
> copal chair from 1836 to 1844, he never ordained a single minister,
> not even a deacon. The second year after his election he requested
> the Baltimore Annual Conference to locate him. Indeed, even after
> his ordination he held charge of the Ellicott Mills Circuit, and
> sometimes of Bethel in Baltimore. In the eighth year of his epis-
> copate he resigned his episcopal authority, although he was able to
> travel as a Bishop, and returned to the ranks of the effective elders
> till his death.[65]

In 1844 William P. Quinn was elected to assist the aging
Morris Brown. Quinn had been most active in establishing the
Church in the West, that is, in western Pennsylvania, Ohio, and
Indiana. His report of his work in the General Conference of
1844 was largely responsible for his election. Morris Brown died
in 1849, leaving Bishop Quinn alone. Two Bishops were elected
in 1852, Daniel A. Payne and Willis Nazrey, giving the Church
three active Bishops.

The growth of the Church gave it increasing importance as an
organization, and it also gave importance to the leaders of the organization. The bishopric was the highest ecclesiastical office in
Protestantism. With the growth of the Church it came to be the
most coveted office. Just before the Civil War the A.M.E.
Church numbered about twenty thousand members. This was the
largest interstate organization among blacks in America, and with
the A.M.E. Zion Church it was one of the two main ones. Moreover, it was an organization largely of free Negroes, who were
naturally the most vocal and influential element in the black population. Thus to be a Bishop in a Methodist Episcopal church

after 1850 was to be in a position of genuine power and national influence.

The Church as it grew became the chief source for the organized expression of black protest and black aspirations. For instance, in 1850, 1854, and 1856 the Church issued formal statements in condemnation of slavery, and set days of prayer and fasting for the eradication of the evil. It thus gave the lie to the claim that Negroes accepted slavery and were patient under it. The Church gave organized rejection to the plans of the American Colonization Society which sought to return Negroes, especially free Negroes, back to Africa, thus depriving the black group in America of its most vocal and active leadership. The Church was able to give organized support to the antislavery movement and to assist in efforts at slave liberation. The fact that the Church spoke for thousands of blacks, mostly free, gave importance to its pronouncements that far exceeded individual voices. For example, when the Baltimore Annual Conference met in Washington in 1834,

> the sitting of this body was attended with unusual success; it being the first colored body that ever convened in the Capital of the United States, caused great excitement. Many hundreds, both of white and colored, assembled at the preaching-house, especially on the Lord's Day, and listened with delight to the ambassadors of the cross . . . the authorities of the city expressed their good feelings toward the Conference, and offered their protection in case any occurrences should require such action. President Jackson was waited upon by the Conference in a body, and His Excellency expressed his warmest approbation of the work, and wished hearty success to the cause.[66]

This meeting with authorities was achieved at a time when the Black Code laws made it impossible for the Conference to meet in Maryland.[67] A further evidence is seen in a visit that Bishop Daniel A. Payne made to President Abraham Lincoln in 1862. In the course of the interview Bishop Payne was able to urge the President to continue his efforts to extirpate slavery from the District of Columbia.[68]

The Church not only made itself felt at home, but was able also to participate in international and ecumenical church gatherings. In these larger assemblies the black protest against slavery was expressed, but what is perhaps more important, Negroes of culture and ability were able to be present and participate, thus giving living evidence of the mental and moral capacities of the race.[69]

With the growth in size and influence, the Church came to play an increasing part in the cultural development of the people. Much of the Church's work in this regard was due to the persistent, wise, and courageous leadership of Daniel A. Payne.

CHAPTER VII

The Second Great Separate: The African Methodist Episcopal Zion Church

THE FOUNDING OF THE African Methodist Episcopal Zion Church was much like that of the A.M.E. Church several years before. The same factors were present, the same causes were operative. In short, the establishment of this second separate black body was due directly to the inability of the Methodist Episcopal Church to work out a satisfactory situation for its Negro or "African" members. There was one striking difference, however. The antagonism and wrangling that marked the separation of the A.M.E. Church in Philadelphia was not as severe in New York. For the most part, the separation of the A.M.E.Z. Church was an amicable development.

As has been previously said, Negroes were part of the Methodist movement from its inception in America. In the beginning they were sought and welcomed into the movement and into the Societies. In the first Methodist service of which there is definite record, which was the service in the home of Philip Embury in 1766,[1] a young Negro servant named Betty was one of the five persons constituting the congregation. In 1768, when the first "meeting house," which later became John Street Church, was built, the names of several Negroes who probably were slaves are found in the list of contributors.

The number of Negro members of John Street Church continued to grow through the years until in 1802 it was 211, or nearly one-third of the total membership of the church, 720. In 1804 there were 268 Negroes.

The large black membership raised a number of problems. The first was the accommodation of the Negro members. The present John Street Church is not a large building, and the earlier buildings were even smaller. The Negro members alone could have filled the building, and with the number steadily growing, the whites could have been crowded out. The simple fact of attending services and finding seats was a disturbing problem.

Second was the fact of social difference. The Negro members were either slave or free. If slaves, they necessarily were on a social level far below that of the whites. But if "free," as many of the black members of John Street Church were, their social status was little higher than that of the slave. Both by law and by custom they were severely suppressed, almost always poor, uneducated, and, according to American standards, unrefined. To be sure, there were among the black members some individuals of high intelligence, good education, and unusual abilities. An example is Peter Williams who, though born a slave, with the help of the Trustees of John Street Church, purchased his freedom by working as a sexton of the church. He later became a successful tobacco merchant, and was one of the most widely liked and influential members in the church. His home was a favorite meeting place for white Methodist preachers and laymen. Although he played a large part in founding the "African" chapel which was organized later, he kept his membership in John Street until his death. Also, there was James Varick, who was both a shoemaker and a schoolteacher. But Williams and Varick, and those like them, were exceptions. The average black man whether slave or free was unlettered, uncultured, and poor. He could hardly be otherwise.

There was no question about Negroes being members of the Church, but the problem of seating them intensified with the years. In the early days when Methodism was primarily an evangelistic drive with meetings held in open air, borrowed halls, or even homes, seating Negroes, especially in the North, was not a major issue. But when Methodism became an established, settled Church with its own church buildings, a resident ministry, and congregations that more and more included people of wealth and status, the seating of the black members became increasingly irritating. Many white Methodists, particularly those who were slaveholders or who favored slavery, as growing numbers did, resented sitting beside and associating on equal terms with slaves or half-slaves. As the liberal ideas of the Revolution faded, and as the slave system became more and more accepted, the practice developed of seating the blacks in special sections of the church buildings, such as the balcony, if there was one, or in the rear of the church or along the walls.

Yet despite their limited and underdeveloped condition many Negroes had an irrepressible sense of their human dignity and of the kind of brotherhood that ought to obtain among Christians. They were disappointed at the forced separation and resented it. It confirmed their growing determination to have meeting places and services of their own.

The Negroes' desire for separate meetings was a factor that further complicated the problem of their presence in Methodism. The conditions under which blacks had to live made it necessary that at some time they should have worship services that would speak to their needs. They needed services that would express their passion for freedom and also give them solace in their sorrows and release from the bitter hurts of the brutal social system under which they had to live.

In the case of the New York Methodists, Negroes at first sought only the right to have occasional prayer meetings by themselves. They participated fully in the life of the church, but they would meet at nights or on Sunday afternoons in the interval of the regular services, for their own services.

In 1780 at the New York Annual Conference the twenty-fifth question asked was:

> Ought not the assistant (Mr. Asbury) to meet the colored people himself, and appoint in his absence proper white persons, and not suffer them to stay so late and meet by themselves?
> Answer: Yes.[2]

This action of the Conference recognized the right of the Negro members to have meetings of their own with, of course, the Bishop or someone appointed by him being present at the meetings.[3] At any rate, the meetings continued and grew both in numbers and popularity among the blacks.

This, however, led to a further complication. The separate meetings soon came to include not only prayers but also preaching. In the last two decades of the eighteenth century Negro preachers began to arise in Methodism. Though limited in education and totally without formal training, they still were effective leaders and gifted, persuasive preachers. Some outstanding examples already mentioned are Absalom Jones, Richard Allen, and Harry Hosier (Black Harry); and among the Zionites Abraham Thompson, James Varick, June Scott, Thomas and William Miller.[4] Several of these were licensed as local preachers by the John Street Church, but the New York Conference, prior to 1806, would not ordain them deacons or itinerant elders. They were preaching regularly, however, in the separate meetings that the black members were holding. Being unordained they could not serve the sacraments or perform the other ministerial functions. Requests for their ordination were repeatedly submitted, but the Conference refused, usually giving as its reason the lack of education and the inability of black preachers to travel as widely as the Methodist itinerancy required.

Perhaps at this point two things should be said. First, it was true that most Negro preachers were uneducated, and a preacher who could not read would only be a source of confusion for the teaching of the Bible and the doctrines of the Church. But the Negro preachers could have been taught. Early Methodism made little if any effort to instruct its black preachers or laymen. Secondly, some Negro preachers did have at least rudimentary educations. This was true for Daniel Coker, Absalom Jones, Richard Allen, and James Varick. Besides, many early white Methodist preachers had very little schooling, for example, Benjamin Abbott. Yet Absalom Jones through the kindly and sympathetic interest of Bishop William White was taken into the Protestant Episcopal ministry with its highly ritualistic services, and became the first Negro priest in America.[5] But at any rate, the Church failed to take a step here which might have been good not only for Negroes but for the entire Methodist movement.

The separate meetings were held in the John Street Church building. But these meetings, although held in "off" hours, because of the steadily growing black membership were straining not only the physical resources of the church, but also the time and strength of the white ministers. To secure some kind of solution a group of Negro members met with Bishop Asbury in 1796. Among the group were men who later were founders of the A.M.E. Zion denomination. They were Francis Jacobs, William Brown, Peter Williams, Abraham Thompson, and June Scott. According to Christopher Rush, the first historian of the A.M.E. Zion Church, the Negro members were given permission to meet "in the interval of the regular preaching hours of our white brethren," and they were to conduct their services "in the best manner they could."[6]

This conference, very much like the one sixteen years before it in 1780, confirmed the right of Negroes to meet, but it did not solve the problem of the attendance of black members at regular church meetings. Clearly additional space was needed, and this could most conveniently be provided in a separate meeting place. This the black members set out to obtain. A cabinetmaker's shop belonging to one of the black members, William Miller, was finally located on Cross Street between Mulberry and Orange. It was fitted with seats, a pulpit, and a balcony. Here prayer meetings were held on Sunday afternoons and Wednesday and Friday nights. The services were conducted by the preachers previously mentioned, Abraham Thompson, William Miller, and June Scott. Visiting Negro preachers from other churches led the services from time to time. This extension of John Street Church was known as the African Chapel. The first meeting was held in

1796.[7] The chapel was under the supervision of a white elder appointed by the New York Annual Conference. He was usually an assistant pastor of John Street Church.

Within three years it was seen that a larger and more permanent meeting place was needed for the Negro group. A meeting was called "of some of the most respectable and intelligent religious colored men of the city, in order to consult upon the best method to proceed in this great undertaking for colored people in the City of New York."[8] They included persons other than the Negro members of John Street Church. Minutes of the meeting were not preserved, but they planned to set up not just a place of worship but rather a new church or congregation that "should be under the Methodist government."

The move was not opposed by the John Street Church or the New York Conference. It was done in a harmonious and cooperative spirit. Rush states: "When our White brethren, the Ministers of the Methodist Episcopal Church, found that we were determined upon becoming a separate body, or society, they appointed the Rev. John McClaskey, at their General Conference, who was one of the stationed Elders for the Methodist Episcopal Church in the City of New York, to make arrangements and effect some articles of agreement with us for our government, in order that the spiritual part of the government might be under the direction of the General Conference of the Methodist Episcopal Church from time to time, and so keep the two Churches or Societies in union with each other . . ."[9]

This cooperative spirit was in sharp contrast to the attitude that had prevailed in Philadelphia. The elder who was appointed to work with the African Chapel in New York was the Reverend John McClaskey, the same person who had had so much controversy with Richard Allen and Bethel Church in Philadelphia. There he had opposed the formation of the separate church and had tried to block the supplemental agreement that gave the Bethelites control of their church property. In New York, by contrast, it was he who worked out the agreement between the African church and the New York Conference which gave the Zionites many of the very rights and privileges the Bethelites had tried vainly to obtain. The reasons for his change of attitude are not known. Perhaps in the years between 1794 and 1801 he had come to accept the formation of separate black Methodist congregations as an inevitable and acceptable development in American Methodism.

The Trustees were successful in raising funds for the new church. Two lots were purchased on the corner of Church and Leonard streets, a frame building, 45×35 feet, was erected, and first services were held in September 1800. They named the new church "Zion." In official documents it is referred to as "The African Methodist Episcopal Church called Zion."[10]

The Reverend John McClaskey helped the new church to work out two legal arrangements, one a charter under the state of New York, and the other an agreement with the General Conference of the Methodist Church.[11] In the charter, the Trustees of Zion Church owned or controlled all the property of the church. Bradley points out that this is in sharp contrast to other Methodist churches in New York City whose property was owned and controlled by the Trustees of John Street Church.

In the agreement with the Methodist Church it was stipulated:

1. That the Church called Zion Church be a corporation with "the style and title" of "The African Methodist Episcopal Church of the City of New York, in the State of New York."

2. The trustees of the Corporation "shall have and hold the said building called Zion and all other properties belonging to the Corporation.

3. That "none but Africans or their descendants shall be chosen as Trustees of the said African Episcopal Zion Church."

4. "That the Trustees and members of the African Methodist Episcopal Church do acquiesce and accord with the rules of the Methodist Episcopal Church for their church government and discipline, and with their creed and articles of faith, and that they and their successors will continue forever in union with the Methodist Episcopal Church in the City of New York . . . except in the temporal right and property of the aforesaid Zion Church . . ."

5. That the elder of the Methodist Episcopal Church for the City of New York shall have the direction and management of the Spiritual concerns of Zion Church "for the time being."

6. No person is to be taken into Zion Church except as recommended by one or more of the Trustees; any member who may

have "walked disorderly" is to be tried by members of the Church; the elder shall nominate the preacher who shall officiate in the services, but the elder himself is "to administer the ordinances of Baptism and the Lord's Supper, as often . . . as he can make it convenient."

The Trustees who signed the Agreement were Francis Jacobs, Thomas Sipkins, George E. Moore, George White, George Collins, Peter Williams, Thomas Cook, William Brown and David Bias. Four of the nine could not write their names and could sign only with an X.[12]

The two agreements seemed to give both groups most of what they wanted. For the blacks, they had the ownership and control of their church property and the right to direct the life of the church. For the white Methodist Church there was the guarantee that the separate church would be under government of the Conference and that it would be fully within the Methodist tradition, this being assured, of course, by the fact that an elder appointed by the Conference would have ultimate direction of the spiritual life of the church.

For the blacks there was one question that the agreements did not settle or even consider, and that was the ordination of Negro preachers. But for the time being this particular issue was not raised.

Under the Agreement affairs moved along quite smoothly for the new church for the next ten years. The congregation soon outgrew the new building. More room was obtained by extending the building twenty feet.[13]

There were, of course, some conflicts, but as far as the progress of the church was concerned, they were minor. For instance, two of the three Negro preachers who served Zion Church were dissatisfied with the financial support they were receiving. A white man, one John Edwards, invited the disgruntled preachers, Abraham Thompson and June Scott, to join him in setting up a new church among Negroes. They did join the new church, which was called the "Union Society." Zion Chapel threatened to expel them. Thompson immediately returned, pleading that he did not know what he was doing. June Scott did not come back but eventually joined another church. The defection did not develop into a split, as they had expected.[14]

There was, however, another separation that resulted in the formation of a second black congregation, but even this was accomplished without serious disturbance. In 1813 Thomas Sipkins, a trustee and leading member of Zion who once was expelled for being "somewhat headstrong and rather ungovernable," undertook to form a separate Negro Methodist church in New York City. He purchased land, put up a building, and got William Miller, an ordained deacon at Zion, to be the preacher. They asked the Reverend Phineas Cook, the elder in charge of Zion, for guidance in setting up the new church under the Methodist connection. The trustees considered the question, and decided that the organization of a second church was good. The new church was called Asbury Church.

The churches continued to grow. In 1819 Zion and Asbury churches together had 791 members. Zion needed a larger building. It was decided this time to erect a stone building, and to include a schoolroom in the basement. The contract was let on July 13, 1819.[15] Since the school would be for all children, an appeal was made to the Legislature of New York for a grant toward the cost of constructing the building. The appeal was not granted, and the congregation undertook construction on their own. Their money soon gave out. The old building had been torn down, and so the congregation had to rent two places for their services, one the "Riding Circus" on Broadway between Hester (now Howard) and Grand streets, for Sunday morning services, and the Rose Street Academy between Pearl and Duane streets for Sunday evenings and weekdays. By mortgaging the old property and by strenuous efforts the funds were raised, the work continued, but the new building was not fully completed for several years. They could worship in it, however, and on August 20, 1820, the Sacrament of the Lord's Supper was served in the new building for the first time.[16]

Between the years 1798 and 1826 the term "African Church" occurs in the minutes of the Common Council of New York City eighteen times. The items include petitions for educational funds, for a burial ground, and for relief on taxes. Four of the entries are complaints against the "unruly" and "riotous" conduct of "Boys and Unruly Persons" who disturbed the worship of the church. Also there are complaints by neighbors against "the extreme late hours of the night to which the exercises in said church [Zion] are continued."

One entry in 1807 was an invitation to the members of the Council to attend a service celebrating "the period which puts a stop to commerce of the human species" [the slave trade], and also asking the Council to provide officers to keep order.[17]

While some of the entries are ordinary business matters, others reveal the opposition and harassment to which the church was subjected, as well as the quiet determination of the Negroes to carry on their constructive activities in spite of public opposition.

SEPARATION

Despite the fact that the A.M.E. Church had separated from the Methodist Episcopal Church in Philadelphia in 1816, there was little talk of or desire for separation in the New York churches in 1820. The Zion and Asbury churches wanted to remain under the New York and General Conferences of the M.E. Church. A few ministers were dissatisfied with the Methodist refusal to ordain black preachers, but the great majority of the members wanted to remain.

Moreover, the "Philadelphia Movement" or the "Allenite Movement" as the A.M.E. Church was called was unpopular. A main reason was Bishop Allen's attempt to set up a church in New York City. As previously stated, the man Allen sent to New York to do this was especially displeasing to the New York churches. He was a former member of Zion who had gone to Asbury Church for ordination. Asbury Church would not ordain him, and sent him to Bishop Allen in Philadelphia. Allen ordained him and sent him back to New York to set up an A.M.E. church there. For Allen to use this man to set up a church in New York they felt was unfair competition, and an effort to take advantage of Zion's building and financial troubles. Both Asbury and Zion churches agreed that they would have nothing to do with the

Allenites, "that we would neither preach for them nor permit them to preach for us."[18] Later in 1820 when Bishop Allen himself visited New York, the opposition was relaxed somewhat but there still was little association with them.

The event that did most to precipitate separation from the Methodist Episcopal Church was the Stillwell secession. Ironically, it was a controversy within the white church, and the black churches were only incidentally involved. For many years prior to 1820 white Methodists in the New York Conference had been dissatisfied over several matters. One serious problem was the control of Methodist church property; another was the authority of the clergy and the lack of representation of the laity in church government; still another problem was the handling of church funds.

John Street Church was the first Methodist church in New York City. Church property was under the control of the Trustees of this church. As new societies were set up, their properties were also put under the control of this Board of Trustees which had become the central Board for the Conference. The newer churches came to feel, however, that too much of other churches' property was being used for John Street and the downtown churches. Then many laymen of the Conference wanted more participation in the government of the Church. They felt that ministers had too much to do with forming the Discipline, and they wanted lay representation in the Annual Conferences. In addition to all this, many persons felt that the collections from class meetings should be used to support preachers, and not for church maintenance.

The issues came to a head in 1820 when the Reverend William Stillwell petitioned the New York Conference for relief. The petitions were rejected, whereupon Reverend Stillwell and several hundred others walked out. Unfortunately, Reverend Stillwell was the elder in charge of Zion and Asbury churches, appointed by the New York Conference. His leaving the Conference meant that he was no longer the pastor of Zion and Asbury churches. On August 16, 1820, Reverend Stillwell announced to the Zion members that he was no longer a member of the Conference. This was sad news for the black churches, for they loved and respected him. They were at a loss as to what to do. Unfortunately, again, the Methodist Presiding Elder did not help matters. Instead of simply appointing a new pastor for the black churches as he should have, he put the decision up to the churches, asking them what they wanted to do. The Negroes, who hardly understood the issues, held several meetings to determine a course of action. They talked with Bishop George, the Presiding Bishop; they talked with white Methodist pastors who had been friendly, such as Joshua Soule, Ezekiel Cooper, and William Phoebus.

There were some aspects of the controversy that caused the Negro members grave concern. For example, they wanted control of their church properties. In the efforts to combat the Stillwellites, the white Methodist preachers wanted all church property put under the control of Methodist preachers. This the Negroes did not want.

Secondly, the Negro members wanted an ordained ministry. Realizing that the New York Conference would not accept Negro ordination, they appealed, at Ezekiel Cooper's suggestion, to the Philadelphia and New York Conferences to set up a separate African Conference that would have its own ordained preachers who would be under the government of the Methodist Church. They proposed a plan that was something like the Central Jurisdiction plan instituted a hundred years later.[19]

The Philadelphia Conference was favorable to the plan, but the New York Conference rejected it, stating that only the General Conference could set up an annual conference; one annual conference could not set up another. They asked the Negro church to wait for the next General Conference and appeal there. They also, in the meantime, would license preachers but not ordain them. This was a crushing blow to the blacks.

Meanwhile, the black members did reach two basic decisions. In a meeting on August 11, 1820, they asked: "Shall we join Bishop Allen?" The answer was no. On the second question, "Shall we return to the white people?" the answer again was no.[20]

With these two answers the blacks were determined to become a separate black Conference under Methodist government with their own ordained ministers.

Thus reluctantly, but almost inevitably, the Zion and Asbury Methodists were moving more and more toward separation.

To secure the special arrangements that they desired, the members of Zion Church saw that it would be necessary to make changes in the Methodist rules of government or Discipline. They decided to have a Discipline of their own. In September 1820 a committee of five was appointed to draw up a Discipline. The title of the document was "The Doctrines and Discipline of the African Methodist Episcopal Church in America." It is interesting that the name of the new body is identical with that of the A.M.E. Church in Philadelphia in 1816, but it is understandable. The title "African" was generally used for Negro enterprises, and they wanted to retain the Methodist Episcopal tradition. The committee selected the portions of the Methodist Discipline that were acceptable, and wrote in their own special regulations. George Collins wrote the preamble. It was adopted by the Zion Church on October 25, 1820, and 1,200 copies were printed.

They had the fact of separation, but they still did not have an ordained ministry. They did not want ordination at the hand of Bishop Allen, because he would not ordain their pastors unless they "would put themselves under his charge." This they were unwilling to do.

They appealed to Bishop Hobart of the Protestant Episcopal Church, but he would not cooperate. Their minister, Reverend Stillwell, informed them that according to his studies, in cases of emergency elders could be elected by the congregation. This was acceptable. Therefore, on October 1, 1820, Abraham Thompson and James Varick were elected elders by the official members of Zion Church. On November 12, 1820, Abraham Thompson and James Varick, elders elect, administered the Lord's Supper. Also in November 1820, Zion and Asbury churches with the help of the Reverend William Stillwell, their elder, worked out an agreement that would govern the cooperation between the two congregations.[21]

The members of Zion and Asbury churches were dissatisfied with the decision of the New York Conference. It meant that they would have to accept the Discipline of the Methodist

Church, which would mean the loss of control of their properties. They, Zion and Asbury, decided to follow the plan approved by the Philadelphia Conference for a separate black conference.

Other separate congregations or societies of black Methodists had been organized in Long Island, New Haven, and other towns. A black church in Philadelphia, the Wesleyan Church, had withdrawn from the A.M.E.'s. These churches met in their own conference in New York City on June 21, 1821.[22] They still considered themselves under the Methodist Church, and selected one of the Methodist bishops as their Superintendent. The Reverend Joshua Soule and the Reverend William Phoebus were present. Since the Bishop could not come, Reverend Phoebus was chosen "President *pro a viso*." Freeborn Garrettson was also present and encouraged them in their effort to get a separate conference. Representatives from the following six churches were present at this meeting:

Zion, New York	(763 members)
Asbury, New York	(150 members)
New Haven, Connecticut	(24 members)
Long Island, New York	(155 members)
Wesleyan, Philadelphia	(300 members)
Easton, Pennsylvania	(18 members)

Total members represented 1,410

The total amount collected for the Conference was $35.08.

The second meeting of the black churches was held in Philadelphia in June 1822. The question of ordination was not only urgent, it was critical. Members were becoming restless and dissatisfied. Also the presence of Reverend Stillwell as elder was confusing since he was not appointed by the New York Conference.

Seeking guidance, the churches appointed committees to talk with Methodist Bishops George, McKendree, and Roberts. The Bishops' reply in essence was that since the Negro Methodists had their own Discipline, they, the Bishops, could do little or nothing without authority from the General Conference.

Getting no help here, the Negroes decided to secure ordination otherwise. They found three white elders who would help them, Dr. James Covel, the Reverend Sylvester Hutchinson, and the Reverend William Stillwell. These three ordained Abraham Thompson, James Varick, and Leven Smith elders on June 17, 1822. In July, in an adjourned session of the Philadelphia Meeting, the three new elders ordained six others: Christopher Rush, James Smith, James Anderson, William Carmen, Edward Johnson, and Tillman Cornish. They were ordained deacons in the morning and elders in the afternoon.[23]

The new church now had its ministry. Since neither a Methodist Bishop nor Dr. Cooper could attend, Abraham Thompson was chosen President of the second yearly meeting.

INDEPENDENT WORK

The failure of the General Conference of 1824 to take some action on the appeal of the black churches left those churches in a state of deep despair. They had appealed to the General Conference not in a spirit of rebellion or threatened secession, but in an honest effort to get that Conference to take some constructive steps that would help the black members to attain a satisfactory arrangement within the Methodist Episcopal Connection. They felt that their life situation required certain special considerations, but given these, they wanted to remain in the Methodist Episcopal fold. When the Conference refused to do anything, they had no alternative except to move out on their own. They had to take up the task of maintaining their churches and spreading the faith among their fellows, both slave and free. Considering their poverty, their limited educations, and, above all, the strangling restrictions imposed on blacks, they knew that this would be a most difficult task.[24]

It is hard to imagine a more black prospect facing a group of Christians who aspired not only to keep the faith but to spread it as well. The number of churches attending the annual meeting, small as it was, had been reduced by the loss of Asbury Church and William Miller.[25] There was some dissension within the group. The New Haven church was divided and some members were demanding to withdraw to return to the Mother Church. Most serious was the competition they were facing from the A.M.E.'s, competition that was vigorous and, as some saw it, unscrupulous.[26]

The fact that the few churches, led by Zion Church of New York City, decided to move out as an independent church body, was due to the determination and dedication of the men who were leading the churches at that time. One of the most outstanding of the early leaders was Abraham Thompson. He was one of the first three Negroes who were licensed to preach in New York,[27] and he was a member of the committee that talked with Bishop Asbury in 1896 when Negroes received permission to have separate meetings, leading later to the establishment of the African Chapel. Thompson continued as a preacher in the Zion Chapel, and he was also active in setting up other churches. His behavior was somewhat erratic, for in 1801 he with June Scott joined John Edwards in setting up the Union Society. He soon returned to Zion, however, and became one of the preachers of the Church and also one of the most influential persons in the early history of Zion. He was a member of many of the committees that attempted to fashion the course for the black members. He was the first person elected an elder in 1822, and was elected President of the second yearly conference of the black churches.[28] He played a great part in fashioning the early form of the Zion body.

Another of the outstanding early leaders was James Varick. Unfortunately, records regarding him are very meager. The date of his birth is uncertain. Bradley makes the remarkable statement that "Varick was born in Newburgh, New York, anywhere between 1750 and 1796. Somewhere between these two dates seems more reasonable."[29] B. F. Wheeler, a biographer, sets his birth on June 17, 1750. He was of mixed parentage. We have little direct knowledge of his childhood, education, or youth. The dates of his conversion and decision to preach are unknown. He is mentioned by Christopher Rush as being one of the persons who talked with Bishop Asbury in 1796. His name was not on the

Charter of the African (Zion) Chapel nor on the Agreement of 1801 with the Methodist Church. In 1806 Varick, along with Abraham Thompson and June Scott, was ordained a local deacon in the M.E. Church.

The name of Varick begins to occur most frequently about 1820. In that year he did the controversial thing of attending and participating in the meeting that Bishop Richard Allen held in New York by opening the meeting. He shared in the first service held in the new Zion Chapel. It was in his home that a committee met to see what should be done as a result of the Stillwell secession. He served on the committee that talked with the Methodist Bishops, with Bishop Allen, and with other influential persons in their search for a working arrangement in the Methodist Episcopal Church and especially in seeking ordination for the Negro preachers. He was active in the yearly meetings of the group of churches that began meeting in 1820. At the first meeting of the group in June 1821, Varick was elected District Chairman.[30]

On October 1, 1820, Varick was elected an elder by the members of Zion Church, the second person elected. Abraham Thompson was first. On June 17, 1822, Abraham Thompson, James Varick, and Leven Smith were ordained elders. In 1822 Varick was elected District Superintendent, the first such officer in the Zion movement.

From his activity in the formative years of his Church, Varick must have been an influential dependable leader. John J. Moore describes Varick as a "man of great firmness, patience, perseverance, forethought, caution, and uprightness. Plain but orthodox in his preaching, his memory is one of the revered relics of Zion Connection."[31] From this quotation, J. W. Hood proceeds to draw an elaborate picture of Varick as a person and as a leader. It is largely inferential, and Bradley feels it exceeds the evidence as presented by the scant records that we have.[32] It is clear, however, that Varick was an active and constructive participant in the early years of the Church. He served as Superintendent from 1822 to his death in 1828. Under his superintendency the Church grew in numbers and in extent.

The man who played the most outstanding part in the early days of the Church was, of course, Christopher Rush. He is generally acknowledged as the guiding spirit of the young organization. He was born in North Carolina of slave parents in 1777. He "embraced religion" in 1793 when sixteen years old. He came to New York in 1798, and joined the Zion Chapel in 1803. He was licensed to preach in 1815, and was one of the six persons who were ordained deacons and elders on the same day in 1822. He served as a pastor and also as a missionary before he was elected General Superintendent in 1828, succeeding James Varick. He served in this position for more than twenty years.[33]

Christopher Rush was eminently prepared for the task of leading the new Church. He was physically strong, mentally keen and vigorous, and of high moral character. Moore says: "Although he was debarred . . . from collegiate training, yet by his extraordinary work of self culture, his scholarly attainments astonished all that came in contact with him"[34] He was able to endure the rigorous conditions facing black preachers and evangelists in his time, and he was able to guide both people and pastors who were mostly unlettered in their efforts to organize and maintain churches and societies in the Methodist tradition.[35] Under his leadership new conferences were formed, the ministry grew in number, and the membership increased many times. He had to retire in 1852 because of blindness, but he continued to be a strong influence in the Church until his death in 1873.[36] He takes his place along with Asbury, Richard Allen, and other early Methodist preachers who built a Church at the cost of self-sacrifice and great labor.

These brief glimpses into the lives of three leaders give some indication of the kind of persons, clerical and lay, who in 1824 set out to develop a new Connection of Methodism in America.

In the annual meeting of 1821, already mentioned, six churches were present. In 1824 only four churches were represented. Asbury Church had withdrawn and gone first to the Methodist Episcopal Church, and then a year later to the Allenites. New Haven was not present because of resentment over the expulsion of one of their members. The meeting of 1825 was still smaller with only the preachers from New York City attending. The only appointments made that year were to Zion Church in New York, to which Christopher Rush was appointed, to the society in Harlem, and to Newark and Elizabethtown in New Jersey. Rush says that this year "there was no extra preaching" and that they "had a flat time."[37] The sixth session of 1826 was somewhat brighter. Nine ministers attended. Of these, two were ordained deacons and one an elder. The seventh meeting in 1827 was brighter still. A representative from a church in Buffalo was present, and Jacob Matthews, who had left to join the Allenites, returned to be an elder in Zion.

The annual meeting of the group of churches in 1828 is regarded by some as the first General Conference of the African Methodist Episcopal Zion Connection. It is significant because at this session Christopher Rush was elected General Superintendent, succeeding James Varick. With the election of Rush the new connection begins its steady but not very rapid growth.

The Church grew very little in its first ten years. In 1821 there were six churches, 1,410 members and twenty-two preachers. In 1831 there were 1,016 members and twelve preachers in the New York Conference, and 673 members and fourteen preachers in the Philadelphia Conference, making a total of 1,689, a small gain for the Church of 279 members and four preachers.[38]

There are several reasons for this slow growth. J. J. Moore, later Bishop Moore, gives acceptable explanations:

Having secured our form of church government [the Zion Discipline], the official members of the church being now fully determined upon gathering into the connection such churches of their colored brethren as were willing to unite with them in the formation of a uniform system of church government, they held a meeting on the subject. It was known at this time [1820] that there were several places open where our preachers might have formed societies or taken charge of those already formed under the White Methodist Episcopal Church, but being inexperienced, they did not succeed very rapidly in organizing societies. This, and the want of means, hindered them considerably in their work of extending Zion's borders. Sometimes, the Allenites did not hesitate to represent themselves to be the same as the Zion preachers, when they found it necessary to make a point . . . At this date information was received by some of the officiary, that there was an African Methodist Society at Flushing that wished to connect with us, but before we could send a preacher, George White, one of Bishop

Allen's preachers, visited the society, and although we sent two preachers, Mr. Miller and George Collins, with whose visit the society seemed pleased, yet through the influence of White, one of Allen's preachers, they were induced to join Allen's connection.[39]

J. W. Hood states that they circulated stories "that Zion is a split from Bethel,"[40] and they also pointed out "Zion has no Bishops," since the Zion presiding officers were called "Superintendents" until 1864.[41]

The A.M.E.'s (Allenites or Bethelites) were first in the field. With their greater experience, with Richard Allen's aggressive leadership, and with their roughshod tactics, they made it difficult for the Zionites to get started or to grow very much for the first ten years.[42]

The growth of the Church was much more rapid in the second and succeeding decades. The leaders of Zion were becoming more confident and more active. Superintendent Rush was giving strong leadership. He was himself a hard working, self-sacrificing, courageous evangelist. The Negro evangelists of that day had to endure the rigors and hazards of travel under segregated conditions; the rude and rough accommodations that were all that a poverty-stricken though willing people could provide; and above all, the ever present danger of being caught and sold into slavery by lawless, brutal slave catchers. These conditions called for men of strength and courage, and they led, among the black Methodist evangelists as well as the white, to early graves for many. Perhaps a representative picture of what preachers and evangelists endured is seen in this statement about J. J. Moore:

> . . . he travelled on numerous circuits and filled stations in various parts of Pennsylvania, Maryland and Ohio. Crossing the Allegheny Mountains as a traveling preacher, he proclaimed life and salvation to the fugitive slaves who had found an asylum in these mountainous regions. Among the coal and iron mines he carried the gospel on foot, walking thirty miles a day and preaching at night . . . During his busy life of religious labor [he] encountered many perils, being three times shipwrecked at sea, and among hostile Indian tribes while the bullets were flying . . .[43]

The Zion missionaries went east into New England; they went north into upper New York State; they crossed Lake Erie into lower Canada; they went south into New Jersey, Maryland, and Delaware and the District of Columbia; and they went west across the Alleghenys into western Pennsylvania, Ohio, and Indiana. Societies were set up and churches were organized or taken over from the white Methodists. They started with the New York Conference. The Philadelphia Conference was added in 1829, the New England Conference in 1845, and the Allegheny Conference in 1849. The Genesee Conference (western New York State) was organized in 1849, and the Southern or Baltimore Conference in 1859. The missionaries did not venture into the South, of course, because of the bans (restrictions) on travel by blacks both free and slave, and because of the dangers of being seized and sold into slavery.

In 1831 there were 1,689 members, in 1840 there were 3,020 members and 52 preachers; in 1860 there were 4,600 members and 105 preachers,[44] of whom 85 were elders.

THE A.M.E. ZION DIVISION

At the middle of the nineteenth century, the Zion Church suffered a division.

It began in 1852 and lasted for eight years. It was due largely to personal rivalry over the superintendency of the denomination.[45]

In 1840 it was deemed wise to elect an assistant for Superintendent Rush. The person elected was the Reverend William Miller, who was one of the first ministers in the African Chapel. His connection with the denomination had been unstable. He it was who withdrew from Zion Chapel to found Asbury Chapel, and who later led Asbury Church back to the Methodist Episcopal Church, then to Bishop Allen's movement, and then again back into the Zion denomination in 1830. He must have been a man of strong personal influence, for by 1840 he had regained sufficient status in the denomination of the elected Assistant Superintendent to General Superintendent Rush.

In 1846 Miller died, and at the General Conference of 1848

George Galbreath was elected Assistant to Christopher Rush who was re-elected General Superintendent. In 1852 Christopher Rush had to retire because of blindness. In the election for the presiding officer, George Galbreath was chosen General Superintendent and William Bishop Assistant Superintendent. However, objection was raised as to the legality of the election, and it was ruled out of order. A second election was held. This time the Reverend William H. Bishop was elected General Superintendent and George Galbreath Assistant Superintendent. Galbreath, however, was dissatisfied. He thought he should have been elected General Superintendent succeeding Christopher Rush and that Reverend Bishop should have been the Assistant. To ease the conflict, the Conference voted to do away with the term "General" Superintendent and to make all Superintendents co-equal. Also a third Superintendent, George A. Spywood was elected. Each Superintendent was assigned to an area.

Galbreath died in 1853. This left two Superintendents, William Bishop and George Spywood. Before Galbreath died he proposed that the name of the denomination be changed from "African Methodist Episcopal" to "Wesleyan Methodist Episcopal." Reverend Bishop, who wanted to reverse the action of 1852 and return to the general superintendency, also adopted Galbreath's idea of changing the name. He was charged with a violation of the Discipline, and was ordered to appear for trial. This he refused to do, and he was consequently suspended. He thereupon withdrew from the denomination and took a large share of the members to form the Wesleyan Methodist Church. A court case in Pennsylvania ruled that the Bishop faction could not take church properties belonging to the parent denomination. The original Zion denomination continued under Superintendent Spywood.

The split in the Church seems to have been regretted by all parties. Efforts were soon made to achieve reunion. In 1856 the Bishop faction indicated to the General Conference that they wanted to reunite. Also Mother Zion Church in New York, the strongest church in the denomination, wanted the breach healed, and suggested that the two sides meet there in 1860. A plan for a basis of reunion had been previously presented to the two factions. Therefore, when the groups met in New York in 1860,[46] they immediately adopted the first statement of the plan which was: "Resolved: That all matters pertaining to former difficulties be laid aside forever."[47]

Thus ended the one great split in the denomination which for a time threatened to sever the Church into two or three factions, but which ended fortunately with little or no damage to the denomination.

THE A.M.E. ZION CHURCH AND SLAVERY

The A.M.E. Zion Church became one of the strongest and most effective antislavery agencies of the time. It served not only as a source of protest, but through its ministry and members it also was active in helping fugitive slaves to make their way to freedom.

An example of organized protest and appeal to the national conscience is seen in a statement issued by the General Conference of 1856 held in New York:

> Whereas, the whole nation is now agitated upon the great sin of American slavery, which is regarded as the sum of all villainies, it is time for every honest hearted man to define his position before the world either for or against this great moral evil . . .
>
> Therefore, Resolved, that it is the duty of the members of this General Conference to take a Gospel stand against the sin of slavery, as against all other sins, in teaching, preaching, praying and voting; and to let the world know that so long as this sin remains . . . we will, through God's help, be found on the side of the slaves, whether they be white or black . . .[48]

The Zion Church through both clergy and laity was especially active in helping slaves to escape and make their way to freedom. Through the work of the Zion missionaries churches had been organized in northern and western New York, particularly in the region around the cities of Jamestown, Rochester, Syracuse, Utica, and Buffalo. This area was one of the main sections of the "Underground Railroad," that chain of friendly homes, churches, and other stopping places where harried and hunted slaves might find food, shelter, rest, and cover in their dash for Lake Erie and

Canada where at last they could be free. Located in the area, the Zion churches naturally had opportunity to be active and helpful.

Among the leaders in antislavery efforts were Catherine Harris, Thomas James, Frederick Douglass, Harriet Tubman, Jermain Loguen, and Sojourner Truth.[49] Catherine Harris lived in Jamestown, New York. Her home was one of the "hottest underground railroad stations in the country." Once "she had 17 slaves in the house at one time and cooked and 'did' for all of them until it was safe for them to go."[50] The A.M.E.Z. Church in Jamestown was started in her home.

The Reverend Thomas James was an outstanding opponent of slavery. Born a slave in New York State, he was separated from his mother by sale when eight years old. At seventeen he escaped to Canada. He returned to New York State after several years and found work on the Erie Canal. He joined the Memorial A.M.E.Z. Church in Rochester in 1823, and in 1833 became a traveling preacher. He became interested in the abolition movement in 1831. He came to be one of the greatest advocates of freedom in the nation. He pastored churches in Rochester, New Bedford, Massachusetts, and Long Island. In each place he conducted antislavery meetings, helped fugitive slaves, and worked with the abolitionists. He is credited with getting *"Jim Crow"* cars on the railroads of the Northeast outlawed.[51]

Frederick Douglass is, of course, the most famous of black abolitionists. In his escape from slavery he found shelter and help in the Zion Church in New Bedford, Massachusetts. James W. Hood says of him:

> Fred Douglass, one of the most remarkable men that the race has produced, admits that he is indebted to the African Methodist Episcopal Zion Church in New Bedford, Mass., for what he is. As sexton, class leader, and local preacher in that Church he got his inspiration, training, and send-off, which have made him the wonder of his time.[52]

Fred Douglass' lifework, however, was not in the ministry of the Church, but in the secular abolition movement in which he became a powerful force.[53]

Another great antislavery worker in the A.M.E.Z. Church was

Isabella Baumfree, who gave herself the name of Sojourner Truth. Born a slave in New York State, she experienced the cruelties of slavery at their worst in her childhood and youth: brutal beatings, sold three times, forced to live in direst poverty and want. After obtaining her freedom under New York's emancipation law of 1829, she felt religiously called to be a liberator of her people. She became an ardent, effective worker in the abolition movement, working beside Frederick Douglass and William Lloyd Garrison. She became noted for one of her remarks. At a meeting when Douglass was speaking, he felt that the only way slavery could be abolished would be through bloodshed. In the midst of his address she called out to him: "Frederick, is God dead?" She was opposed to violence.

A brief but touching picture of her is given in Bishop Walls's book *The African Methodist Episcopal Zion Church.*[54]

Jermain Loguen, who became one of the Bishops of the Church, was born a slave in Tennessee. When about twenty-one years of age he escaped to Canada. A passage from a letter that he wrote to his friend Frederick Douglass in 1856 gives a revealing picture of the plight and the triumph of the fugitive slave:

Twenty-one years ago—the very winter I left my chains in Tennessee—I stood on this spot [in Hamilton, Ontario] penniless, ragged, lonely, homeless, helpless, hungry and forlorn—a pitiable wanderer without a friend or shelter, or place to lay my head. I had broken from the sunny South, and fought a passage through storms and tempests, which made the forests crash and the mountains moan, difficulties new, awful, and unexpected . . . There I stood, a boy twenty-one years of age (as near as I know my age) the tempests howling over my head, and my toes touching the snow beneath my worn-out shoes—with the assurance that I was at the end of my journey—knowing nobody, and nobody knowing me or noticing me . . . I can never forget the moment. I was in the last extremity. I had freedom, but nature and man were against me. I could only look to God, and I prayed . . . an earthly father took me to his home and an angel wife who became to me a mother. He thought a body lusty and stout as mine, could brave cold, and cut cord wood, and split rails, and he was right . . . They paid me better than I asked, and taught me many lessons of religion and life. I had a home and place for my heart to repose and had been happy but for the thought that ever torments the fugitive, that my mother, sisters and brothers were in cruel bondage, and I could never embrace them again.

Hamilton . . . is now an Underground Railroad Depot, where [the fugitive] is embraced with warm sympathy. Here is where the black man is disencumbered of the support of master and mistress, and their imps, and gets used to self-ownership. Here he learns the first lessons in books, and grows into shape. Fortunately for me, I gained the favor of the best white people . . . They took me into the Sabbath School at Hamilton, and taught me letters the winter of my arrival; and I graduated a Bible reader at Ancaster, close by, the succeeding summer . . .[55]

After several years of farming in Ontario, Loguen returned to western New York State. He pursued further education, joined the A.M.E.Z. Church, was ordained by Superintendent Christopher Rush in 1843, and served as a pastor in Syracuse. With regard to his antislavery activities, J. W. Hood says: "It is doubtful if any one man did more than Bishop Loguen in aiding those who were in search of liberty; hence he was called the "Underground Railroad King."[56] It was largely because of his prominence as a freedom worker and abolitionist that he was elected a Bishop of the Church in 1864, and again in 1868.

Harriet Tubman is one of the truly great women of American history. Fortunately, the story of her life has been well preserved and written, much more so than for most black historic personalities. Her exploits as a leader in the Underground Railroad are almost incredible. She helped hundreds of fugitives to freedom. One biographer writes:

Sometimes Harriet and her slave collections took shelter in a Rochester Church. That was the African Methodist Episcopal Zion Church at Spring and Favor Streets. Fugitives by the score hid in its pews. Here also was her spiritual home while in Rochester.[57]

Equally thrilling is the story of her work in the Northern army, in which she served as a scout and intelligence officer. After emancipation she continued to work in the women's suffrage movement, and in providing for poor and elderly Negroes. She was a faithful member and worker in the A.M.E.Z.

Church, and deeded her home and land to the Church in 1903 to be used as a home for the poor. It was formally opened in 1908, and in 1974 the home was designated a National Historic Landmark. The home is located in Auburn, New York.

A DATE FOR THE A.M.E. ZION BEGINNING

It is difficult to fix upon a date for the actual founding of the A.M.E. Zion denomination. At no time was there a single corporate action by the group of churches setting themselves apart as a new church body or denomination, such as the action taken by the A.M.E.'s in Philadelphia in 1816. Indeed, the separation of the Zionites from the Methodist Episcopal Church was a long, tortuous, reluctant process resulting as much from neglect or indifference on the part of the white church as from any specific act by the blacks. Some writers take 1796 when the Negro members of John Street Church received permission to meet by themselves as the beginning of the denomination. They overlook the fact, however, that the Negroes were all members of John Street Church and remained so for five years thereafter. The "African" or Zion Chapel which was later built was simply a mission branch of John Street Church. Also, the Zion Chapel until 1820 was under the supervision of an elder appointed by the New York Annual Conference.

The agreement made between Zion Chapel and the M.E. Church in 1801 did give the trustees of Zion Chapel special control over their church property and over some other aspects of church life, but the same agreement also provided that

> the Trustees and members of the African Methodist Episcopal Church do acquiesce and accord with the rules of the Methodist Episcopal Church for their church government and discipline, and with their creed and articles of faith, and that they and their successors will continue forever in union with the Methodist Episcopal Church in the City of New York, subject to the government of the present Bishops and their successors, in all their ecclesiastical affairs and transactions . . .

The agreement provided further "that the elder of the Methodist Episcopal Church . . . in the City of New York, appointed as aforementioned, shall have the direction and management of the spiritual concerns of the said Zion Church . . ."[58]

It was under this arrangement that both Zion and Asbury Chapels continued in the Methodist Episcopal Church until the Stillwell controversy of 1820. The two Chapels were separate and distinct units or congregations enjoying certain special privileges, but they were fully within the Methodist Episcopal Church in faith and polity and were willingly subject to its government. They were not in any sense a separate denomination or church body.

When the Reverend William Stillwell in 1820 withdrew from the Methodist Episcopal Church he automatically would have lost his place as elder of Zion and Asbury Chapels, for it was provided in the agreement of 1801 and had been the custom for years that the elder in charge of these churches should be appointed by the New York Conference. It was the vacillation of the Methodist Bishops and the presiding elder of New York City in failing to appoint a successor to Reverend Stillwell that led to certain actions on the part of the black members that tended toward complete separation, but did not reach that point for several years.

In trying to find their way through the Stillwell controversy and its effects on them, the black members of Zion Church decided, first, not to go to Bishop Allen, for he would not take them unless they submitted to his control. They decided, secondly, not to "return to the white people," that is, to put themselves wholly under the New York Conference, for this would mean loss of control over their church properties and the other special privileges that they enjoyed. To further protect these privileges, they wrote and adopted a new "Discipline" which stipulated their patterns of property control and also provided for more lay participation in church government. They gave themselves a name, "The African Methodist Episcopal Church in America.") But they were still part of the Methodist Episcopal Church. At no time had they announced separation from it or abjured its jurisdiction.

As a constructive solution to their plight they did make in 1821 a proposal to the Philadelphia and New York annual conferences.

At the suggestion of Ezekiel Cooper, a distinguished and venerable Methodist preacher, they proposed that a special black annual conference be set up in the New York area composed of all the Negro churches and societies, with its own *ordained* Negro preachers and officers who would minister only to the black membership. It was to be a special conference *within* the Methodist Episcopal Church, and fully under the government of the Bishops and General Conference except in such matters as stipulated in the Zion Discipline. The plan proposed was much like the Central Jurisdiction in the Methodist Church which was formed a hundred years later. But again, it was not to be a new denomination. It was to be a special arrangement *within* the Methodist Church.

The Philadelphia Conference liked the plan and recommended its adoption. The New York Conference rejected the plan, pointing out that one annual conference could not set up another. Only the General Conference could set up an annual conference, and they advised the Negro members to await the General Conference of 1824.

The Zionites were willing to wait, but in the meantime they had to have ordained preachers. This they obtained through Reverend Stillwell and other friendly white ministers.

In the three years from 1821 to 1824, Zion and Asbury were joined by other black churches in holding annual meetings. These meetings were really an implementation of the plan proposed to the Philadelphia and New York conferences. The black churches met by themselves, to be sure, but they elected a Bishop of the Methodist Church as President. When he could not attend, a white minister, the Reverend William Phoebus, was chosen in the Bishop's place. The second year, 1822, the same procedure was followed. When no whites could attend to preside, Abraham Thompson was chosen President. Again, these meetings were separate, but they were still regarded as within the Methodist Episcopal Church.

In the session of 1821, Wesley Church from Philadelphia was pressing for the formation of a new denomination altogether separate from the mother church. On the other hand, Asbury Chapel in New York City, which up to then had been the faithful companion of Zion Chapel, withdrew from the group and returned to the Methodist Episcopal Church, and then a year later went over to Bishop Allen's group, the A.M.E.'s.

The second session of the group in 1822 first met in Philadelphia. It did not complete its work, however, and an adjourned session was held in New York City in July 1822. It was at this adjourned session that the six preachers were ordained deacons in the morning and elders in the afternoon. It was also at this session that James Varick was elected "Superintendent."

The group met in third session in New York on May 21, 1823. Wesley Church in Philadelphia did not send a representative and Asbury Chapel had withdrawn from the group. It was not an encouraging prospect. They were hoping for favorable action from the General Conference which was to meet in the next year.

It was not until after the General Conference of 1824 that it became clear to the black churches that they would have to be on their own. The General Conference decided that the special arrangements requested by the black churches were unacceptable. If these churches wished to continue in the Methodist Episcopal Church they would have to be fully under its government like other churches. They could not have their own Discipline nor their own exceptional arrangement as they proposed. It was in the face of this refusal that the little group of black churches met in New York July 15, 1824. The issue was clear. They would either have to submit or separate. They reluctantly proceeded with their already established organization. Perhaps 1824 is the clearest time for marking the complete separation of the African Methodist Episcopal Church in America from the Methodist Episcopal Church. The name Zion was added later.

CONCLUSION

And so by 1860 the Methodist Episcopal Church in America had spawned two black offshoots, the African Methodist Episcopal Church of Philadelphia, and the African Methodist Episcopal Zion Church of New York.

In 1860 neither group was very large. The A.M.E.'s had only 19,963 members, and the A.M.E.Z.'s had only 4,600. This was because both groups were able to work only among Negroes in the North whose number was comparatively small and where Negroes were mostly free. But both churches were well organized and had high potential for growth.

Each organization had a complete hierarchy of Methodist Episcopal clerical offices ranging from Bishops and General Superintendents at the top to local preachers and exhorters at the bottom.

Each organization had a growing number of church buildings and other properties. Despite the poverty of their members, they were steadily growing in financial resources.

Each had an increasing, loyal laity who were growing in their appreciation of black church membership and of the prestige and dignity it bestowed upon the members. Within their church groups they could move without the humiliations of segregation and discrimination, and without embarrassment at their obvious deficiencies in white culture.

They had their own Books of Discipline, but these were adapted from the Discipline of the parent white church and differed mainly on points of organization and polity. In faith, doctrine, and pattern of Christian life they were thoroughly Methodist and faithful followers of Wesley.

The separation of these black bodies from the mother Church was originally due to the failure of that Church to work out an acceptable place for its black members within the Church body. But in the years since 1816 the clergy of the black bodies had had a taste of the prestige and power of clerical office, and they were determined to keep it by remaining separate. Indeed, they were reluctant to do anything that might curtail their powers, even the consideration of union between the two black bodies themselves.

CHAPTER VIII

Continuing Methodism

WHEN THE SEPARATE black Methodist denominations were formed, some Negroes left the Methodist Episcopal Church to join them, but the number was not as large as is often believed. As a matter of fact, only a few left.

In 1816 there were 42,304 black members in the M.E. Church. Only 1,066 withdrew with Richard Allen, and four years later only 1,406 were in the five churches that formed the A.M.E. Zion denomination. Despite a great deal of propagandizing by the black bodies, at no time was there a wholesale rush out of the Methodist Church.

This is seen in the slow growth of the black bodies and also in the steady growth of the black M.E. Church membership. After ten years, in 1826, the A.M.E.'s had 5,637 members, the Methodist Church had 54,065 black members. In 1840 the A.M.E.'s had 9,223 members, the Methodists had 87,197. Thus, down to 1844 the time of the great split of Methodism into North and South, it is clear that most Negro members remained in the Methodist Episcopal Church.

Figures for the black membership of the Northern Methodist Episcopal Church after 1844 are not available, and only the Northern membership can be compared with the African Methodist churches, since these churches could not operate in the South. But the overall growth of black members in the Methodist

Episcopal Church was heavy, and continued to grow. The Bishops of the Methodist Episcopal Church in their address to the General Conference of 1856 stated the black membership in the Northern Church was about 100,000 (members and probationers). This included 28,000 black members in the border states of Maryland, Delaware, Kentucky, and Missouri.[1]

As to why most Negroes preferred to remain in the "mother" Church there are a number of reasons. First of all, in their beginnings the black denominations were small and unimpressive. Five little churches with fourteen hundred members are not impressive or promising beginnings for denominations. So small was the beginning of the A.M.E.'s that the first annual conferences were held in homes. Daniel Payne, the first historian, is not sure that any annual conference was held in 1817, and he could find no record of the General Conference in 1820.[2] At the start the black denominations were not only small but they seemed trivial and impermanent. They had little appeal for persons seeking a permanent church connection. Payne says: "This then was the origin of the African Methodist Church. Poor and lowly, an outcast and despised of men, it thus entered feebly into being; . . ."[3]

Secondly, the efforts at ecclesiastical independence on the part of the two black groups to many persons white and black seemed ludicrous, to say the least. To have black men, some of whom had been slaves and could hardly read calling themselves Bishops, General Superintendents, Presiding Elders, General Officers, and other high-sounding titles was almost comic audacity. Even the members of Zion Church in New York City spoke deprecatingly of the "Allenite" or "Bethelite" movement as they called it.[4] Only the personal prestige and devoted leadership of such truly outstanding men as Richard Allen, James Varick, and Christopher Rush kept the early churches from being widely regarded as ridiculous.

Another reason for remaining in the white Church was that separate meetings among Negroes, even religious ones, were publicly disapproved and often legally forbidden. Even though the young churches courageously went ahead with their activities, they had to move with caution. They were often subjected to harassment, and sometimes they were unable to act at all. For instance, in the Baltimore Conference of 1819, Payne says: "we find in two instances how utterly futile were the 'Ways and Means' adopted by the Conference of 1819 to prevent the dreaded 'discord, schisms, tattling and tale-bearing.' "[5]

Or again, as late as 1832 Payne says "our churches in certain quarters were quite seriously threatened" and that in Delaware the "Ambassadors of the Cross were not allowed to itinerate."[6]

On several occasions records indicate that Zion Church in New York City had to ask for police protection against "Boys and unruly Persons."[7] Such difficulties did not increase the attractiveness of the black bodies.

One main reason why many blacks preferred to remain in the Methodist Episcopal Church was that this provided an opportunity for wholesome association with whites, at least the most wholesome association possible at the time. If they worshiped in the same churches with whites they were in most cases segregated, especially where the Negro membership was large, but they were still members of the congregation. Or if they worshiped in separate congregations of their own, they were separate to be sure, but they still had much in common with their white fellow Methodists. They all held a common faith, their lives were ordered by the same religious ideals, and in a real if limited way they were brothers and sisters in Christ. These relationships in the church naturally carried over into the workaday world. And here any kind of brotherly concern or kindred feelings were highly helpful.

When people were politically helpless, economically strangled, and legally defenseless as Negroes were both slave and free, one of the surest survival resources a disadvantaged person could have was a friend in the power structure or dominant group. For example, Richard Allen was once saved from being sold down South into slavery by an outlaw slave catcher through the strong and kindly efforts of a white sheriff. Membership in the white Church provided opportunity for contacts and associations that touched many areas of life besides the religious. These contacts were often the source not only of security but of economic advancement, and sometimes they were the source of manumissions.

Another reason why blacks remained in the M.E. Church was that this Church was one of the friendliest of all the major Protestant bodies toward Negroes, and was one of, if not the most vigorous and effective spokemen for Negro rights and freedom. Some other bodies, such as the Quakers, were strong in their antislavery and abolitionist pronouncements, but they were reluctant to take Negroes into the societies.[8] Methodists by contrast openly sought Negroes and took them readily into the societies and into the churches, conforming as time passed, however, to prevailing patterns of racial discrimination and segregation.

Of course, as has been previously said, in a large nationwide organization such as the Methodist Church there was not just one attitude on the Negro question, there were many. There were some who felt that the withdrawal of the Negroes into separate bodies was good riddance. There were others who regretted that Negroes would leave, but felt that it was not a complete loss since they still were Methodists. As Nathan Bangs put it, "We cannot do otherwise than wish them all spiritual and temporal blessings in Christ Jesus. Though formally separated from us in name, we still love them as our spiritual children, and stand ready to aid them, as far as we may, in extending the Redeemer's Kingdom among men."[9] With regard to slavery and abolition, the attitudes in the Church ran the whole scale. It may be said in general that at one end was the North which was antislavery and abolitionist, especially New England. On the other end was the South which not only accepted slavery, but defended it. It was the North, however, with its agitation for the abolition of slavery that made Negroes look upon the Methodist Church as friendly, and to look upon such men as James O'Kelly, Freeborn Garrettson, Orange Scott, and George Storrs as their champions.[10] Of course, as time passed and the slave power grew the Church softened its protests and compromised its Wesleyan ideals. It seems safe to say, however, that the overall attitude of the Church toward Negroes was one of friendly helpfulness. Even in the South where the Church defended slavery, the Mission to the Slaves expressed a spiritual and mildly humanitarian interest.

For reasons such as these the great majority of the Negro members remained in the M.E. Church until the Civil War. Yet to stay in the Church did not mean peace or freedom from problems. It may have meant more problems since the black members were thence beset from two sides. From the outside they were cajoled and taunted by the African Methodists who accused the M.E. members of being voluntarily submissive, of lacking in independence, in manhood, and in self-determination. In his *History of the A.M.E. Church,* Daniel Payne devoted a chapter to "the beneficial results of separation from the M.E. Church." The chapter was aimed, of course, at the black brothers who did not separate. He says:

> In 1792 the number of the colored members constituted but about one-fourth of the whole Methodist fellowship in the states. In 1828, about thirteen years after, it constituted still about one-fourth. In 1840, about twelve years later, it formed less than one-seventh, of the whole church, and in 1845, it formed about one-tenth. So, viewed in whatever light you please, the existence of the colored man as a factor in the M.E. Church, always was, still is, and ever must be a mere cipher. The tendency of all this was to prove that the colored man was incapable of self-government and self-support. But is not the existence of the African Methodist Episcopal Church a flat contradiction and triumphant refutation of this slander, so foul in itself and so degrading in its influence?[11]

There were also problems coming from the inside. In particular there were the three old problems of discrimination in church membership, the refusal of the Church to ordain black preachers, and its refusal to set up black annual conferences. For forty years prior to 1864 memorials or petitions had been presented to the quadrennial General Conferences requesting these three actions. Each time the petitions were kindly received but persistently turned down. When the Church split into North and South in 1844, it was hoped by the black members of the North that their Church would now grant the three requests. Strong memorials both in writing and in person were presented to the General Conference of 1848, only to be turned down with the statement that such actions at that time would be "inexpedient." To the black members, this was disheartening. They felt that it strengthened the hands of the black churches. One black M.E. member bitterly complained that the black denominations increased by one-fourth between 1844 and 1866 because of the M.E. Church's refusal to ordain black preachers or to set up black conferences, and thus give its black members fuller self-expression.[12]

And yet the negative attitude of the Church toward Negro ordinations and separate conferences must not be taken as indicative of a completely anti-Negro feeling. In terms of the times the Northern Methodist Church was still quite liberal and genuinely concerned in Negro welfare and progress. There were several actions that indicated a steady growth in liberalism. In 1852 and 1866, for instance, the M.E. Church, North, elected two black bishops. They were elected for work in Africa, to be sure, but they had all the rights and privileges of other Methodist bishops.

The first of these, Francis Burns, was elected a missionary Bishop for Liberia. He was an American Negro who was sent to Liberia as a missionary, and in 1858 was called back to America to be consecrated a Bishop. It was said that his ordination sermon would have been creditable to any of the Methodist bishops. He was the first black Bishop in the Methodist Episcopal Church.[13]

The second black Bishop, John W. Roberts, who succeeded Bishop Burns, was also a native American, but when a child he was taken to Liberia by his mother along with his two brothers under the American Colonization Society. The three boys grew up in Liberia, all joined the Methodist Church, and all became distinguished men. One son, Joseph J. Roberts, became President of Liberia. The youngest son became an outstanding physician, and the middle son, John, was elected missionary Bishop of Liberia in 1866. He too was consecrated in America, and served nine years until his death in Liberia in 1875. The election of these two black Bishops was a highly advanced step for a major American denomination.

In 1864, again in response to urgent appeals, the General Conference at last authorized the ordaining of black preachers as traveling elders and the organizing of two black annual conferences, the Washington and Delaware Conferences. These permitted black Methodists to have their own congregations and their own preachers and such management of their own affairs as an annual conference affords.[14]

A further indication of benevolent interest is seen in an educational effort that the M.E. Church undertook in 1856. The Ohio Annual Conference, meeting in Cincinnati, Ohio,

> decided to "establish a school for the benefit of the African race." The site selected for the school was Tawawa Springs (Sweet Water), which is three miles north-east of Xenia, Ohio. The school opened in September, 1856, with Dr. Richard S. Rust as President. The institution ran successfully until the spring of 1862, when it was forced to close its doors. This was due to the pressure of the Civil War which forced the patrons of the institution, who were chiefly slaveholders in the South, to cease supporting it.[15]

The school had incurred a debt of $10,000. In 1863 President Rust informed Bishop Payne of the A.M.E. Church that his Church could have the property for the amount of the debt alone. This was almost a gift, for the state of Ohio would have paid a much higher price in order to develop an asylum on the property.[16] Bishop Payne by strenuous effort purchased the school, and thus, through the generosity of the M.E. Church, Wilberforce University came into being.

There is one other phase of Methodist interest in the Negro which must not be overlooked, and that is the tremendous and heroic part that the Northern Church played in the Civil War. The Church was concerned not only to preserve the Union, but it was also concerned to drive human slavery from the nation. In recognition of the great contribution of the Methodist Church in this regard, President Abraham Lincoln said:

> Nobly sustained as the government has been by all the churches, I would utter nothing which might in the least appear infidious against any; yet, without this, it may be fairly said that the Methodist Episcopal Church, not less devoted than the best, is, by its greater numbers, the most important of all. It is no fault in others that the Methodist Church sends more soldiers to the field, more nurses to the hospitals, and more prayers to Heaven, than any. God bless the Methodist Church! Bless all the Churches! And blessed be God, who, in this our great trial, giveth us the Churches![17]

Of course in fighting to preserve the Union, to defeat the South and for the extirpation of slavery, the Church was championing the Negroes' cause and it was also expressing its continuing interest which came to fullest flower in the missions to the freedmen following the War.[18]

Facts such as these enabled the Negro members to stay in the Methodist Church with dignity and pride, to love it, and to feel as one black member felt, "The colored man from one end of this country to the other had always recognized the Methodist Episcopal Church as a friend to him and his, a friend whose sympathies were worth a great deal."[19]

SUMMARY

Thus in its first fifty years, Methodism had come face to face with and had begun to struggle with America's severest human problem, the race problem, and the Church would continue to struggle with this problem for a hundred and fifty years.

The Church began nobly in true Christian spirit. The early preachers demanded freedom for the slaves and an end to the horrible brutalities of the slave system. The men who preached this doctrine in the beginning and who continued to preach it down to the Civil War were heroes of the highest kind, paying for their preachments with pain, privation, and in some cases death.

The Church was soon to learn, however, that evil does not yield easily, even to righteous declarations, especially when the declarations come from a comparative handful of uninfluential preachers who were looked upon as overzealous enthusiasts of a strange if not fanatical faith. The Church was also to learn, sadly for some such as Asbury and Coke, that church members are human. Not all are heroes. Thus compromise and concession are as integral in church people as protest and struggle.

The Church learned, too, that its race problem was not a simple one capable of a quick and single solution. Instead it was complex and confusing, making direct action difficult and sometimes questionable. This was true even for the black churchmen. On the one hand they wanted to be members in full standing in the main Church without segregation. On the other hand they wanted and needed religious services that would speak to their particular life situations and meet their spiritual needs. This dual if not paradoxical attitude, when complicated with human prejudice and caste feelings, made a problem that was difficult of solution, and led to withdrawal by the blacks.

Thus by 1816 and 1820 two separate denominations were springing from the parent body and would not be reunited even until our own time. The Church, however, continued to struggle, and even underwent severe pains for its concern.

CHAPTER IX

The Mission to the Slaves

FROM ITS BEGINNING in America, the Methodist movement was interested in the Negro's religious welfare. They preached to and converted large numbers of Negroes and took them readily into Methodist membership. In 1787 Negroes were 15 per cent of Methodist membership. By 1800 they were 20 per cent or 13,500.[1]

It soon developed, however, that there was a great difference between membership in the denomination and membership in a local church. Segregation of Negroes began to appear in earliest days when Methodism consisted mainly of preaching services in loosely organized "Societies." The earliest preachers were disturbed by the fact that Negroes, mostly slaves, were not always permitted to attend the services, and when they did attend they had to sit in separate sections or hang about windows and doors. Preachers were often able to reach blacks only in separate services held in kitchens or outhouses or in meetings after the regular services. Then later, as Methodism became an established church with church buildings and a resident ministry, patterns of segregation in church life not only continued but crystallized. In the North it became customary to seat Negroes along the walls, or in the rear, or in the balcony if a church had one. In the South slave balconies became regular features of church buildings, and in places where there were blacks in large numbers, such as on the larger plantations, there might even be a special house for slave meetings.

In the North these discriminations were irritating and humiliating to the black members, who often were free Negroes.[2] Such discriminations in Methodist churches in Philadelphia, Baltimore, and other cities had led to the withdrawal of blacks into separate congregations, and later to the formation of the African Methodist Episcopal denomination in 1816, and the African Methodist Episcopal Zion denomination in 1824.

A second source of disturbance to black members was the refusal of the Methodist Church to ordain black preachers as itinerant elders, the highest order in the Methodist ministry. It was not until 1800 that the General Conference permitted Negro preachers to be ordained local deacons, and Richard Allen was the first black preacher to be so ordained in the Methodist Church.[3] But a local deacon could only serve in the location where he resided. He could not travel to evangelize or to preach in other churches, and he lacked other rights and privileges of the traveling ministry.

While the discriminations offended Negroes, they were almost to be expected. The Negro's social status as a slave or half slave made it almost impossible for whites in the North to accept him as a social equal even in the Church. In the South the Negro's status as a slave made such acceptance out of the question. In churches both North and South the names of black members were carried on the church rolls, but there were sharp restrictions on the participation of the black members.

In considering the Methodist Church, it is not to be regarded as a unit with all members thinking and acting alike. In American Methodism, as in all large bodies, attitudes varied widely. As a general rule, most Methodists were conservative in racial matters and followed the prevailing social patterns of their areas, both in secular life and in church life. Since segregation in varying forms was the prevailing social rule all over the nation, most Methodists followed their localities. The great majority of Methodists were also conservative in their attitude toward slavery, and many were slaveowners. But while this was the majority, at each end of the scale there were the radical exceptions. In the North there were the abolitionist Methodists who were completely opposed to slavery and demanded its elimination from American life. Such persons were Orange Scott, George Storrs, and LaRoy Sunderland. The abolitionists were also opposed to discrimination and segregation of Negroes especially in the Church, but also in secular life.[4] Some of these Methodists became leaders in the national abolitionist movement.

At the other end there were the Southern Methodists who not only tolerated slavery, but openly defended it and tried to justify it from Scripture and history. Yet the Southerners were Methodists, and it was the Methodist aim to preach the Gospel to every creature. To fulfill this aim, Southern Methodists developed the *Mission to the Slaves*. This mission, apparently so noble, and yet in many ways so morally blind, was a direct result of the interest of Southern Methodists in the Negro's religious welfare.

One result of the evangelistic movements that swept across America after the Revolutionary War was the emphasis on missions, that is, on reaching the unreached and taking the Gospel to every creature. Congregationalists, Episcopalians, Presbyterians, and Baptists, as well as Methodists, were all moved with this purpose. In 1812 the American Board of Commissioners for Foreign Missions [5] sent out their first workers. In 1814 the Baptists organized the Convention for Foreign Missions.[6] The American Colonization Society had as one of its major objectives the "Christianizing of the Africans." Methodists organized their own national mission society in 1819 under the leadership of Nathan Bangs.[7]

One fertile field for missionary activity, of course, was the large and growing number of Afro-American slaves in the South. Some of these people had been taken into the Methodist Church through its regular evangelizing efforts. In 1826, for example, 40 per cent of all Methodists in Georgia and South Carolina were blacks. But the number in the Methodist Church, or any church at all, was very small in comparison with the vast hordes who were untouched. Some Methodists in the South were concerned. One of these was the Reverend James O. Andrew. He pointed out that the number of slaves who were in the church simply pointed to the larger number who ought to be.[8]

In 1824 the South Carolina Conference created a separate department to deal with the Negro's spiritual welfare.[9] Several South Carolina ministers joined in publishing a weekly paper devoted to a mission to the slaves.[10] One thing that did much to further the mission idea happened in 1829 when Charles Cotesworth Pinckney, a wealthy planter and later governor of South Carolina, requested the South Carolina Conference to send missionaries to his plantation. He had found religion to be a helpful influence in controlling his slaves and in improving the moral quality of their lives. This appeal from such a prominent person led other slaveowners to accept the mission idea and to permit the religious instruction of their slaves. In response the South Carolina Conference sent two missionaries into the "low country" on the Santee and Ashley rivers.[11]

It was in 1829 that the man who did most to develop the Mission, and who in many ways was the slave's most sympathetic spokesman, was called into leadership of the mission cause. He was William Capers, who in that year was appointed Superintendent of Missions in the South Carolina Conference. In 1840, eleven years later, he was made Secretary of the Southern Department of Mission Work, and also was made editor of the *Southern Christian Advocate*.[12]

In a remarkable paragraph, Professor Donald G. Mathews gives an accurate and appreciative sketch of Capers:

> Capers was a slaveholder of Huguenot descent who had rejected Blackstone for the Bible, entered the Methodist ministry, and became a pastor to Negroes and a missionary to Indians. A dignified, thoughtful, and moderate man who served the Church far better than most of his fellow Southerners, he was a lifelong "Apostle" to the Negroes. One of his first churches was in the Negro district of Wilmington, N.C.; as a minister in Charleston he had sent out Negro preachers to the slaves despite the illegality of his action. Later as a prominent pastor he fought a hard and bitter fight with cynical whites in his congregation who wished to degrade and segregate the Negro members. To him the slave was a soul to be valued, a human being ultimately equal to the master, even if "uncontrollable circumstances" effaced that equality in society.[13]

Under the leadership of William Capers and with the strong support of men like the Reverend James O. Andrew, the mission grew until it extended over the entire South. The number of missionaries reached 80 in 1844. About 22,000 slaves were listed as members of the missions, but a much larger number heard the preaching and were touched in various ways.

The growth of the mission was not without opposition. Many masters felt that conversion made slaves harder to manage; it would increase their desire for education. Attending meetings caused slaves to lose time from work. Also, the official position of the Methodist Church was that slavery was an evil and should be discontinued as soon as possible. Many slaveholders, therefore, resented Methodism and distrusted the missionaries. They often made it difficult if not impossible to work with their slaves.

This put the mission workers on the defensive and made it necessary for them to prove to the slaveowners that the mission was not against the slave system. William Capers said that the mission led to "superior contentment, improved morals and worthy obedience of Negroes."[14] Capers and other workers had to point out that what they were interested in was the Negro's immortal soul. Reverend Andrew wrote that Negroes were fellow heirs of immortality as were whites, and masters should care for their souls as well as their bodies.[15] This is why the action of Charles Cotesworth Pinckney in 1829 in calling for the instruction of his slaves was such a helpful act to the mission. In an address before the Agricultural Society of South Carolina, Pinckney said: "Nothing is better calculated to render a man satisfied with his destiny in this world than a conviction that its hardships and trials are as transitory as its honors and enjoyments." By improving the slaves' morality, the missions would improve slavery, thus giving the South the "advantage in argument over . . . our Northern Brethren."[16]

Arguments such as these along with the increasingly conservative position of Southern Methodists on the question of slavery[17] eventually brought slaveholders to tolerate the mission if not to enthusiastically welcome it, permitting the missionaries to go forward with their work of converting slaves.

But the opposition of planters was only one problem that the Mission had to face. Another was lack of funds. The national Missionary Society of the Methodist Church made each annual conference financially responsible for its work with slaves. At first large contributions were received, but later funds came from collections raised among slaves, the preachers, laymen, and Sunday School children.[18] In 1844 a total of $22,000 was spent on the Mission. This sum, however, was inadequate for a program as extensive as was the Mission, reaching from Texas to Virginia. It probably is one reason why the number of slaves who were members of the Mission was always comparatively small. The ratio of black to white members in the Methodist Church remained the same despite the work of the Mission.[19]

Some of the severest problems, however, were those faced by the missionaries as they tried to carry on their work. For one thing, it was difficult to get at the slaves. Most of them had little time or opportunity for attending meetings. Another great handicap was that the instruction had to be entirely oral. It could not be supplemented by reading, since reading was prohibited to slaves. Thirdly, so much of the moral teachings was meaningless. For instance, the teachings on duties of husbands to wives and parents to children were worthless since slave marriages and slave families had no legal protections and could be broken up at any time. Teachings on love and brotherly kindness were ironic and meaningless in the presence of the brutal treatment to which many slaves were subjected.

One hardship for the missionary was that he had little help in his work. In the interval of visits to his stations, which might be as much as two or three weeks, the missionary would use local Negro preachers or some faithful black laymen. But the local preachers could not administer the sacraments and the lay teachers who could not read were very limited in what they could teach. The task of instruction fell wholly on the missionary. Teaching under such conditions required great patience as well as great devotion.[20]

This devotion was seen in the determination of the missionaries to carry on under the most adverse conditions. Professor Donald G. Mathews in a few vivid sentences has aptly described the setting of the Mission. "No number of stars in a minister's 'crown' could make it very pleasant to risk health and life in miasmic swamps for the honor of being called a 'nigger preacher.' " Capers wrote a friend that few men could be a servant of slaves literally—treated as inferior by the proprietors, as hardly equal to the overseers, half-starved sometimes, suffocated with smoke, sick with the stench of dirty cabins and as dirty negroes, sleepless from the stings of . . . musquitoes [sic] and all in the very centre . . . of the kingdom of disease . . .[21]

These missionaries were Southerners, members of annual conferences to which they answered. Their purpose was not emancipation, but conversion, and pastoral care . . . [they revelled] in the look of wonder in children's faces, the gratitude of the adults, the prayers of confidence from a dying grandfather. Theirs was not a pleasant task, as Capers had said. For a pittance they would cover broad circuits, perhaps tending 23 congregations in three weeks, always straining to explain their message in plain language and short sentences. After the exhaustion of their patience they might complain of the slaves' "depraved ignorance, blind superstition, and extreme stupidity"—and turn back once again to do their work.[22]

From the 1841 Report of the Missionary Society of the Methodist Episcopal Church, "Missions to the Colored Population":

In no portion of our work are our missionaries called to endure greater privations or to make greater sacrifices of health and life, than in these missions among the slaves, many of which are located in sections of the Southern country which are proverbially sickly, and under the fatal influence of a climate which few white men are capable of enduring even for a single year. And yet, notwithstanding so many valuable missionaries have fallen martyrs to their toils in missions, year after year are found others to take their places, who fall likewise in their work, "ceasing at once to work and live." Nor have our superintendents any difficulty in finding missionaries ready to fill up the ranks which death has thinned in these sections of the work; for the love of Christ and the love of the souls of these poor Africans in bonds, constrain our brethren in the itinerant work of the Southern conferences to exclaim, "here are we, send us!" The Lord be praised for the zeal and success of our brethren in this self-denying and self-sacrificing work.

Since the slaves could not read the Bible or anything else, it was only natural that they knew very little about the Christian faith. Their religious knowledge is described in Chapter II.[23]

It was hard for them to understand much of the preaching without a background of doctrine and knowledge. Therefore, the missionaries had to do as much teaching as preaching. What the slaves were taught was embodied in a catechism which William Capers wrote out in 1833, entitled "A Catechism for Little Children and for Use on the Missions to the Slaves in South Carolina." It consisted of a series of questions and answers which the slaves memorized and repeated back to the teacher, since all of the instruction was oral. The questions dealt with the basic tenets of the Christian faith. These were (1) God so loved the world that He sent His Son into this sinful world to offer new life; (2) the new life could be entered here and hereafter; (3) when converted, people entered the new life here, and if they lived righteously, they would receive eternal life in the last judgment. The Ten Commandments were taught, and selected passages of Scripture were quoted to point out what constituted the good life. (4) Christians should love their enemies, be faithful in marriage, never steal, lie, swear, or break the Sabbath. The slaves were reminded that they were slaves, and that the Scriptures taught obedience to earthly masters as well as to the heavenly Master.[24]

It was generally agreed among the Southerners that the Mission was helpful to slaves and masters. Missionaries reported that slaves were more clean and honest and less thieving and adulterous. The slaves in turn were helped spiritually. "The gospel which the Methodists preached gave some slaves purpose, hope and love in a purposeless, hopeless, loveless world—such as it had to some whites."[25] But the Mission did not at all touch the system of slavery or the Negro's status as a chattel slave. Its purpose was to convert the Negro, not to emancipate him. The catechisms showed that the Mission was neither subversive nor revolutionary.

In summarizing the Mission to the Slaves, on the positive side it can be said first that it was a widely extended work, covering the entire South, but the number of members was comparatively small: 22,000 at the height of the Mission. Yet while only 22,000 were members, the Missions doubtless touched thousands of other persons directly or indirectly.

Secondly, as a source of instruction, the Mission was better than nothing, but its effectiveness was greatly limited because slaves could not read and the instruction was entirely oral. The slaves simply did not have and could not get the background understandings needed for an enlightened appreciation of the Christian religion.

Thirdly, the Mission was the work of earnest, devoted persons who were doing what they could to help the slaves. They could do little for the slaves materially, but they were trying to help them spiritually. By converting the slaves, they felt they were helping them to attain eternal life, which, as the missionaries saw it, was the completely compensating value.

Fourth, the dedicated and sometimes heroic work of the missionaries came to be regarded by Southern Methodists as a symbol of the deep concern that the Southerners had for the slave and his religious welfare. The Mission stood as a symbol of noble service. It assuaged the Southern conscience on the issue of slavery, and it served as a reply to the abolitionists who charged the South with being inconsiderate of the Negro's moral and religious welfare. It enabled the South to appeal to Northern conservatives. In much of the Southern literature of the period the Mission became almost a glorified myth.

Fifth, the Methodist Mission was by far the largest of all work among the slaves. The Episcopalians, Presbyterians, and Baptists all had some mission activities, but none was as extensive or as intensive as the Methodist.[26]

But despite the glorified image of the Mission published by the Southerners, the Mission had its failures, or negative aspects. First was the fact that the Mission did not and possibly could not attack or question the slave system. This deliberate hands-off policy to the moral wrong of slavery was perhaps the only way the missionaries could have carried on their work. They restricted themselves, therefore, to "preaching the Gospel." As the report of the Missionary Society of the South Carolina Conference for 1841 put it:

> So to preach this Gospel that it may be believed; and being believed, may prove "the power of God unto salvation," is the great object, and we repeat it, the *sole* object of our ministrations among the blacks. This object attained, we find the terminus of our anxieties and toils, of our preaching and prayers.[27]

Thus the Mission's inability to challenge the slave system meant that they could never get at the cause of the trouble, which was the slave system itself, and thus the Mission was morally handcuffed.

The Northern abolitionists saw the weaknesses of the Mission. They said it was an attempt to impose religious sanctity on slavery; that one can't teach Christianity without reading the Bible; and that it was wrong to make a mutilated Gospel an instrument of bondage. Orange Scott said that Christianity sought to make a man a bold soldier of Jesus Christ, not a slave.[28]

One scholar, after careful study, concludes: "As a great moral cause the Mission was a noble effort to give men new life; but it also reinforced an ignoble effort to keep men in bondage."[29] It reveals, what we can only see with sadness, the inability of the Church to rise above the thoughts and practices of its time and place.

CHAPTER X

Early Black
Methodist Preachers

THE FIRST METHODIST preachers proclaimed the Gospel to all men, white and black, bond and free. Many slaves welcomed the message and came as they could to hear it. The Methodist Gospel and pattern of religious experience was simple, personal, and readily comprehended by blacks as well as whites. Richard Allen, himself a Methodist convert and preacher, said that the Methodist form of faith was the best for his people.[1] A further reason for the popularity of Methodism among the slaves was the fact that the early preachers actively sought the slaves, made them welcome at the preaching services, and took them into the "Societies."

In the beginning, Methodist preachers were few, and those few were traveling evangelists. They aspired to convert a continent. They covered vast "circuits" that extended often into several counties and sometimes into more than one state. Travel was slow and hazardous and there might be several weeks between a preacher's appearances at a given point.

In the interim between the preachers' visits, the converts were kept "in the way" by local leaders. Among whites these leaders were heads of "classes," which were the basic units of Methodist organization. Among blacks the leaders were often volunteer

Christian workers, persons who had heard the Methodist message, who had felt its saving power in their own lives and were anxious to impart it to their fellows.

Unfortunately we do not even know the names of most of these early black leaders, to say nothing of the story of their lives. We do know that they were largely responsible for the preservation of the faith and its transmission among slaves in the early days. A few examples will show their significance.

On one of his trips through South Carolina in 1788 Bishop Asbury saw a slave fishing on the bank of a stream. "Do you ever pray?" asked the Bishop. "No sir," the slave replied. Bishop Asbury alighted from his horse, sat down by the slave's side, instructed and exhorted him. The poor man wept; the Bishop sang a hymn, knelt with the astonished slave in prayer, and left him.

Forty-eight years after this interview, a Methodist itinerant visited a plantation where it was reported there were many black but unrecognized Methodists. He found between two and three hundred members in a Society. The itinerant asked to see the leader. He was taken to a hoary-headed old black man with palsied limbs but a smiling face, leaning on a staff. "He looked at me a moment in silence, then raising his eyes to heaven, he said, 'Lord, now lettest Thou Thy servant depart in peace, for mine eyes have seen Thy salvation.' He asked me to have a seat. 'I have,' he said, 'many children in this place. I have felt for some time that my end was near. I have looked around to see who might take my place when I am gone. I could find none. I felt unwilling to die and leave them alone, and have been praying to God to send someone to take care of them. The Lord has sent you, my child, and I am ready to go.'

"It was Punch. The Bishops' passing word had raised up an apostle who had, through all these years, been ministering to his neglected people."

People at first would gather at Punch's door for conversation and prayer. Eventually crowds came. The overseer opposed these meetings, and Punch had to work with small groups in homes. But despite opposition from overseers and masters, Punch continued to give religious leadership for near half a century to his fellow slaves. The only name we have for this saint is "Old Punch."[2]

In the mission to the slaves conducted in the first half of the nineteenth century, the volunteer black workers played a large and important part. White preachers or missionaries did the preaching and catechizing, but it was the local black leader, male and female, who kept groups together and made the teachings a part of everyday life. In his work in a mission in Beaufort, South Carolina, a missionary reported that the two or three hundred Negro children whom he catechized "were kept together under the care of an elderly female." He did not give the name of the "female" who performed this important and doubtless wearying work.[3]

A similar instance of volunteer leadership is recorded about the mission on a Louisiana plantation. "Agreeable surprises sometimes awaited a missionary . . . [He would find] a society, rudely organized . . . there before him, with its stated times of worship, its rules, and its members. By purchase or partition of estates, or by immigration, a religious negro or family of negroes was thrown like leaven, into an ignorant mass of his fellow beings, and became a source of instruction and a center of life which took form and grew, even under unpropitious surroundings. One missionary to such a sugar plantation in Louisiana found over thirty 'members': he had these to begin with."[4]

We do not know the number of these humble workers. There must have been many hundreds. They were found in all denominations. We do know that they were largely responsible for making the Christian faith a living fact in the lives of slaves and free black people in America in their day, and thus were responsible for its transmission to later generations.

Very early in the evangelical movements, beginning in the latter half of the eighteenth century, men began to appear who were not satisfied to be just unordained lay workers. They aspired to the full Christian ministry. They wanted to preach the Gospel to all who would hear, and to be leaders of regularly organized congregations. They arose in all of the evangelical bodies. Among Baptists there were such men as David George (c. 1775), preacher of the first Baptist church at Silver Bluff, South

Carolina; George Liele, of Burke County, Georgia, an eloquent preacher to blacks and whites; and Andrew Bryan (1737–1812), founder of the first African Baptist Church of Savannah. There was John Chavis (c. 1801), who was made a missionary to slaves by the Presbyterians; and, most unusual, Lemuel Haynes, a man of learning and eloquence who through all of his life pastored only white congregational churches in New England.[5] The account here, however, is concerned mainly with Methodism, which had its full share of the early black preachers.

Among the earliest black preachers in the Methodist Episcopal Church were Harry Hosier, Absalom Jones, Richard Allen, Daniel Coker, Abraham Thompson, James Varick, Christopher Rush, and Henry Evans. All of these men began their preaching careers in the M.E. Church. With the exception of Harry Hosier and Henry Evans, however, they all later withdrew from the M.E. Church and joined other denominations. It is in connection with the other bodies that their names became best known. Absalom Jones, for example, left the Methodist Church to become the rector of the African Episcopal Church of Saint Thomas in Philadelphia, the first black Episcopal priest in America. Richard Allen was a preacher in the M.E. Church for thirty-six years until the founding of the A.M.E. denomination in which he became the first Bishop. They all began, however, in the Methodist Episcopal Church.

The main reason these men left the Methodist Church was the reluctance of that body to accept them fully into its ministry. The Church did recognize their preaching and organizing abilities, especially in the work with blacks, and used them as exhorters and local preachers, the lowest orders in the Methodist hierarchy. But despite repeated appeals over a long time, the Church would not ordain them as deacons, the middle rank, and certainly not as elders, the highest rank. It was not until 1800 that the General Conference agreed to ordain even black local deacons.

The reasons usually given were first, that the black men were uneducated, which was true. Most could hardly read or write, if at all. Also blacks had difficulty traveling freely enough to meet the demands of the Methodist itinerancy. Yet against these reasons is the fact that these same men made phenomenal contributions to the new denominations that they joined and in some cases helped to start. The thought cannot be downed that these men could have done within the Methodist Church what they did outside it, had the Church decided to utilize their abilities and given them the necessary training.[6] Also, some of the black preachers were striking exceptions. Daniel Coker was not only well educated, but he taught school in Baltimore and published what is perhaps the first pamphlet produced by a black man in America.[7]

For the lives of the earliest preachers records are few and fragmentary. Only in one or two cases do we have anything like adequate biographies or autobiographies. In most cases we only have passing references or comments by interested persons. But even these records indicate that the early black preachers, though lacking in education, were men of intelligence and dedication, and were possessed of remarkable preaching and organizational powers. All were converted in true Methodist fashion; they believed and preached the true Methodist doctrine; and they were aflame with the passion to spread the good news of the love of God, the saving power of Jesus Christ, and the need to flee from the wrath to come by accepting Christ as personal savior.

Most famous among the early Negro Methodist preachers, of course, was Harry Hosier, or, as he was popularly known, "Black Harry." He was a truly remarkable man. Unfortunately we do not have a full biography of him, but we do have allusions to him in contemporary writings and more comments on his great preaching than on any other early Negro preacher. He is mentioned nine times in *Asbury's Journal;* as many times and at greater length in Garrettson's writings; and several times in Coke's Journal. He was the first Methodist preacher white or black whose preaching was commented upon in a New York newspaper, the *Packet.*[8]

Hosier served as Bishop Asbury's traveling servant. He also traveled with Bishop Coke, Freeborn Garrettson, and Richard Whatcoat. Physically he was "small in stature, and perfectly black, but had eyes of remarkable brilliancy and keenness." He was uneducated. He could neither read or write, but "he had a

quick mind, a most retentive memory, and such an eloquent flow
of words, which he could soon put into almost faultless English."
His natural marvelous oratorical gifts made him one of the won-
ders of his time. Dr. Benjamin Rush, the distinguished Quaker of
Philadelphia, said, making allowance for Harry's illiteracy, he
was "the greatest orator in America."[9] Bishop Coke with whom
Harry traveled in 1784 said that he was one of the best preachers
in the world. "I have now had the pleasure of hearing Harry
preach several times," he wrote in his journal. "I sometimes give
notice immediately after preaching, that in a little time he will
preach to the blacks; but the whites always stay to hear him.
Sometimes I publish him to preach at candle-light, as the negroes
can better attend at that time. I really believe that he is one of the
best preachers in the world—there is such an amazing power as
attends his word, though he cannot read, and he is one of the
humblest creatures I ever saw."[10]

Harry "acted as servant or 'driver' for the eminent intinerants,
but excelled them all in popularity as a preacher, sharing with
them in their public services, not only in black, but in white congregations. When they were disabled by sickness or any other
cause, they could trust the pulpit to Harry without fear of un-
favorably disappointing the people. Asbury acknowledges that
the best way to obtain a large congregation was to announce that
Harry would preach; the multitude preferring him to the Bishop
himself."[11]

Harry preached frequently in Maryland, but mostly in the
North. He was very popular in Philadelphia. Bishop Asbury
wrote in his Journal that if Harry would go with him to Virginia
and the Carolinas to preach to the blacks and they could spend
six months there, "it would be attended with a blessing." But
Harry was unwilling to go.[12]

In 1790 Harry traveled with Freeborn Garrettson. At Hudson,
N.Y., Garrettson says:

> I found the people very curious to hear Harry. I therefore
> declined preaching, that their curiosity might be satisfied. The
> different denominations heard him with much admiration, and the
> Quakers thought that as he was unlearned he must preach by im-
> mediate inspiration.[13]

At another town in the same area Garrettson writes:

"I rode in the afternoon and preached in Salisbury, in a part of the town in which I had never before been, and I think I have never seen so tender a meeting in this town before, for a general weeping ran through the assembly, especially while Harry gave an exhortation. The Lord is carrying on a blessed work here.[14]

Harry accompanied Garrettson on his pioneering excursion into New England, going as far as Boston. In all of the cities Harry preached regularly, his audiences numbering hundreds, and on one occasion in Providence, more than a thousand. He was not entirely free from the rebuffs that the early evangelists received, however. In Hartford, Connecticut, the people received him "very uncivilly." Asbury relates that in Maryland "certain sectarians are greatly displeased with him, because he tells them they may fall from grace, and that they must be holy."[15]

This latest statement by Asbury is the best indication that we have of *what* Harry preached. All the other statements are about *how* he preached, and the powerful effects of his messages, but we have no clear examples of his sermons or his theology or his social opinions. Since his messages were received with such rapturous praise by nearly all who heard him, it can safely be concluded that he preached the typical Methodist form of the Christian Gospel and that he was noncontroversial in his social preachments.

It is said that near the end of his life, Harry became addicted to drink. In the opinion of his peers, he "fell from grace." Abel Stevens, the Methodist historian, says: "Though he withstood for years the temptations of extraordinary popularity, he fell, nevertheless, by the indulgent hospitalities which were lavished upon him. He became temporarily the victim of wine, but had moral strength enough to recover himself. Self-abased and contrite, he started one evening down the Neck, below Southwark, Philadelphia, determined to remain till his backslidings were healed. Under a tree he wrestled in prayer into the watches of the night. Before the morning God restored him to the joys of his salvation. Thenceforward he continued faithful. He resumed his public labors, and about the year 1810 [1806] died in Philadelphia, 'making a good end,' and was borne to the grave by a great procession of both white and black admirers, who buried him as a hero, once overcome, but finally victorious."[16]

But despite any weakness or limitations in thought or training, for a black man and a slave, or near slave, to rise to the top of a respected profession, equalling or excelling the greatest in the field, proves that here we are in the presence of a truly rare human being who used his great gifts as best he could for the betterment of his fellow men.

In their religious work Richard Allen and Daniel Coker are known first as leaders of the separate black Methodist congregations in Philadelphia and Baltimore respectively. They are much better known, however, for founding the A.M.E. Church in 1816. Coker, a brilliant, erratic man, was elected first Bishop of the new denomination, but for unknown reasons declined to serve. He soon left America for Africa and died there after establishing several churches in Liberia and Sierra Leone. Upon Coker's declining, Allen was immediately elected and ordained, thus becoming the first effective Bishop in the new denomination, and the first black Bishop in Protestantism. He filled the office of Bishop with efficiency and distinction, giving to the new Church stability, respectability, and growth. A brief sketch of his life and work is recounted in Chapter VI.

Many other able men were drawn into the ministry of the A.M.E. Church. Chief among them are Morris Brown, William Paul Quinn, and that most remarkable man, Daniel A. Payne. All of these men became bishops in the Church. Descriptions of their work are found in the chapter on the A.M.E. Church.

The ministerial leaders in the founding of the A.M.E. Zion Church were Abraham Thompson, June Scott, William and Thomas Miller, William Carman, Leven Smith, James Varick, and Christopher Rush. Except for Christopher Rush, biographical information is meager indeed. We do know that all of these men were zealous for freedom of worship among their people; they were active in founding the Zion and Asbury churches in New York City and separate black congregations in New Haven, Long Island, and Newark, New Jersey. The name of Varick occurs most frequently comparatively late. He was active in forming the association of churches that led eventually to the creation of the new denomination. He was elected Superintendent of the associated congregations in 1822.

Abraham Thompson was the central figure in organizing the Zion congregation and in carrying on the negotiations with the parent church. The most powerful figure in the early Zion denomination, however, was Christopher Rush. He was the preacher, evangelist, organizer, and leader who led the Church in its early formation and into its early growth. He also gave to the Church its first history, which still is the basic source of essential information. (See Chapter VII.)

In addition to these men of whose lives we know a little, there were the great number of other men on the plantations of the South who played a most important part in keeping the faith alive among their fellow blacks. In the Mission to the Slaves we hear much about the heroic, self-sacrificing service of the white missionaries or preachers. Indeed, the Mission was almost glorified in Southern writings as an example of Christian service at its best. We hear almost nothing of the black workers who were "assistants" to the missionaries in their work and who were largely responsible for the wide acceptance and intimate application of the faith in the daily lives of the blacks. Once in a while their names are mentioned in the contemporary literature, often with appreciation for what they were doing. Emanuel Mack, Silas Phillips, Nace Duval, and Sancho Cooper are a few of the names mentioned.[17]

William Capers, the founder of the Methodist Mission to the Slaves, has much to say about the black religious leaders. He had great appreciation for their work and for them as persons. He said he always had a group of them about him. Among those he mentions are Castile Selby, Amos Baxter, Thomas Smith, Peter Simpson, Smart Simpson, Harry Bull, Richard Halloway, Alex Harlston, "and others." Some of these were devout laymen, some were unordained local preachers and exhorters. All were used as "assistants in the work with the slaves. Yet despite the fact that history has passed them by, it was these little-known persons, men and women, who took to their fellow blacks whatever healing and strength religion held for a soul under bondage.[18]

Greatest of the Southern Methodist preachers by far was Henry Evans, the founder of the Methodist Episcopal church in Fayetteville, North Carolina. Evans was a contemporary of Harry Hosier. Hosier died in 1806, Evans in the year 1810. Evans was fully as great as Hosier, and possibly greater in some ways. While Hosier enjoyed almost unbroken popularity and eager reception, Evans at first encountered severe opposition and persecution and at least three times risked his life. Hosier was a traveling evangelist who thrilled varying crowds. Evans, with equal popularity and power as a preacher, stayed in one community and built a lasting church. Hosier's work was limited to preaching. Evans was also a pastor who had a visible effect on the morals of his community. Hosier preached to whites and blacks in the North where it was permitted. Evans preached to whites and blacks in the South where it was socially disapproved and later legally forbidden.

Thanks to William Capers, we have more biographical information on Evans than on any other preacher of his time except Richard Allen. Capers writes in his autobiography:

The most remarkable man in Fayetteville when I went there, and who died during my stay, was a negro, by the name of Henry Evans. I say *the most* remarkable in view of his class; and I call him negro with unfeigned respect . . . I have known and loved and honored not a few negroes in my life, who were probably as pure of heart as Evans, or anybody else . . . Remarkable . . . I use the word in a broader sense for Henry Evans, who was confessedly the father of the Methodist Church, white and black, in Fayetteville, and the best preacher of his time in that quarter; and he was so *remarkable* as to have become the greatest curiosity of the town; insomuch that distinguished visitors hardly felt that they might pass a Sunday in Fayetteville without hearing him preach. Evans was from Virginia; a shoe-maker by trade, and I think, was born free. He became a Christian and a Methodist quite young, and was licensed to preach in Virginia. While yet a young man, he determined to remove to Charleston, South Carolina, thinking that he might succeed best there at his trade. But having reached Fayetteville on his way to Charleston, and something detaining him for a few days, his spirit was stirred at perceiving that the people of his race in that town were wholly given to profanity and lewdness, never hearing preaching of any denomination, and living emphatically without hope and without God in the world. This determined him to stop in Fayetteville; and he began to preach to the negroes, with great effect. The town council interfered, and nothing in his power could prevail with them to permit him to preach. He then withdrew to the sand-hills, out of town and held meetings in the woods, changing his appointments from place to place. No law was violated, while the council was effectually eluded; and so the opposition passed into the hands of the mob. These he worried out by changing his appointments, so that when they went to work their will upon him he was preaching somewhere else. Meanwhile, whatever the most honest purpose of a simple heart could do to reconcile his enemies was employed by him for that end. He eluded no one in private, but sought opportunities to explain himself; avowed the purity of his intentions; and even begged to be subjected to the scrutiny of any surveillance that might be thought proper to prove his inoffensiveness; anything, so that he might but be allowed to preach. Happily for him and the cause of religion, his honest countenance and earnest pleadings were soon powerfully seconded by the fruits of his labors. One after another began to suspect their servants of attending his preaching, not because they were made worse, but wonderfully better . . .

It was not long before the mob was called off by a change in the current of opinion, and Evans was allowed to preach in town. At that time there was not a single church-edifice in town, and but one congregation (Presbyterian), who worshiped in what was called the State-house, under which was the market; and it was plainly Evans or nobody to preach to the negroes. Now, too, of the mistresses there were not a few, and some masters, who were brought to think that the preaching which had proved so beneficial to their servants might be good for them also; and the famous negro preacher had some whites as well as blacks to hear him. From these the gracious influence spread to others, and a meeting-house was built. It was a frame of wood, weatherboarded only on the outside, without plastering, about fifty feet long by thirty feet wide.

Seats distinctly separated, were at first appropriated to the whites, near the pulpit. But Evans had already become famous, and these seats were insufficient. Indeed, the negroes seemed likely to lose their preacher, negro though he was, while the whites, crowded out of their appropriate seats, took possession of those in the rear. Meanwhile Evans had represented to the preacher of the Bladen Circuit how things were going, and induced him to take his meeting-house into the circuit, and constitute a church there. And now, there was no longer room for the negroes in the house when Evans preached; and for the accommodation of both classes, the weatherboards were knocked off and sheds were added to the house on either side; the whites occupying the whole of the original building, and the negroes those sheds as a part of the same house.

Evans' dwelling was a shed at the pulpit end of the church. And that was the identical state of the case when I was pastor. Often was I in that shed, and much to my edification. I have known not many preachers who appeared more conversant with Scripture than Evans, or whose conversation was more instructive as to the things of God. He seemed always deeply impressed with the responsibility of his position; . . . And yet Henry Evans was a Boanerges, and in his duty feared not the face of man.

I have said that he died during my stay in Fayetteville this year (1810). The death of such a man could not be but triumphant, and his was distinguishingly so. I did not witness it, but was with him just before he died; and as he appeared to me, triumph should express but partially the character of his feelings, as the word imports exultation at a victory . . . His last breath was drawn in the act of pronouncing I Corinthians xv. 57: "Thanks be to God, which giveth us the victory through our Lord Jesus Christ." It was my practice to hold a meeting with the blacks in the church directly after morning preaching every Sunday. And on the Sunday before his death, during this meeting, the little door between his humble shed and the chancel where I stood was opened and the dying man entered for a last farewell to his people. He was almost too feeble to stand at all, but supporting himself by the railing of the chancel, he said: "I have come to say my last word to you. It is this: None but Christ. Three times I have had my life in jeopardy for preaching the Gospel to you. Three times I have broken the ice on the edge of the water and swam across the Cape Fear to preach the gospel to you. And now, if in my last hour I could trust to that or to any thing else but Christ crucified, for my salvation, all should be lost and my soul perish forever." A noble testimony! Worthy not of Evans only, but of St. Paul. His funeral at the church was attended by a greater concourse of persons than had been seen on any funeral occasion before. The whole community appeared to mourn his death, and the universal feeling seemed to be that in honoring the memory of Henry Evans we were paying tribute to virtue and religion. He was buried under the chancel of the church of which he had been in so remarkable a manner the founder.[19]

Another most remarkable early black Methodist preacher was John Stewart, who spent his entire ministry as a missionary to the Wyandot Indians in northwest Ohio.

Stewart was born free in Virginia in 1786. When he was thirty he was converted at a camp meeting in Ohio. Before conversion he was a drunkard and a wastrel, and once considered suicide. His conversion changed his life. He joined a church, felt a desire to preach, and became a licensed exhorter. He was a man of "no learning but a melodious voice."

Once, after a severe illness, he heard voices telling him, "You must declare my counsel faithfully." The voices "seemed to come from a northwest direction." In obedience to the voices he set out on a northwest trek and eventually came to the Wyandot reservation near Sandusky, Ohio. With the aid of Jonathan Pointer, another Negro, who served as interpreter, Stewart began his work among the Wyandots. He converted many, including Pointer and several chiefs. Bishop George licensed him a local preacher. His ministry was highly effective but tragically short, only about six years. He died of "consumption" in 1823.

The Indians loved and respected him. After his death they moved his remains to the site of the Wyandot mission and placed over his grave the inscription EARTH FOR CHRIST.[20]

THE EARLY PREACHERS—AN EVALUATION

In the current emphasis on black history, which is an effort to appreciate better the contribution of black people to American life, much attention is being given to black religion and, of course, to the black preacher. Several studies have recently appeared.

Many factors need to be taken into account if the judgment of history is to be fair to the early preachers. First, care must be taken to see them in the light of the times in which they lived.

Secondly, all aspects of the ministers' work must be considered, not just preaching. Thirdly, the stereotype of "slave preacher" must be discarded. The preachers must be seen for what they were, a highly varied group of men serving under different conditions in different ways.

As to the times of the early preachers, they lived in a day when men saw God, Jesus, heaven and hell as real, the most real things in life. To have the favor of God, obtained through belief on His Son, Jesus Christ, meant the assurance of heaven and eternal blessedness, which was the chief end of living. And by contrast, the worst fate for any life was to merit hell and eternal damnation. This was the faith as the early preachers received it and believed it. It was the reality of this faith that enabled the preachers, white and black, to endure the worst of sufferings and to face even death time and again as they proclaimed it.

It is difficult now for many moderns to sense the reality of this faith, especially educated persons. The nuclear bomb, the impending possibility of human extinction, the teachings of modern science, and contemporary cosmology all tend to make belief in heaven and hell difficult and to make Christology and soteriology inexplicable if not irrational. The grounds of faith for moderns are being steadily eroded. But the early preachers lived before all this. For them God and heaven were real, as real as sunshine and as certain as sunrise. The reality of their faith gave them the strength to live through the worst of persecution, human slavery, and gave them hope that a better day would somehow come. Failure to sense the reality of their faith, or to judge them in the light of our weakened beliefs, is unfair to the men who suffered to take the faith to their fellows. Thus Henry Evans, after a lifetime of sacrificial service to his people could say: "None but Christ. Three times I have had my life in jeopardy for preaching the gospel to you. Three times I have broken the ice on the edge of the water and swum across the Cape Fear to preach the gospel to you. And now, if in my last hour I could trust to that, or to anything else but Christ crucified, for my salvation, all should be lost, and my soul perish forever."

In contemporary studies of black preaching much emphasis is placed on the oratorical performance of the preachers. It seems to be assumed that black preaching contains some esoteric charismatic element peculiar to it alone. This has yet to be shown. To be sure, black preaching was and is remarkable in many ways. For one thing, the early preaching was highly imaginative, filled with beautiful, fanciful figures painted in flights of oratory by men who were natural masters of attractive delivery, often in their voices, often in their persons, and always in histrionic impressiveness. The imagination, of course, was due to the preachers' illiteracy. Many could not write or read even the Bible. They were dependent upon what they were told and upon their own reconstruction and interpretation of things. Untrammeled imagination was inevitable.[21]

To accompany their imaginary meanderings many preachers would use big or sesquipedalian words which often were their own creations. Big words were a sign of intellectuality, to be sure, but the words the preachers used actually were the result of illiteracy. Being unable to read, they had very limited vocabularies. Yet the ideas of religion and philosophy called for extraordinary words and expression. What, therefore, could be more natural than to invent them. Thus Daniel Payne after hearing a preacher preach commented: "Brother Baker preached in his usual vague and indefinite manner. This brother, I believe, is a good man and means to do well, but he is one of the most unintelligible preachers I have ever heard. He makes use of words which cannot be found in any language under the sun."[22]

Secondly, black preaching spoke to the hopes and hurts of the people both slave and free. Being one of them and suffering with them, the black preacher elicited a rapport which the white preacher could seldom attain. The preacher often had to speak, of course, in covert terms, especially in slave country, when speaking of freedom, or justice or retribution for wrongs. Sometimes just a look or a gesture could say as much as many words. They became masters of innuendo.

Among Methodists, Baptists, and the other evangelical churches, when the black preachers preached they aroused shouts, "crying aloud," and often tears among their hearers. They also produced other effects, such as stiffening in their seats, or jumping over benches, or running up and down the aisles. But such demonstrations usually ended with the sermon. This kind of emotional response is sometimes regarded as an indication of a uniquely charismatic aspect of black preaching. But it would hardly seem so, first because these effects were not peculiar to black preaching, and secondly because they were mild. Indeed, the reactions aroused by the black preachers were mild when compared to the excessive reactions aroused by early white preachers or to the phenomena that occurred at camp meetings. For instance, even of Harry Hosier it is said that "a general weeping ran through the assembly" when Harry exhorted. Or as at a meeting conducted by Daniel Payne, the Lord "seemed to have manifested himself to every soul. Some rejoiced aloud, and some merely sighed, and some or nearly all were in tears."[23] But there is almost no mention of the paroxysms, prostrations, and other violent emotional "exercises" aroused by such men as Benjamin Abbott or Thomas Rankin, or even John Wesley. For instance, Abbott reports:

> At my next appointment, the Lord made bare his arm of almighty power in such a manner that many fell to the floor; their cries were very great, the sinners sprang to the doors and windows, and fell over one another in getting out: five jumped out at a window; and one woman went by me and cried, You are a devil! A young man cried out, Command the peace! but the magistrate answered, It is the power of God. Another with tears in his eyes, entreated the people to hold their peace; to which an old woman replied, They cannot hold their peace, unless you cut out their tongues. Glory to God! this day will never be forgotten in time or eternity! I was as happy as I could contain.[24]

Or to quote Abbott again:

> Next day, being the Sabbath, I preached there again; in the morning I met the black class in the barn, many fell to the floor like dead men, while others cried aloud to God for mercy; but I had to leave them as it was time to attend my next appointment.[25]

William Capers gives this description of emotional reactions at a camp meeting in South Carolina:

> But what was most remarkable . . . was the strange and unaccountable bodily exercises which prevailed there. In some instances, persons who were not known before to be at all religious, or under any particular concern about it, would suddenly fall to the ground,

and become strangely convulsed with what was called the jerks; the head and neck and sometimes the body also, moving backwards and forwards with spasmodic violence, and so rapidly that the plaited hair of a woman's head might be heard to crack . . . In other cases, persons falling down would appear senseless, and almost lifeless, for hours together; lying motionless at full length on the ground, and almost as pale as corpses. And then there was the jumping exercise, which sometimes approximated dancing; in which several persons might be seen standing perfectly erect, and springing upward without seeming to bend a joint of their bodies.[26]

If the ability to arouse emotional response is an indication of a unique charismatic quality, it certainly was not limited to black preaching, and it was not as pronounced in black preaching as in white.

In looking at the early preachers, there is one phase of their work that must not be overlooked, and that is their pastoral activity. It is fully as important as pulpit performance if not more so. Human slavery is a terrible ordeal for any people who happen to suffer it. It hurts the body and it hurts the soul. It was the early preachers and volunteer religious workers who spoke words of strength and comfort against the hurts of the social systems in which blacks were bound, whether they were in the slave quarters of a Southern plantation or in the poverty-stricken ghettos of "free" Negroes in the North.

The brutal and brutalizing aspects of American slavery need hardly be recounted here. For a man to be unable to give his wife, daughters, sons, sisters, or even his mother any protection against designs of masters or predatory whites; for a woman to have her children torn from her side and sold away forever beyond her reach and care—such violations of deepest human ties occurring daily could easily have broken the spirits of adults and children alike.

In cases like these it was a psychological as well as spiritual service of inestimable value for a person of respect and position (unofficial, of course) to come and speak a word of comfort and hope, and to give assurance that there was "a better day a-coming." Since formal preaching by blacks was illegal in the South, the counseling services mentioned here were rendered by the unnamed volunteers and the unknown exhorters and local preachers who were used as "assistants" by the missionaries in the mission to the slaves. They were black persons who had held on to their own faith in spite of slavery and shared it in time of need with their burdened brethren.

Among the free Negroes of the North it was men like Richard Allen, Absalom Jones, and Christopher Rush who proved to their people by word and example that they could survive their handicaps and that they could and should "overcome." Without vision in some situations people do perish. It was the early preacher who kept vision alive in the oppressed black hearts, and thus maintained a cardinal element in racial motivation.

There is another area in which the pastoral or counseling work of the early preachers was vitally important. On the plantations the slave quarters were little more than slave pens—large numbers crowded together under rudest conditions with minimum provisions for privacy, decency, or physical comfort. It was almost the same in the ghettos of the cities. These communities had all of the vices common to people in similar social situations: disintegration of character; little respect for persons or property; theft almost a way of life; sexual immorality and abuse; drunkenness; fighting, often over trifles; and talebearing or tattling to overseers and masters. To worsen matters, law enforcement was lax and indifferent except where the offense affected a white person or the master's property.

Such behavior is not racial; it is the result of social situations. Even today in the slums of American cities, the rate of crime by blacks against blacks is distressingly high. Thus in the slave quarters and in the free ghettos where law enforcement was lax and criminal proclivities ran rampant, moral control by each individual was one of the main hopes for reasonably secure living. Therefore, when the early preachers were urging love of neighbor and adherence to the teachings of the Christian faith, it was much more than just a religious exercise. It was an effort to counteract the destructive effects of the conditions in which American slavery and prejudice were forcing black people to live. It was an expression of the passion for decency which survived slavery and expressed itself so fully when freedom finally came.

With regard to social leadership, the early black Methodist preachers varied widely. This was especially true of their attitudes toward methods of attaining the freedom and progress of their people. They ran the whole scale. There were some who were highly aggressive, even revolutionary. Morris Brown, for example, was accused of being implicated in the Denmark Vesey conspiracy of 1822 and of using his church as a meeting place for the conspirators. He was later absolved of the charge, but it is true that he helped many slaves to attain their freedom through normal ways. At the other end of the scale there were men like Henry Evans who simply did not attempt to fight slavery directly, but gave their attention to other areas of need, and used their influence through religion to make daily life better in any ways possible for the slaves.

The great majority of the early preachers, slave and free, were men who hated slavery and wanted it destroyed, but they wanted to achieve this end through more orderly and nonviolent means. Many were active and even aggressive. Absalom Jones, for instance, in 1800 signed a petition with other free Negroes calling upon Congress to restrict the slave trade and modify the fugitive slave law; the petition also expressed the hope that there would eventually be a day of general emancipation for all slaves.[27] The petition raised a storm of protest, especially from Southern congressmen. Richard Allen's home was a haven for escaping slaves, and he gave generously to help them. In the North many preachers were active in the antislavery movement, and many used their churches as stations on the "Underground Railroad." A number of A.M.E. Zion preachers were especially active in this way. The Reverend Thomas James, for instance, conducted antislavery meetings in Rochester, Syracuse, New Haven, Long Island, and New Bedford, Massachusetts. On several occasions he was instrumental in rescuing captured runaways from their captors.

Jermain W. Loguen, later Bishop, was a friend and co-worker of Frederick Douglass, and was most active in the antislavery and abolitionist movements. His reputation as an abolitionist was so widely known that when he was elected a Bishop in the Zion

Church in 1864 and was assigned to the South, he would not go and resigned the bishopric for fear of being seized in the South.

All of the early preachers were fully committed to the advancement of their people in every essential way. They wanted freedom from slavery, of course, but they also wanted the mastery of American culture. Efforts in this latter direction were possible, however, only among the free preachers in the North. Thus toward economic progress Absalom Jones and Richard Allen founded the Free African Society in Philadelphia in 1787. It was much like a mutual savings club. Allen later helped to found the Free Labor Society, purchasing only goods that were made without slave labor. In its new church building in New York in 1820, the A.M.E. Zion congregation provided for a public school room in its basement. Daniel Payne encouraged public education in schools conducted by A.M.E. churches, and he insisted upon training for the ministry. Such efforts indicate the dedication to progress and to the preparation of the people for freedom, which they believed some day would surely come. They were not mistaken.

Of course, the few persons mentioned here are the outstanding examples. In some cases they are striking exceptions. The rank and file of the early preachers were men of lesser gifts and cruder methods. In the A.M.E. General Conference of 1856 a resolution was introduced that would require ministers to "put off all superfluity and costly apparel," or face suspension from their Annual Conferences. In the debate that followed, a number of glimpses are given of ministerial conduct of that day. One member, Dr. Bias, opposed the resolution on the ground that it would only promote hypocrisy since the ministers would not observe it. He said, "Some men's alimentiveness is so very large that all their moneys are spent to fill their bellies." Also, they like to wear "shad-belly" coats.

Another member spoke for the resolution. He said, "Our backs and stomachs are robbing us of much money, so that we are not able to acquire property. This is also why our periodicals are not sustained, and also why our children are not well educated." He averred that many of the preachers on the Conference floor were wearing more costly apparel than Nicholas Longworth. By contrast, Brother E. Weaver was opposed to the measure because it was unnecessary. He said he did not see any more superfluity in wearing an extravagant coat than in wearing a long beard. "If the one was a superfluity, so was the other."

One of the most vigorous statements in support of the resolution was made by one Elder Moore. He disapproved the extravagance of the "young men who dress more like gamblers than like ministers of Him who wore a seamless garment. He was equally opposed to men going into the pulpit with their mouths full of tobacco, spitting and squirting out the filthy juice like a squirrel. "It is a shame!"[28]

But whatever differences there may have been between the leading and the average early Methodist preachers, there is one respect in which they all were one: they were all true Methodist preachers in true Methodist tradition. They believed that religion was a *feeling* experience. If you were saved, you could feel it; and if you felt it, you knew it. Therefore, they preached to attain this joyful feeling of blessed assurance in season and out of season wherever two or three or more could be gathered together. Though black, in a very real sense they were John Wesley's spiritual progeny, and they gloried in that heritage.

PART III

Reconstruction and Expansion

CHAPTER XI

The A.M.E. Church

THE END OF THE Civil War and the defeat of the South meant different things to different Americans. To those in the North it was a noble, hard-won victory that fully justified the terrible cost in lives and national resources. Through Northern valor and sacrifice, secession had been prevented, the Union had been preserved, and the anomalous, unbearable blot of human slavery had been eradicated from the economy of the nation, a nation founded to provide liberty and justice for all. They believed that God was on their side.

To most white Southerners the crushing defeat was an undeserved tragedy which had been inflicted upon them by a stronger, misguided opponent, an opponent obsessed with fanatical abolitionist ideas and the determination to destroy the Southern way of life. To those Southerners who were religious it seemed to be an unexplainable act of desertion by God, the God in whom they had trusted and who, they had brought themselves to believe, approved human slavery and their way of life.

To blacks both North and South, the Southern defeat was the righteous judgment of an Almighty God who through the blood and violence of war was wreaking just retribution for all the suffering His black children had known; a God who, as Lincoln had said, was exacting a drop of blood by the sword for every drop that had been drawn by the lash. For blacks it was the marvelous fulfillment of hopes and dreams and prayers. Thus one black churchman could exult:

> O thou King of Kings, thou Lord of Lords! God of the races! Loving Father of humanity! how marvelous are thy dealings with the nations, with the governments, with the races, with the families of the earth, with individuals! . . . Only the sword of the Lord and of Gideon could, within the life of a single generation, bring to pass such wonderful changes![1]

In practical terms, the defeat of the South meant for blacks the opening of doors to larger life and service which the Southern slave power had so brutally kept closed. Immediately after the Emancipation Proclamation, while the guns were still sounding, the black churches began to move into the South. But the black churches were not alone. The Methodist Episcopal Church, North, had already begun its southern thrust to effect what came to be one of the brightest pages in the history of Christian missions.[2] (See Chapter XIV.)

On April 27, 1863, the Reverend C. C. Leigh, a local preacher in the M.E. Church and a financial officer in the National Freedmen's Aid Association, visited the Baltimore Annual Conference and requested Bishop Payne to send two itinerant preachers "as missionaries to care for the moral, social and religious interest of the freedmen in South Carolina, who were then as sheep without a shepherd, left in that condition by their former white pastors, who had fled before the advancing and conquering army of the Union." He asked that they be sent within ten days. Bishop Payne immediately named the Reverend James Lynch, of the Baltimore Conference, and the Reverend James D. S. Hall of the New York Conference to undertake this work. They willingly responded, and on May 20, 1863, they sailed from New York for Charleston on a government steamer, the *Arago*. On the boat also were four white women who were going as missionary teachers to the freedmen in the South.[3]

Incidentally, Reverend Lynch on the Sunday before leaving New York preached his farewell sermon in Sullivan Street A.M.E. Church. His sister was so impressed by the work he was going to do that she, too, applied to Bishop Payne to go as a missionary teacher. Shortly afterward her wish was fulfilled. She was sent to teach in Beaufort, South Carolina, supported by the women of a white Baptist church in New York City. The two preachers, of course, had military permission and protection. They began their work in Port Royal, Edisto, and Beaufort, South Carolina, where Union forces were in control, and as soon as the Union troops entered Charleston and Savannah, they followed and started work in those cities.[4]

On May 13, 1865, Bishop Payne, himself, accompanied by three preachers, landed in Charleston harbor, "Just about thirty years and four days from the hour he was exiled by the force of Carolina's laws for the crime of teaching colored children how to think and check." Their ship was the *Arago*, the same one that had carried the first two black missionary preachers. For Payne this was an occasion of deepest personal significance and victory.[5]

On Monday morning, May 15, 1865, Bishop Payne organized the South Carolina Conference. At the opening only five ministers were present, two elders, two traveling licentiates, and one local preacher. Later in the session others arrived: Elders R. H. Cain, Anthony S. Stanford, and George S. Rue from the New York, Philadelphia, and New England Conferences, respectively; and four native South Carolina "brethren," namely, Charles Bradwell, N. Murphy, Robert Taylor, and Richard Vanderhorst. The last named, Vanderhorst, subsequently became a bishop in the Colored Methodist Episcopal Church, organized in 1870.[6]

At its organization the South Carolina Conference included North Carolina and Georgia. Through the work of the missionaries and the ministers who joined at that session, four thousand members came into the A.M.E. Church. The Conference discussed temperance, missions, and education, organized a historic and literary society, and set up a society for preachers' aid. The Conference at its inception "was like a ship sent to conquer other lands in the South."[7]

In 1866, at Savannah, Georgia, the South Carolina Conference held its first annual session. At this time forty itinerant preachers were ordained of whom fourteen were elders. Seven superintendents were appointed "to plant and train mission churches."[8] They were Anthony L. Stanford and Henry M. Turner for

Georgia; George W. Broadie and Samuel B. Williams for North Carolina; Augustus T. Carr and R. H. Cain for South Carolina; and Charles H. Pierce for Florida and Alabama. Meanwhile, the Reverend John M. Brown had been stationed in Virginia where his labors were most fruitful. Henry M. Turner was remarkably successful in the state of Georgia. Some of these men were soon drawn off into politics and other fields. For example, Broadie served as a banker among the freedmen; R. H. Cain became a senator in the South Carolina Legislature; Pierce did the same in Florida, and Turner in Georgia. The reason was, as Payne says, that "for intelligence and organizing power their equals could not be found in the laity, hence politics laid hold of them, and by a kind of conscription forced them into the army of politicians."[9]

At the same time that the Church was expanding on the southern eastern seaboard it was also expanding toward the west. In 1863 Bishop Payne was invited to Nashville, Tennessee, by two congregations of black Methodists who formerly belonged to the M.E. Church, South. They wanted to join the A.M.E. Church. A Committee of seven presented the following resolution to Bishop Payne on December 15, 1863:

> Whereas, It is the opinion of us whose names are here unto subscribed that a vast majority of the ministers and members of the Methodist Church, South, have proven themselves disloyal to the Constitution and government of the United States by identifying themselves with those who are now in open rebellion against it; and
>
> Whereas, We believe it our duty as Christians and citizens to bear our testimony against such unjustifiable conduct, as also to testify our own loyalty to the country which gave us birth and the constitutional government which controls as well by deeds as by words; therefore
>
> Resolved, 1st. That we now, by our own voluntary act, do transfer our membership and Church relations to that ecclesiastical organization known by the name and title of the African Methodist Episcopal Church in the United States of America.
>
> Resolved, 2nd. That a committee of several be appointed to invite the Rev. Bishop Payne to organize us into a branch of the said A.M.E. Church, and take us under his episcopal care.[10]

Bishop Payne, of course, took them in and changed the names of the congregations from Capers' and Andrew's Chapels to St. John's and St. Paul's A.M.E. Churches.

The acquiring of these two churches is a good example of how the black Methodist denominations grew in their first years of Southern mission. As has previously been seen, the black Methodist bodies, prior to the Civil War, were not permitted to work in the South. Therefore, the only black Methodists in the South were members or former members of the white M.E. Church, South. Sometimes the blacks had been segregated members in white congregations. Sometimes in the cities the blacks would constitute separate congregations with their own buildings or chapels pastored by white preachers, as was the case in the two Nashville churches. Also there were the slave missions which with the end of slavery left groups without churches or pastors. In many cases the white preachers either because of the war or because they were not in sympathy with Negro freedom, simply abandoned their black charges. Many blacks, in turn, were anxious to get out of everything that looked like white direction or control, and through race pride wanted to be associated with black institutions. On this racial basis the black bishops and ministers exercised strong appeals. Thus there were large numbers of black Methodists having no church connection or leadership, and they were natural targets for the pioneering black missionaries. While the black preachers did some preaching and evangelizing among unchurched individuals, their main drive was for the former congregations of the M.E. Church, South.

In some cases, whole congregations asked to be taken into the black bodies as was the case with the Nashville churches, or with a large church of eight hundred members in Norfolk, Virginia, or of a church in Augusta, Georgia, of over two hundred members. In other cases the approach was made by the black denominations, always with persistence and at times with pressure. Wesley J. Gaines, who was one of the first and most active preachers in Georgia, and who later became a Bishop, writes:

The Lord had blessed us. The connection was growing with what might be termed a healthy growth—that is, the churches to which the right hand of fellowship was offered made no unseemly haste for affiliation, but after mature deliberations, which were at many times lengthy and critical, transferred themselves to the fold of African Methodism. This deliberation was wise, for it gave assurance of the future stability of a union which must possess this important characteristic for successful increase in strength.[11]

Or again he writes:

This year was one of trying labor . . . There was much to contend against from both white and colored. The former noted a movement [the A.M.E. Church], the independence of which grated harshly upon them under so recent defeats and losses, and the inexperience of our own ranks led to varying results. Then there was a prejudice born of generations of the recognized dominion of the whites which we had to meet and overcome in leading the bodies of Negroes to seek a church where they could be free and untrammeled in their religious worship.[12]

Taking over churches resulted in very rapid growth. Thus the South Carolina Conference, which included North Carolina and Georgia, at its second session was able to report a membership of between forty-eight and fifty thousand. Also the ministry of the black churches was becoming more and more popular and was attracting young men. Thus H. M. Turner was able to take to this session fourteen men who were applicants for the ministry. More remarkable, forty-six were ordained as deacons or elders at that session.

The Church grew rapidly, but figures on rising membership and geographical expansion do not tell the whole story. Here was a Church composed of people who were culturally and economically limited attempting to spread the Christian Gospel among the great mass of their fellows who were even more limited still. It was a noble effort, but a very homely one. Some insight into the nature of things may be gained from this statement of the Reverend Andrew Brown, a preacher in Georgia when the work began:

I am not so superstitious as to claim to be a prophet, nor the son of a prophet, but I saw the A.M.E. Church in 1844 as bright as I see her tonight. I then prayed that I might outlive the surrounding circumstances, and see the church in reality as I then saw it in my mind. The day the M.E. Church, South, split from the M.E.

Church, while in the woods upon my knees, God showed me this church. The day was dark, but, thank God, we waited on and on. God's horse was tied to the iron stake. For a long time he failed to prance in Georgia and South Carolina. The day the first fire was made at Sumter, I saw the Gospel Horse begin to paw. He continued to paw until he finally broke loose and came tearing through Georgia. The colored man mounted him and intends to ride him. He is not particular where he goes, for he has practiced until he can and does ride him in the white man's pulpit. In 1866 I was in Dalton. In 1865, I a poor, bare-footed, bare-headed man, had met in Atlanta a man named James Lynch; he told me of the A.M.E. Church. The first of September the M.E. Church, South, held their Conference and sent a preacher to preach to the colored people in Dalton. He sent for me and told me he was sent there. I told him we could not comply with his request; we must look for ourselves. He said if I was going to take the people, to take them and leave. I thanked him and we left. We were in a sad plight, for there was not an ordained minister from Chattanooga to Atlanta.

In 1866 we met in Savannah for the first time as a Conference. There I met Dr. Turner, who gave me the Marietta District. Turner threw me on the right wing, Stanford [was] on the left and he held the centre . . .

What did we know at the first Conference?

When I was Presiding Elder of the Marietta District, there was but one colored man that could write his name and read the hymn-book. We had to get little white boys and poor white men to act as Secretaries of the Quarterly Conference. Now (1880) we cannot call a dozen men together unless there are several scribes among them. At the Conference in Atlanta, only one Secretary could be found, and he had to read his writing while it was hot, for if it ever got cold he could never have read it in the world. After the rising of the adjourned Conference, which met in Macon, Ga., we commenced to grow, and have advanced steadily on until now.[13]

Before 1870 there were two, and after then there were three black Methodist denominations working avidly among the freedmen of the South. There often was rivalry between them, and sometimes open conflict. A congregation of black Southern Methodists ready to be taken over was a prize. Often the representatives of two if not all three of the denominations would be working on the same congregations at the same time. Since the

A.M.E.'s were the oldest, largest, and most aggressive of the three, they were most frequently accused of unfair and overriding tactics. The church that Henry Evans founded in Fayetteville, North Carolina, was the object of contention between the A.M.E.'s and the A.M.E.Z.'s, with the latter finally winning the church.[14]

A further and greater source of contention was the matter of church property. Some of the Southern Methodist black congregations owned church buildings and other properties. When these congregations joined the black denominations, what should happen to the property? To whom did it belong? Should it remain with the parent body, the Methodist Episcopal Church, South, to which the congregations had originally belonged? Or should it go with the congregation into the black denomination and become property of that body? Or should the properties pass down to the Colored Methodist Episcopal Church which after 1870 was the recognized and legal successor to the black section of the M.E. Church, South?

Such questions over property naturally aroused bitter feelings, and led to court fights. It caused the bishops of the C.M.E. Church in 1872 to appeal to the A.M.E. Church to turn back to the C.M.E.'s properties which the A.M.E.'s were unlawfully occupying. "Your ministers have been very hostile to us in the past," the statement said, "forbidding us preaching in our houses of worship, that are occupied by your congregations . . ."[15] In most cases, however, the black bodies paid little attention to claims or laws. If a congregation had a building the new denomination would simply claim it and put its name on the door, and proceed with its worship and evangelizing, holding possession until evicted by physical force or law.

The A.M.E. Church continued southwestward and west, especially into the black populous regions of Alabama, Mississippi, Louisiana, Texas, and Arkansas. Bishops were elected, consecrated, and sent out to direct the burgeoning work; annual conferences were organized and churches were either taken over or rapidly built. Bishop James A. Shorter directed the work, or as C. S. Smith says, "led the forces," in Tennessee, Texas, and Mississippi; Bishop J. P. Campbell in Arkansas; and Bishop J. M. Brown in Alabama.[16]

The needed ministers for the work were found among the men who had been exhorters, local preachers, or missionary assistants in the M.E. Church, South, and also among aspiring laymen who were quickly licensed, ordained, and put into service. Like the early Methodist Church in Wesley's time, the black denominations in the first years had to utilize men of little education and practically no professional training for the ministry. The very few of them who had high school educations, and the one or two who had attended college were widely acclaimed as "scholars." Fortunately through the influence and efforts of Daniel Payne and his required courses of study, which unfortunately were often taken lightly, and through the increased opportunities for learning provided by the white missionary teachers who had recently come South, the level of education steadily improved.

The growth of the Church in the first years after Emancipation, while rapid, had its hardships. Charles S. Smith, one of the historians of the Church says:

> When we take into account the trying circumstances of the times in which they acted, that they were a part of a despised and feeble people, strong only in faith and hope, and inspired by the Holy Spirit, we can, to some extent, realize how marvellous were their accomplishments in the face of unrelenting opposition, bitter persecution, and obstacles which were intended to be insurmountable . . . Verily these men sowed in tears, and endured privations and sufferings which it is not possible for those of this generation to sense. They labored without thought or hope of earthly reward. No titles followed their names . . . They exacted no promises from the appointing power. They were willing to go wherever sent. They rendered cheerful and loyal obedience to their superiors, which was largely the cause of the successful progress of the work. One of the problems they had to face was the Ku Klux Klan.[17]

Smith gives the names of many of these men and pays tribute to their sacrificial and often heroic labors.

The Church also extended its reach to the West Coast. In 1859 the Reverend John M. Wilkerson was sent as a missionary into Kansas. He organized a church at Leavenworth City, the first A.M.E. church in Kansas. By 1889 the Kansas Conference had grown to 1,321 members with twenty appointments and eighteen pastors. Churches were also established in Nebraska and Colorado. Previously, in 1854, the Reverend T. M. D. Ward had been sent to California, in the midst of the gold rush. Through trying experiences he succeeded in establishing churches in San Francisco and Los Angeles, and organized societies in thirteen other California cities. He also built a chapel in Denver, Colorado. Daniel Payne says he accomplished his work in California despite the persistent opposition of the Reverend J. J. Moore, an elder of the A.M.E. Zion Church.

The rapid growth of the A.M.E. Church required development in internal organization to manage properly the nationwide structure. Through the years the Church has responded faithfully, if sometimes turbulently, to this need for change.

In 1868 the "Dollar Money Plan" was adopted for meeting the costs of the General Church. Under this plan each pastor was required "to secure from or pay for each of his members" one dollar per year. Until recently this plan was an adequate source of income. At present, however, with greatly increased costs and increased general church activities, especially the educational program, the Church operates on a general budget fixed quadrennially by the General Conference. The amount of the budget is apportioned among the episcopal districts. For 1972 the annual budget was $3,107,402. More than one-third of the total, or $1,210,000 is allocated to the Church's eight colleges and two seminaries.

In 1872 the Financial Department was established. This Department centralized and controlled the receipt and disbursement of funds which now were coming from all across the nation. The head of the Department, formerly titled Financial Secretary, is now called the Treasurer of the A.M.E. Church. He directs the Department from the office in Washington, D.C.[18]

THE YOUNG PEOPLE'S PROGRAM

From its beginning the church was concerned with the education of its young people, both religiously and academically. In the first two decades of its history, annual conferences began requiring pastors to maintain both Sunday schools and day schools for their youth. They required this of pastors who themselves had little if any formal education. Daniel Payne, the apostle of education, constantly prodded the Church into action. (See Chapter VI.)

After the War, as the Church expanded among the freedmen, the instruction of the vast number of young people became an imperative concern.

In 1881 the Reverend C. S. Smith submitted a proposal for a connection-wide Sunday School Union. Under the plan the work of instruction would be standardized, thus helping the preachers and leaders of limited education. The plan was adopted by the Council of Bishops in 1882, and Reverend Smith became the first Secretary of the Union.

When Reverend Smith began, the Church had two publications, one for youth and one for adults with a combined circulation of about 10,000. Within five years he was issuing five publications, three for youth and two for adults with two quarterly instructional booklets. The total circulation of these was 225,000. This enormous production was possible because the publishing house of the Methodist Episcopal Church, South, did the printing. The production was also profitable. With the profits Reverend Smith purchased a building and eventually set up his own printing facilities. Bishop Payne said that it was the most successful activity in the history of the A.M.E. Church. In its early years it was the finest and largest program of religious education among the Black Methodist bodies.

The succeeding secretaries, especially Dr. Ira T. Bryant, 1908–36, carried the work to higher levels.

In 1896 the Christian Endeavor Movement, which was spreading rapidly throughout the nation, was adopted by the Church and made a connectional program. It is now called the Allen Christian Endeavor Fellowship.

The Church now has a Department of Christian Education which embraces many agencies or services, such as Christian Family Life, Youth Work, Vacation Week-day Church Schools, Campus Religious Life, Boy Scouts, Audio-Visual Education and Adult Work. The Reverend Andrew White is Secretary of the Department.

The Church has a Division of Educational Institutions which gives some measure of support to eight colleges and two theological seminaries. These schools are mentioned in Chapter XIV. More than one-third of the budget of the Church is devoted to educational institutions, in 1972 $1,210,000.00. This is a worthy effort but a burdensome one. With education costs rising so rapidly, it is a question as to how long the Church can continue to aid significantly this large number of schools with only three of them accredited. Dr. Sherman L. Greene, Jr., heads this work.

The Church has four publications: the *Christian Recorder*, the *A.M.E. Review*, the *Voice of Missions*, and the *Woman's Missionary Recorder*. There is a Department of Publications which is responsible for these and other publications, particularly those of the Sunday School Union.[19]

EXPANSION ABROAD

The A.M.E. Church, like most American bodies, early became imbued with the missionary impulse. There were many who felt that the Black churches could be especially effective in the effort to "redeem" Africa. Daniel Coker, the first Bishop-elect of the Church, went to Africa in 1820 and set up churches in Liberia and Sierra Leone. He went on his own initiative, however, and was partly sponsored by the American Colonization Society. He was not an official missionary of the A.M.E. Church. Coker's work did not survive.[20]

The first A.M.E. missionary to Africa was the Reverend J. R. Frederick. He developed work in Sierra Leone. In 1891 Bishop Henry McNeal Turner went to West Africa. He was deeply interested because he was an ardent emigrationist. Bitterly disillusioned by the treatment American Negroes were receiving during the Reconstruction period in the South, he regarded emigration to Africa as a partial if not complete solution to the Negro's plight. He was for years a vice-president of the American Colonization Society. During his visit the Bishop organized annual conferences in Sierra Leone and Liberia.[21] In 1898 Bishop Turner also went to South Africa to organize work that had been started there by indigenous African Christians, and appointed an African, James M. Dwane, "Vicar-Bishop." This appointment was rejected by the General Conference, however.

Bishop Turner was unquestionably the most active of the A.M.E. bishops in the African cause. He founded the "Voice of Missions," the publication which is still in existence. Bishop J. A. Gregg and R. R. Wright were also active in South Africa, the latter founding the Bible School that bears his name. In 1938 Dr. J. R. Coan, most outstanding of the A.M.E. missionaries, went to Africa to serve as Dean of the Bible School.

Today the A.M.E. Church has eighteen annual conferences in Africa in four episcopal districts. One of these districts embraces the West African work. The remaining three are in the south. It is generally agreed that the A.M.E. Church is the leading black Church in Africa. A rough estimate of the membership is about 10,000 in West Africa and 200,000 in the south. The work could be much larger if it were more faithfully developed. The lack of resident leadership, the failure to elevate indigenous leadership, the lack of funds and personnel have all resulted in small growth and ineffective service in an area where the Church could be a great source of spiritual and social progress.

In the half century from 1865 to 1915 the A.M.E. Church grew from a struggling, limited institution aspiring to speak for the black people of America, into a well-established, highly organized nationwide institution of about a million members, when the Sunday School enrollment is included. It came to have great prestige and influence, and it played a significant part in Negro development. This was especially true in education. Some of the further developments in the Church's history are discussed in a later chapter.

CHAPTER XII

The A.M.E. Zion Church

THE SOUTHERN EXPANSION of the A.M.E. Zion Church was much like that of its older sister, the A.M.E. Church. Long before the end of hostilities the black churches were ready to move into former slave country to spread the Gospel among the liberated slaves.

In 1863 Superintendent and later Bishop J. J. Clinton was appointed to the Southern and Philadelphia Conference. At that time this Conference embraced the whole of the South. The choice of Bishop Clinton was most fortunate. He was completely dedicated to his Church, and he had been an excellent administrator in the work of the Northern conferences. In addition to his great energy and indefatigable working ability, he was favored with a gracious, magnetic personality. He could call men into service and hold their allegiance.

When Clinton was assigned to the Southern work at first he hesitated to accept. There had been no previous activity by his Church in the South, and the Church had neither funds nor resources for opening the work. It was at this point that a woman member of the Church in Washington, D.C., rendered a strategic service. She was Mrs. Melvina Fletcher, a governess in the home of Postmaster General, Montgomery Blair. "She was," to quote Walls, a loyal church woman, and had heard of the dissatisfaction that had overtaken Bishop Clinton, who had written his resignation. One memorable night, during the fall of 1863, she went to his stopping place, called him out of his sleep at 3 o'clock in the morning, and had the famous conference that changed his mind. When he complained that he had not a single minister or dollar to take a delegation as missionaries to the South, she remonstrated with him to tear up his resignation, promising that she would help raise the funds for his cause. Clinton needed $300, which she promised to raise. She went to her friends in the Blair orbit and the churches of Washington and raised it, and presented the $300 in gold to him as the fulfillment of her promise, to meet the need of his mission.[1]

This deed restored Clinton's confidence. Within a year he found and sent into the South five men, some of whom became outstanding leaders in the Church. The five were James W. Hood, Wilbur G. Strong, John Williams, David Hill, and William F. Butler. Hood worked in North Carolina, Strong in Florida and the far South, and Butler in Kentucky. Through Hood's great work and aggressive leadership, North Carolina became the strongest state in the Zion connection.[2]

The denomination plunged at once into the struggle for Southern churches. J. W. Hood went to New Bern, North Carolina, which was then, January 14, 1864, tenuously in the hands of Union forces. Hood found a large, well-established church in great confusion. Two white denominations, the Methodist Episcopal Church (North) and the Congregational Church, were each trying to get the church to join them. Then, on the same day that Hood arrived, two A.M.E. preachers from Virginia came and tried to get the congregation to join the A.M.E.'s.

Hood, however, was the most skillful maneuverer of them all. On the next Sunday, Easter, he preached with "incentive vitality" to an overflowing crowd. At the close of the "highly spiritual" service, he presented a letter from Secretary of War Stanton which he had obtained on a special trip to Washington. It stated, "The congregation of colored Methodists worshipping in Andrews Chapel in New Bern, North Carolina, shall have the right to decide their own church relations and select their own pastor."[3] This greatly impressed the people. They took a vote deciding to enter the A.M.E. Zion Church. The people really wanted a church and a preacher of their own race. Also, Christopher Rush, the second General Superintendent of the Zion denomination, was a native of New Bern and was highly regarded.[4]

Hood followed his success in New Bern with equal success in other cities. In 1864 he "received into Zion" a church at Beaufort, North Carolina, and another in Wilmington. In Wilmington two churches had already gone into the A.M.E. Church. But "Hood, being an adroit maneuverer and experienced mason, worked ardently and manipulated matters so that the St. Luke church withdrew from the compact with Bethel and came with Hood into Zion."[5]

Bishop Clinton himself came to North Carolina in 1864. He arrived at New Bern on May 14. His appearance in the South was a source of inspiration and rejoicing. "Great was the joy of the people," writes Hood, "at being permitted to see a bishop of their own race, and especially a bishop who was willing to become all things to all men."[6] Through the work of Hood, a number of men were ready to be licensed or ordained on this trip by the Bishop. Hood was appointed pastor of the church in New Bern, renamed St. Peter's, which is the Mother Church of Zion Methodism in the South.

Bishop Clinton organized the North Carolina Conference in 1864 with 12 ministers and 400 members. It embraced mainly the strip of land between New Bern and Beaufort which was then in Union hands.[7]

One of J. W. Hood's most outstanding achievements was saving the church in Fayetteville that had been founded by Henry Evans for the A.M.E. Zion denomination. Bishop Walls says:

> The Lord was in Hood's appointment to Fayetteville in 1866. He found a scattered membership there of 78. In three years, he increased the membership of the church to over 500. By going to Fayetteville, he was elected to the Reconstruction Constitutional Convention, and built up a good reputation among the people in 14 counties . . . The Reconstruction Constitutional Convention in North Carolina also laid the foundation for the public school system of that day, and he became Assistant Superintendent of Education of the State.[8]

With the end of the war the Church spread rapidly all over the state. Men of exceptional ability were found and put into service with the remarkable growth as the result. For example, the Reverend William J. Moore, one of the twelve ministers who composed the first Conference, organized 68 congregations, built 11 churches, improved many others and licensed 54 local preachers.[9] The names of the men and descriptions of their work is given by Hood in his contemporaneous history of the time, *One Hundred Years of A.M.E. Zion History*.[10]

A second person who became a highly influential leader was Wilbur G. Strong. Bishop Clinton met Strong when he was teaching school in Newark, New Jersey. Impressed with Strong's abilities, Bishop Clinton persuaded Strong to give up his teaching position and join the Zion ministry. Clinton ordained Strong in Washington, D.C., and sent him to organize a church in Key West, Florida, where the Bishop said a minister was urgently needed. Strong arrived in Key West in October 1865 and soon had a church of seventy-five members, "which," says Hood, "was the nucleus of all our work in the far off South."[11] Strong also took charge of a school in Key West which he said was very much needed among the freedmen. Incidentally, a few days after Strong arrived in Key West, he experienced a typical Florida hurricane.

Much damage was done to property and fruit, but fortunately no lives were lost. We never witnessed such a storm and blow in our life. It was terrific. We thought at one time that our own little domicile would be blown down, but Providence preserved it and us.[12]

Bishop Clinton sailed from North Carolina to New Orleans where he organized the Louisiana Conference on March 13, 1865. The Bishop had Strong to come from Key West to New Orleans to help in organizing the Conference. There were fifteen preachers present. At its organization the Conference embraced all of the territory south of North Carolina. Later, however, the Louisiana Conference was divided into the Oklahoma, Florida, Georgia, Texas, and North Louisiana conferences. The work in Louisiana grew until at one time it reached 15,000 members.

Leaving New Orleans, Bishop Clinton went to Mobile, Alabama. Strong traveled with him. Friends advised Strong not to go for travel for blacks at that time was dangerous. Southern reactionaries resented the activities of the freed Negroes, especially their efforts in education. Bishop Clinton had declared at the Louisiana Conference that it was the aim of the Zion Church to "take ignorance by the neck and choke it to death."[13] Strong, however, went with the Bishop and helped in setting up churches in the Gulf states.

Bishop Clinton left Alabama for a while to supervise the growing work in the upper Southern states. In 1866 the Virginia Conference was organized at Petersburg. There were twenty-five preachers in attendance, but many of them were visitors from other conferences. This conference grew steadily and eventually came to include three presiding elders' districts.[14]

The South Carolina Conference was organized by Bishop Clinton on March 24, 1867. He was assisted by the Reverends I. C. Clinton and D. I. Walker. The Bishop made a profound public impression. "His dignified and genial bearing, in connection with his executive ability, enabled him to govern [the Conference] without assistance." Both white and black citizens came to hear him preach.[15] This Conference, the South Carolina, was the first one in the Zion Church to use the presiding elder system with an elder over a district. By 1872 there were four of these districts.

The growth of this Conference, the South Carolina, was due in large part to personal evangelizing. The men who joined the ministry were earnest, dedicated, hard-working men who carried on their labors often at personal sacrifice. An example is the Reverend C. A. King. He joined the Conference in 1867, and organized a church at Yorkville,

> and sixteen other churches principally in York, Chester, and Kershaw Counties. He also built most of these church buildings. "In many cases Brother King cut logs for these buildings and helped with his own hands to erect them." He was one of the great pioneers in the upbuilding of the South Carolina Conference.[16]

The other three pioneers were I. C. Clinton, D. I. Walker, and A. M. Moore. All became presiding elders. Hood states that within ten years these four men built eighty churches and paid for them.

From South Carolina, Bishop Clinton went back to Alabama. Again he sent for Wilbur G. Strong to join him at Mobile. The Alabama Conference was organized there in State Street Church in 1867. The Bishop traveled throughout the state, supervising the work and himself organizing churches. He organized Clinton Chapel, later known as "The Old Ship Church," in Montgomery, which became one of the most outstanding churches in the state and in the denomination.

The Church in Alabama grew very rapidly. In 1877, just ten years after the organization of the Conference, there were 8,954 members. A year later there were 12,590 members with four hundred preachers, local preachers and exhorters.[17] This growth was due to the caliber of men that came into the Church's ministry. One writer, Hood, says that they "were all stalwart men of zeal, piety and courage." They needed the courage for these were days when the "Ku Kluxers were ranging in that section, whipping, shooting, hanging, and burning churches and schoolhouses." One A.M.E.Z. pastor in Mobile was arrested and sent to the Alabama penitentiary for "refusing to bow to a rebel preacher."[18] Another preacher, the Reverend Solomon Derry, when pastor of Derry's Chapel at Union Springs, Alabama, and teacher of the school that met in the church, was visited by the Klan and

ordered to leave the place, but he refused to obey men, choosing rather to obey God by holding his ground; he remained six years, and was the means of sending out seventy-five local and traveling preachers and brought in six hundred and twenty-five members—a total of seven hundred.

Reverend Derry was not only courageous. He was a remarkable organizer and a farsighted leader. In 1873, when he was pastor of Butler's Chapel at Tuskegee, Alabama,

he built a schoolhouse out of his own pocket and gave it to the church. The normal school at Tuskegee [Booker T. Washington's Tuskegee Institute] began in that schoolhouse.[19]

Another outstanding organizer and leader in Alabama was John W. Alstork, who later became a Bishop. As a young man he was pastor of Old Ship Church in Montgomery; he served as Financial Secretary of the denomination; and he was national grand

master of the A. A. York Masons. His influence did much to
spread the work in Alabama.

From Alabama Bishop Clinton went to Georgia. Here in
Augusta on June 15, 1867, he organized the Georgia Conference.
Wilbur G. Strong again traveled with him. Trinity Church in
Augusta which was reputed to be one of the finest black
churches in the South, was taken into the Zion denomination in
the first year. However, the Reverend Edward West, who
headed the Augusta church, changed his mind during that first
year and went back into the Methodist Episcopal Church
(North), taking with him 1,160 members. This was a severe loss
to Zion. In 1868 the membership of the Georgia Conference was
2,032, and ten years later it was only 4,317, a steady growth but
slow.[20]

The Kentucky Conference was organized on June 6, 1866, by
Bishop Samson D. Talbot, assisted by Bishop Clinton. It was the
third Conference in the South. As a result of the work of the
Reverend W. F. Butler, who was one of the five men sent into
the South by Bishop Clinton in 1864, when the Conference met
in its first session 1,841 members were reported. A year later the
membership had grown to 3,253.[21]

Despite this promising beginning, the Kentucky Conference
soon ran into difficulties. Dissension developed among the
members. The Reverend W. H. Miles, who had been appointed
to the leading church in Louisville, resigned from the denomination. A number of other leading men followed him not only
from Kentucky, but from Tennessee and Georgia also. They, of
course, took their members with them. These dissidents a year
later, in 1870, helped to form the Colored Methodist Episcopal
Church, and Reverend Miles was elected a Bishop of the new
Church. The number of ministers left in the Kentucky Conference went down to nine.

In 1869 Bishop S. T. Jones was appointed to the Kentucky
Conference. With consummate skill he healed the disturbances,
restored confidence, and built up the work of the Conference.
Among the ministerial leaders who were most influential in the
work of rebuilding and expanding were the Reverend E. H.

Curry, the Reverend James Bartlett Johnson and the Reverend Anthony Bunch.[22]

As the Church continued to grow in the South, further conferences were organized: the Florida Conference in 1869, the West Tennessee and Mississippi Conference in 1869, and the Arkansas Conference in 1870, all organized by Bishop Clinton. Through the self-sacrificial work of devoted men the conferences grew steadily.

At the same time that the Church was expanding in the South it was also moving toward the West. An example of how the church expanded is seen in the work of the Reverend Jeremiah M. Washington. Born in Maryland in 1852, at the age of nine he ran away from his owner who was "a cruel taskmaster," and served as waiter to a captain in the Union Army for two years. He witnessed some of the War's worst battles. He was converted at sixteen, licensed to preach at twenty-one, and joined the Kentucky Conference in 1875.

When he joined the Conference he had already formed a congregation of 180 members. In 1877 he was sent to St. Louis to organize a Zion church there. There had been several unsuccessful prior attempts. He found a congregation of "14 members worshipping in a hall over a stable." Within three and a half years he built a large church with a membership of over 900. He organized five other churches in Missouri. He was subsequently moved to Knoxville, Tennessee, and later to Little Rock, Arkansas, where in each city he was highly successful in expanding the work. He was appointed Presiding Elder over the Louisville District in 1885.

In 1889 he was appointed to Chicago. He started with a mission church of 35 members and raised it to a metropolitan church of over 800 members. W. J. Walls who provides a brief biography says:

> He was, indeed, one of the most skillful financiers, successful revivalists and efficient pastors of the church, and a most popular singer of the race who could hold audiences spellbound under the magic influence of his sweet voice. He wrought well for Zion in this Midwestern territory. He died in 1899.[23]

The Missouri Conference was organized in 1890. Bishop George L. Blackwell was assigned to this Conference in 1908. Having a strong missionary zeal, he expanded the Church throughout the Midwest area, setting up churches in the leading cities of Michigan and Missouri. Walls relates how Bishop Blackwell would at times "cash his salary check and distribute it to all his ministers to keep them able to continue service on his mission field."[24]

Before the Church had moved into the South, it had already in 1852 ventured into the far West. The westward drive was the enterprise of one man, John J. Moore who later became a Bishop and who, Walls declares, was "one of the half-dozen greatest leaders our Zion has produced."[25] Moore joined the Philadelphia Conference in 1839. He became a traveling evangelist, serving circuits in Maryland, Pennsylvania, and Ohio. He crossed the Allegheny Mountains to preach to the fugitive slaves who had settled in that region. Among the coal and iron mines he carried the Gospel in true Methodist fashion, not on horseback but on foot, "walking thirty miles a day and preaching at night."[26]

In 1852 he left the East for California. He conducted revival meetings, set up a school, the first school for black children on the Pacific Coast, and in San Francisco built a church costing $50,000, "the colored people in this country having none which excelled it."[27] When Bishop Clinton went to California in 1868 to organize the California Conferences he found churches in three cities and ten preachers.

John J. Moore was elected Bishop in the General Conference of 1868 and transferred to the East. Under the leaders who followed the Western work declined until it reached the three original churches. At the General Conference of 1880 it was reported that the people took advantage of the lag in leadership to "fly to the A.M.E. Church."[28] In 1881 the Reverend Alexander Walters was sent to the West Coast. He was followed by the Reverend C. C. Pettey. These men began a revival of the western work, so that by 1900 there were sixteen preachers and 350 members and thirteen churches. The California Conference included Oregon and Washington as well as the territory of Arizona.[29]

Thus at the beginning of the twentieth century the A.M.E.

Zion Church, like the A.M.E., covered the country, serving as an effective instrument for spreading the Methodist pattern of faith to the masses of black Americans wherever they were found.

THE CHURCH IN THE RURAL AREAS

Most Negroes in the South before the Civil War had been the slaves on the cotton, sugar, and other plantations. Following the War, most of the former slaves or freedmen, since they were destitute, remained on Southern farms as "sharecroppers." They did not have land, but they did have labor, and this the white landlord needed. The Negroes rented land, and paid the rent with a share of the crop that was produced. Hence the term "sharecropper." During the year the landlord would advance to the tenant food, seed, fertilizer, and other necessities to be paid for at the end of the year by the landlord's share of the crop.

This could have been an equitable, cooperative pattern of farming that could have benefited both landlord and tenant. It turned, however, into one of the most vicious, exploitative systems in the history of American agriculture. Most tenants were illiterate. They could not keep accurate accounts. Under the violent white reactionism that developed in the Reconstruction era, Negroes were excluded from all political participation, landlords were in control of the courts and law enforcement, and in many communities landlords became literally lords of the land and life. Poor farmers, black and white, had little recourse against exploitation. Sheriffs were mere enforcers of the landlords' will. A preacher could not last in a community without the landlord's sanction. The result was that poor farmers were reduced to near peonage and lived under repressions that were almost as severe as under slavery.

One of the greatest sufferers was the land. The constant planting of cotton without concern for refertilization; the indifferent care of the land by resentful, exploited tenants, all served to erode the top soil, ruin fertility, and thus to bring down on the rural South an era of poverty as severe as any this nation has known.[30]

The Zion Church, like the A.M.E. and others, moved into the

rural masses, taking the hope and inspiration of the Christian faith to a people who could have easily become discouraged. Among other services the churches sought to provide education which they realized was one of the most basic requirements for progress. A good example is the one-teacher school taught by Lewis Adams in a building provided by Butler's Chapel A.M.E.Z. Church in Tuskegee, Alabama. It was Adams who wrote to General Armstrong at Hampton Institute in Virginia asking that a teacher be sent for the little school. Booker T. Washington was the young man who was sent. It was here that he began his renowned and highly essential program of teaching the children of former slaves the skills, the arts, the culture of the society in which they would have to live, a culture which under slavery and after they were being systematically denied.

FOREIGN MISSIONS

One of the great aims of Methodism was to Christianize the world, or, as it was often put, to "save the world for Christ." This would literally mean taking the Gospel to every creature on earth, and to this high aim the Methodist movement enthusiastically set itself. The black Methodist churches were heirs to this impulse. They wanted to share in saving the world. They realized that because of their limitations they could not save the whole world, but they aspired to save part of it, the black part. Their efforts, therefore, were centered mainly on Canada, that is, on black settlements in Canada; on the West Indies, and especially on Africa which they euphemistically referred to as "the Fatherland."[31]

The Dominion of Canada, especially southern Ontario along the shore of Lake Erie, was the northern terminus of the "Underground Railroad," that chain of towns and friendly sources over which escaping slaves made their way to freedom. The towns of Windsor and Hamilton in Ontario were focal points. (See Chapter VII.) The Zion churches, especially those in New York State, were active in helping runaway slaves. They naturally had an interest in the Negroes who reached Canada and made their homes there.

In 1829 the Reverend Hamilton Johnson from Prescott, Ontario, came to the meeting of the New York Annual Conference and requested that his Canadian mission church be taken into the Zion connection and thus begin work of the Zion Church in Canada. The church was taken in and Zion's foreign missionary work began. At the same time that Negroes were settling in Ontario, a number had settled in eastern Canada in the provinces of New Brunswick and Nova Scotia, and had organized their own churches. In 1856 the Zion General Conference set up the British North America Annual Conference embracing New Brunswick, Nova Scotia, Bermuda, and Cape Breton. The work was small. Three churches were taken in, the largest, Halifax, Nova Scotia, had 86 members; another church had 38, and the third had 9. There were also 130 Sunday School scholars.[32]

The Canadian work did not grow. One reason was the inability of Zion to develop the work due to lack of funds and preachers, and another was that because of Canada's severely cold climate, many Negroes migrated to the West Indies or Africa or returned to the United States after the Emancipation. In 1864 the British North American Conference was merged with the New England Conference, and in 1877 the work in Ontario was joined to the Michigan Conference. The Church decided to concentrate its work on Africa and the West Indies.[33]

The person who planted the A.M.E. Zion Church in Africa was the Reverend Andrew Cartwright. He had been a successful pastor in Virginia and North Carolina, but like many Methodists of the day, he aspired to "redeem Africa." He sailed for Africa in 1876. He organized a church at Brewerville, Liberia, in 1878, Zion's first on the African continent, and by 1880 he had set up two others. He asked the Board of Bishops in 1883 to give him the authority to organize an annual conference and to appoint preachers. He was given this right. Also, at the General Conference of 1880 the Woman's Home and Foreign Missionary Society was organized for the purpose of supporting the work in Africa.

In 1892 Cartwright was made a Presiding Elder over the African work, which was really his own work. He had hoped to be appointed a Superintendent of African missions with powers equal to those of a Bishop.[34] In the General Conference of 1896, however, a special committee on his status reported that he was a "missionary to Africa acting in the capacity of a Presiding Elder" under the appointment of a Bishop.[35] It was recommended that a Bishop should visit the African work at least annually. It was felt that there was not enough work for a missionary Bishop resident in Africa.[36]

This same Conference elected John Bryan Small a Bishop and "assigned him to Africa and the West Indies with the home conferences of North Alabama, West Alabama and Mississippi." He was ideally suited for the assignment. He was a native of Barbados. As a youth he had spent several years in Africa and had learned one or more African languages. He felt "divinely called" to visit the Continent for his Church. He arrived in Monrovia, Liberia, on August 8, 1897. He found that the work begun by Reverend Cartwright was suffering for lack of workers. Cartwright was the only American worker. The natives felt that there should be a Zion Bishop on the field as the other denominations had, but the Church in America could not decide "whether to have a bishop on the field or a bishop at a distance for the field."[37] The work also needed financial assistance.

Bishop Small traveled widely throughout the central west coast, preaching, recruiting workers, and founding and restoring churches. At one time he had five students whom he was supporting at Livingstone College in training for work in Africa. Two most outstanding of his recruits were James E. K. Aggrey and Kobina Osam Pinanko (Frank Arthur).[38] Under Small's administration churches were established in the Gold Coast (now Ghana) through the work of Reverend Pinanko whom Bishop Small had recruited. At the General Conference of 1908, Pinanko reported 15 churches, 527 members, and a school of 207 scholars, as well as a second school, Varick Memorial Institute, of eight teachers.

Bishop Small died in 1905. He was succeeded by Bishop Alexander Walters who first went to Africa in 1910. He organized the Liberia Conference in 1910. Under Reverend Pinanko the West Gold Coast Conference was organized in 1909 and the East Gold Coast Conference in 1910. Bishop Walters stimulated the work during his time on the field. He served until 1917 when he retired because of ill health. Bishop George C. Clement succeeded Walters, but because of the First World War, Bishop Clement was not able to get to Africa. Three missionary workers were sent to the field, however.

At the General Conference of 1920 the Corresponding Secretary of Foreign Missions, the Reverend W. W. Matthews, recommended that the Church send to Africa a *resident* Bishop, "one who is willing to live among them, to sympathize with them, to supervise and direct Zion's destinies in the Fatherland."[39] In response, Bishop Cameron C. Alleyne was assigned to Africa as the first resident Bishop. He found the work in deterioration in places, but with the aid of faithful coworkers it was rebuilt.[40] In 1932 under Bishop W. W. Matthews the Nigeria Conference was added. It had 28 churches, 11 native preachers and 2,345 members. The total number of members in all West African Conferences in 1932 was 18,000.[41]

The African work continued with varying success through the following years. Glowing reports of expanding work would be made to the General Conferences, but realistic accounts would give an up and down picture. In 1924 Bishop Alleyne found the churches of the West Gold Coast Conference "divided and the flock scattered." This was the work so brilliantly begun under Bishop Small and Reverend Pinanko. Bishop Pope in 1954 had to restore the Cartwright Memorial Church in Brewerville, "which had decayed and been removed entirely, the membership having temporarily joined the Methodist Church."[42]

One of the most helpful developments in the African work was the etablishment of the African Memorial Banks, a project initiated by the First Episcopal District in 1959 under the leadership of Bishop W. J. Walls. The first project of the Banks was the restoration of Zion's first church at Brewerville. In 1952 the General Conference also took some progressive steps. Thenceforth the Bishop who would be sent to Africa was to be the best suited person for the work, and not just the last person elected. Also, he was to reside in Africa during the period of his assignment. Had the Church had the advantage of resident episcopal leadership earlier, it is quite likely that its work might well have been larger, more stable, and on a higher level.

The coming of independence to the African colonies presented new opportunities for the Church, but it also presented problems. The fact of Civil War in Nigeria created new problems. Yet despite the war Bishop Alfred G. Dunston was able to establish 10 churches, one of 80 members in the capital city, Lagos. In 1972 the whole of the African work was assigned to Bishop Ruben L. Speaks.

THE WEST INDIES

At the same time that the Church was attempting to get a foothold on the African continent, it also was working in the closer islands of the West Indies. In 1861 an attempt was made to start work in Haiti. The Reverend J. W. Lacy went there in 1861. He formed a union with the A.M.E. Church, but it did not last long. In 1869 Lacey returned to the United States and no further work was attempted in Haiti by Zion.[43]

Bishop John B. Small visited Santo Domingo in 1899. He found several missions there that had been organized by the Reverend Carl H. Williams, but because of the constant revolutions the work could not grow. Later, however, in 1908, it was reported to be growing. Bishop Small also established a mission in British Honduras, his birthplace. Others were started in Jamaica and British Guiana, and in Demerara, Zion's first church in South America. An effort was made to establish a church in Brazil, but this was abandoned after a year, with the feeling that "there was no place in Brazil for a race church."[44]

In 1940 Bishop C. C. Alleyne opened work in the Virgin Islands, and in 1948 set this work apart as a separate Conference. It was expanded under Bishop Stephen G. Spottswood. Also Bishop Spottswood received churches in South Africa into the Guyana Conference.[45]

In 1877 the Bahama Islands Conference was organized. There were churches in eight towns with 206 members. The work was maintained until 1920 when "it seemed to have gone down to a low ebb through lack of a sufficient ministry."[46] In 1959 the work was revived by Bishop Herbert Bell Shaw. He had to reclaim church properties and rebuild congregations. Through his deep interest in foreign missions this work is now going well. In 1965 there were nine churches with a membership of 322.[47]

The United Holy Church of Jamaica, an independent Christian body, in 1966 requested to be taken into the A.M.E. Zion Church. Bishop Herbert Bell Shaw, the Presiding Bishop, received them, and organized the Jamaica Conference with five churches and ministers. It is one of the fastest growing conferences in the connection.

With the recent influx of colonial citizens into England, communities of West Indians and Africans have been formed in many English cities. The Zion church has followed them and, under the lead of Bishop H. B. Shaw, has established churches in London, Birmingham, Bristol, and Manchester with a combined membership of 400. This is called the London-Birmingham Conference, which was organized in 1971.[48] The establishment of A.M.E. Zion work in England was like the return of a child to its native home.

INTERNAL DEVELOPMENT

The growth of the Church in members and geographical extent, especially after the movement into the South, required development in internal organization for the effective management of the burgeoning structure. This called for the introduction of general secretaryships, general officers, and connectional departments.

The first general officer in the Zion denomination was the General Secretary, authorized and elected by the General Conference of 1872. His duty was "to record the ensuing General Conference, take charge of all the books and papers, and other property of the General Conference not otherwise provided for . . ."[49] Prior to 1872 the minutes of the annual and general conferences had been kept by men who served gratuitously and faithfully. Bishop Walls says:

> These men kept the records faithfully of all proceedings of quadrennial sessions; local statistics, Sunday school pupils, finances raised, important records of church property, and annual confer-

ence records before the church began to organize a records department connectionally. They also helped to revise the Discipline,
keep up correspondence with fraternal organizations, and issue resolutions on important church actions.[50]

This was a vital service remarkably well performed. But since the
Church had grown so widely and so rapidly, it needed more
specific and more responsible handling.

In 1876 Reverend William Howard Day was elected first General Secretary. He was an ideal choice. The first black graduate
of Oberlin College, he was one of the best-educated black men of
his day. He was a strong abolitionist, and was President of the
School Board of Control of Harrisburg, Pennsylvania, his home-
town. With the exception of eight years, he served until 1900,
the year of his death.

In the succeeding years the office of General Secretary was
tied into fiscal and auditing functions but these have been reduced or eliminated, and the work now consists primarily of record keeping and statistical functions that mean so much to the
history of the Church.

In 1872 the General Conference levied the first general claim
or assessment. The amount was from twenty-five to fifty cents
per member for the support of the bishops. In 1880 the amount
of fifty cents was fixed, and a new financial officer, the General
Steward, was authorized to receive the payments from the annual
conference and district stewards. The assessment was raised in
1904 to one dollar per member, and the money was used not only
for the salaries of bishops, but also for schools, missions, and
other benevolent causes. The title of the General Steward was
changed to Financial Secretary. The connectional budget for
1972 was $1,650,000.[51]

Through the years several women's organizations have been
formed to assist in carrying on the mission, educational, and
other programs of the Church by raising funds and rendering
other services. The first such group was the Female Benevolent
Society, organized in 1820 to give aid to the sick and distressed,
bury the dead, and to assist in supporting the orphans of their de-
ceased members.[52]

One of the greatest of the women's groups, the Daughters of

Conference, was organized in 1821. Its purpose was to assist the ministers in their mission work and in the erection of new churches. In the early days of the denomination when funds for pastoral support, ministerial travel, and church buildings were scarce if not totally lacking, the work of these women was highly important. On at least two occasions, they played a major part in erecting the church buildings of the Zion congregation in New York.

SUNDAY SCHOOLS AND YOUTH WORK

Early in its history the A.M.E. Zion churches began conducting Sunday Schools for the training of the young people. In 1872 the work was connectionally organized when the General Conference of that year authorized the formation of the Sunday School Union. In 1880 the International Uniform Lessons were adopted as the literature for the Union. In 1888 the Reverend Robert R. Morris was elected General Superintendent of Sunday Schools. The General Conference of 1888 also provided that a Sunday School Convention should be held each year in each annual conference district. The purpose was, of course, to promote the work. Ministers not attending or supporting the conventions would "be dealt with for 'gross neglect of duty.' "[53]

Dr. Morris held the office of General Superintendent until his death in 1895. The office was not filled from 1896 to 1916, the editor of Sunday School literature directing the work for the intervening twenty years. In 1916 Dr. James W. Eichelberger was elected General Superintendent, and served until 1924 when he was elected Corresponding Secretary of the Department of Christian Education. This Department was organized to correlate and to promote more vigorously the several branches of young people's work which had been set up in the Church. Dr. Eichelberger, both as General Superintendent and Corresponding Secretary, soon became a most outstanding leader in young people's work. Bishop Walls states that "he became a symbol for black Protestants in the field of Christian Education." He served until his death in 1967.[54]

Meanwhile the Zion Church joined in the Christian Endeavor Movement.[55] The first C. E. Society in the Zion Church was organized by the Reverend Richard H. Stitt in his church in Brooklyn, New York, in 1893. Through his efforts the General Conference adopted the Christian Endeavor plan for the entire denomination, naming it the Varick Christian Endeavor Society.[56] It soon became an important phase of the Church's young people's program. Plans of organization were devised to suit both the larger and smaller churches.

The development of Zion's Christian Education program was largely due to the concern and efforts of two men, the Reverend W. J. Walls, who in 1924 was elected a Bishop, and Dr. Eichelberger, previously mentioned. Their writings, speeches, and personal leadership resulted in 1924 in the formation of the Christian Education Department. Under the direction of the Department a large variety of educational activities could now be promoted with economy and efficiency and without duplication. For example, funds could in this way be raised and dispensed to schools and colleges without a multiplicity of separate drives or "days." The work of the institutions could also be supervised by the general church.[57] The work with children, youth, and adults expanded rapidly, and engaged persons who became nationally known leaders. Zion's educational program became one of the most outstanding among the black Methodist bodies. Zion's representatives at national and internationl Christian education meetings made significant contributions to the work of these bodies.

MINISTERIAL TRAINING

The need for training among the ministers was recognized early in Zion's history. A minister who could not read even the Bible would be greatly limited in his service to his people, and in the long run he would be a handicap. Prior to the Civil War, getting an education was difficult for the average Negro, even among the free Negroes in the North. Yet it could be done, and persons who aspired to leadership needed to be prodded to do it. Thus, says Walls, before the spread of the Church South, . . . there was a cooperative effort in the six northern conferences on the education and training of their ministry and people. To have reasonable assurance that the preacher was suitably equipped for his task, the conferences early adopted courses of studies for graduates to holy orders. For deacon's orders, the courses included grammar, arithmetic, geography, rules and doctrines of Discipline, scripture doctrine, historical events of scripture, isms [sic], Baptism, and sacrament or the Lord's supper. For elders orders, a review of the previous studies, theology, church government, ancient and modern history, and rhetoric were the prescribed courses of study. Textbooks were recommended in pursuing these studies.

As early as 1858, the Genesee (Western New York) Conference resolved that it would not recommend any person for holy orders who had "not a sufficient knowledge of the English language to speak with tolerable accuracy, and whose knowledge of theology does not enable him to distinguish between Arminianism, Calvinism and Universalism.[58]

The prescription of this list of courses represented an ideal of ministerial instruction, an ideal to which few of the preachers could or did attain. Perhaps a more realistic picture of the average preacher is given by J. W. Hood, himself a well-educated man:

> The ministers of the period were, as a rule, good preachers; few of them were what would be called brilliant men, but a large portion of them could preach a good sensible sermon. Some were powerful, awakening preachers; sinners could not listen without being affected to such a degree that it was impossible for them to hide it.[59]

Among other significant developments in the histories of the black Methodist denominations are the establishment of schools and colleges and the nature and power of the bishopric or episcopacy. These are discussed in later chapters.[60]

CHAPTER XIII

The Christian Methodist Episcopal Church[1]

THE FOUNDING OF THE Christian Methodist Episcopal Church was in some ways quite different from the founding of the other black Methodist denominations. In the first place, the C.M.E. Church did not begin in conflict with whites or in ill feeling. It began in the mutual recognition of a changed situation which called for a new organizational relationship.

The white members of the Methodist Episcopal Church, South, realized that most of the Negro members in their new, liberated status would not want to and could not be expected to remain in the Church in the subordinate, segregated membership that had obtained under slavery. This was evident in the fact that two-thirds of the black members left the M.E. Church, South, between 1860 and 1866. Most of them went, of course, to the independent black bodies, the A.M.E. and A.M.E.Z., and also to the churches that were being organized by the M.E. Church, North, which was now avidly working among the freedmen of the South along side the black churches.[2]

Both the black and white members of the M.E. Church, South, realized that something must be done and done quickly if any of the black membership of the Southern Church was to be held.

This could best be done, they felt, in a separate organization. Under this arrangement the white Church could maintain a fraternal relationship with the black body, and also express a helpful concern which the whites felt they owed the blacks from having been part of the slave system. As for the blacks, many left the white Church with regret. They were indebted to it for their Christian awakening. Although on the unequal relationship of master and slave, the Church, South, had provided for many Negroes a certain amount of "Christian" fellowship. The Church had been also the main voice calling for more humane treatment of slaves and protesting the more brutal aspects of slavery, such as the separation of families.[3] Under the slave system these were very considerable services, and for them many Negroes were grateful. As is now known, friendly, helpful relationships did exist between individual white and black Methodists in the South during slavery.

This complex of feelings and the resulting actions are well expressed by C. H. Phillips, who later became one of the bishops of the C.M.E. Church:

> While Bishop Andrew owned slaves, and thus indirectly, if not directly, gave a tacit assent to the perpetuation of the "peculiar institution" of slavery, which John Wesley declared to be "the sum of all villainies," yet he was a man of warm and tender heart, and frequently rose to sublime heights of eloquence when pleading for the religious instruction of the slave. The services of Dr. Lovick Pierce and James E. Evans; of Bishops George Pierce, John C. Keener, and Holland N. McTyeire shall never be forgotten. They labored assiduously for the Christian civilization of our race.
>
> Thus the religious nature of the slave was developed; thousands took on the civilization by which they were environed, and thousands more cast their lot with the Methodists. It was not unnatural that the Southern Methodist Church should, after the war, have shown a disposition to do what was best for her colored contingent. Gradually this contingent was either going into the African Methodist Episcopal Church and the African Methodist Episcopal Zion Church, or into the Methodist Episcopal Church. Such were the persecution, misrepresentation, ridicule, and stratagems brought to bear against the Church, South, and especially its colored com-

municants, that many were toled away; for out of the 207,000 on the roll before the Civil War, only 78,000 were found at its close. To save this remnant was the supreme thought of the leaders of the Church, South. To organize them into an ecclesiastical body occurred to them as the only feasible thing to be done. Consequently, when the General Conference in 1866 asked, "What shall be done to promote the religious interests of the colored people?" that same body wisely resolved that "when two or more Annual Conferences shall be formed, let our bishops advise and assist them in organizing a separate General Conference jurisdiction for themselves, if they so desire and the bishops deem it expedient, in accordance with the doctrine and discipline of our Church, and bearing the same relation to the General Conference as the Annual Conferences bear to each other."[4]

Thus in a spirit of friendly helpfulness, and in the determination to keep the black members of the Church, South, intact in an organization of their own, the idea of the C.M.E. Church was born.

On December 15, 1870, the first General Conference of the C.M.E. Church (not yet named), met in Jackson, Tennessee. Bishop Robert Paine, Senior Bishop of the M.E. Church, South, presided. Three ministers of that Church were also appointed to assist in the work of organization. The Reverend James A. Beard, pastor of the First Methodist Episcopal Church, South, of Jackson, acted as Secretary, pro tem. Representatives from eight annual conferences which had been organized among the black members were present. Those conferences were the Memphis, Mississippi, Alabama, Georgia, Kentucky, Arkansas, Texas, and South Carolina. Among the delegates were men who were destined to play a great part in the subsequent history of the newly formed Church.

After opening the Conference with divine service, Bishop Paine "made a few impressive remarks. Dr. Green read the actions of the General Conferences of 1866 and 1870 relating to the organization of our Church. This done, our fathers then proceeded to found a Church against which the 'gates of Hell should never prevail.'"[5]

Dr. Samuel Watson, a white minister who was interested in the black members of the Church, South, wrote:

It was a most interesting occasion . . . I have never seen a more harmonious Conference of any kind. There was a good degree of intelligence among its members. A distinguished judge, who attended the Conference daily, said it would compare favorably with the Tennessee Legislature.[6]

Committees were appointed. The first of these, the *Committee on Church Organization,* suggested the name for the new Church, and also the plan of organization:

Whereas the Methodist Episcopal Church in America was the name first given to the Methodist Church in the United States; and

Whereas we are a part of that same Church, never having seceded or separated from the Church, but in the division of the Church by the General Conference in 1844 we naturally belonged to the South, and have been in that division ever since; and now, as we belong to the colored race, we simply prefix the word "colored" to the name, and for ourselves adopt the name, as we are in fact a part of the original Church, as old as any in America; therefore be it

Resolved, 1. That our name be the "Colored Methodist Episcopal Church in America."

2. That while we thus claim for ourselves an antiquity running as far back as any branch of the Methodist family on this side of the Atlantic Ocean, and while we claim for ourselves all that we concede to others of ecclesiastical and civil rights, we shall ever hold in grateful remembrance what the Methodist Episcopal Church, South, has done for us; we shall ever cherish the kindliest feelings toward the bishops and General Conference for giving to us all that they enjoy of religious privileges, the ordination of our deacons and elders; and at this Conference our bishops will be ordained by them to the highest office known in our Church. No other church organization has thus been established in the land. We most sincerely pray, earnestly desire, and confidently believe that there will ever be the kindliest feelings cherished toward the Methodist Episcopal Church, South, and that we may ever receive their warmest sympathy and support.

3. That we request the bishops to organize our General Conference on the basis of the Discipline of the Methodist Episcopal Church, South, in its entire doctrine, discipline and economy, making only such verbal alterations and changes as may be necessary to conform it to our name and the peculiarities of our condition.[7]

A second step of the Conference was to authorize the creation of a publishing house, a Book Agent, and an editor of Church publications. A "Publishing Committee" was appointed to see that the plans were carried out and to receive funds.

On the sixth day the Committee on Episcopacy reported. It recommended the election of two bishops. After an address by Bishop Paine on the kind of men who should be elected, and solemn prayer, the balloting began. Forty votes were cast; 21 were necessary for election. William H. Miles received 27 votes on the first ballot and Richard H. Vanderhorst received 26 on the third. They thus became the first two bishops of the Colored Methodist Episcopal Church.[8] They were consecrated by Bishops Paine and McTyeire in the First Methodist Episcopal Church, South, in Jackson, Tennessee, on the night of the same day of their election.

Both of these men were outstanding persons and well worthy of the bishopric. The second person, however, R. H. Vanderhorst, was broken in health and lived only eighteen months after his election. He was born a slave in Georgetown, South Carolina, in 1813. He was fortunate to have kindly owners. "At the request of his parents, he was put to learn the carpenter's trade, and, as an apprentice under Sampson Dunmore, he became very well versed in the carpentry business." Vanderhorst early became noted for his piety.

> He cared little for worldly amusements; he was "never found on the dancing floor or in the barroom, and was strictly a temperance man from his boyhood to his grave." One of the best evidences of his good training and the godly example of pious parents was his sound conversion. At the age of twenty he sought the Lord, received pardon of his sins, and at once joined the Methodist Episcopal Church, South, at Georgetown.

He later moved to Charleston, became a class leader in a church there, and in 1840, because of his leadership abilities and his outstanding oratorical powers, he was licensed to preach "so far as the laws of the State and the Discipline of the Methodist Episcopal Church, South, would at that time allow."[9]

In 1865 Vanderhorst joined the A.M.E. Church which came into South Carolina under Bishop Daniel Payne.[10] He soon left them, however, to return to his own church, the M.E. Church, South, to help in organizing the Negro members into annual conferences. He was elected from the Georgia Conference as a delegate to the first C.M.E. General Conference in 1870, and there he was elected a bishop.

C. H. Phillips gives this personal picture of the second Bishop of the Church:

> Bishop Vanderhorst held the Georgia Conference, which met in December, in Milledgeville. The writer was only thirteen years old, but he remembers that the Bishop preached a great sermon . . . We do not remember the outlines—but we do recollect that his sermon was eloquent, powerful, and pathetic, and made a great impression upon the people. The intonation of his voice, his graceful gestures, his beautiful cadences, his anxious look, his elegant diction, and his native eloquence marked him an orator of the purest type. He was a tall, erect, dignified black man. Dr. Watson, when describing the two bishops at one time, said: "Bishop Miles is *bright*, but Bishop Vanderhorst, as a Kentucky brother said in the General Conference, is black enough for any of us.[11]

Isaac Lane, in a biographical evaluation says:

> Bishop Vanderhorst may never be regarded as an executive, parliamentarian, or organizer on the order of Bishop Miles; but as a Gospel preacher and as an evangelist, he had no superior. Eloquent and logical, his sermons would stir the hearts of men. Although short as to time, his services were very valuable to the Church. As long as the Colored Methodist Church lives the name of Bishop Richard H. Vanderhorst will be remembered, loved, and revered.[12]

William Henry Miles, the first Bishop, was in full health and strength and was forty-two years old at the time of his election, fifteen years younger than Vanderhorst. He was born in 1828 in Springfield, Kentucky. He was manumitted in 1854, but because of a contested will he was not given his freedom until 1864. While a slave he was distinguished for his "fidelity, integrity and intelligence." He joined the Methodist Episcopal Church, South, in 1855, and was granted a license to preach in 1857. He was ordained a Deacon by Bishop Andrew in 1859. He was already noted for his superior preaching powers and his piety.

In 1865 Miles heard that the M.E. Church, South would soon

cut off its Negro members. Believing this, he joined the A.M.E.
Zion Church which had just come into the state of Kentucky. In
the Zion Church he was appointed a traveling missionary in Kentucky. He did not like the appointment. Also he learned of the
plans that the Church, South, had for organizing its colored
members into a separate body. He therefore resigned his connection with the Zions and returned to his first love, the Church,
South. He was appointed to organize work in Kentucky. To the
first General Conference which was to meet in 1870 he was
elected a reserve or alternate. He was appointed to preach a sermon before the Conference, and it was this that revealed his remarkable qualities and led to his election.[13]

With the General Conference ended, two bishops elected, and
details of organization completed, the new Church plunged at
once into the work of evangelizing on the one hand, and recover-
ing lost members on the other. It started against strong and sometimes ruthless opposition from three Methodist bodies, two black
and one white. The chief mode of attack against the new Church
was by disseminating false impressions and arousing popular prejudices. The C.M.E.'s were depicted as being in league with former slaveholders and as being opposed to black independence and
black progress. Sometimes the feelings against the new Church
actually resulted in violence.

C. H. Phillips describes the situation aptly:

> No easy field lay before these consecrated men. The Church was
> in its infancy; it was maliciously misrepresented, wantonly
> maligned, and frequently calumniated by stronger religious
> denominations. The relation of our Church to the Methodist Epis-
> copal Church, South, was the prolific cause of most of the misrep-
> resentations heaped upon us. The Church was called a "Rebel
> Church," "Democratic Church," and "the Old Slavery Church."
> These were powerful weapons used against us, for the reason that
> our people were naturally credulous, especially concerning any-
> thing that might be said about those who had kept their forefathers
> in slavery for more than two centuries. Some were odiously in-
> clined to the Church, South; others refused social relations with
> those who in any way affiliated with that Church. Thus the
> credulity of the ignorant was played upon with ease . . .[14]

For the men who were doing the work on the field, these were difficult if not dangerous days. In 1873 Bishop Miles, one of the most intrepid of the evangelists, wrote: "The Missouri and Kansas Conference met in first session near Santa Fe, Missouri. The church having been burned just before the Conference, we held the session in the woods. We had a very pleasant time."[15]

In a similar vein Bishop Holsey wrote the church in Thomasville, Georgia:

> The church in this place has been burned by our enemies, but a new one has been erected on the smoking ruins. The present building is in debt, and has only a few members; but these are faithful and true. Their African brethren are still waging an unholy war of persecution and slander against the innocent few because they choose to worship God according to the dictates of an unfettered conscience. What a crime to divide churches and then burn the building![16]

Yet despite opposition and "persecution," the early leaders pushed forward assiduously to spread their Church. Bishop Miles was the ideal leader for the time. Possessed of great physical strength, abundant energy, and an indomitable will, he dedicated himself completely to the Church. His sufferings and privations are reminiscent of St. Paul.

In the midst of these early efforts Bishop Vanderhorst died. It was clear that the new Church, rapidly extending, was too much for one man to supervise. Bishop Miles, therefore, called a General Conference to meet in Augusta, Georgia, on March 19, 1873.

With the Conference assembled, Bishop Miles presided. J. W. Bell of Kentucky was elected Secretary. Bishop George F. Pierce and five elders attended as representatives of the Church, South.

Bishop Miles delivered the Bishop's Address. It was an impressive statement. He first paid tribute to Bishop Vanderhorst. Secondly, he presented statistics showing the size and growth of the Church. He reported 14 Annual Conferences, 635 traveling preachers, 583 local preachers, and a membership of 67,888. "In view of the opposition from certain quarters," he said, "these results are very inspiring. Let us thank God and take courage."[17]

He next recommended the election of three bishops. "The territory in our conference is very large. One or two men in the episcopacy can only make transient visits to the chief points. A more thorough personal oversight is necessary to an intelligent and effective administration."

Then followed an expression of thanks to the Methodist Episcopal Church, South, for "the Christian kindness and consideration toward us as a people . . . The brethren of the Church, South, have shown us great favor; and their debtors we are for sympathy and encouragement, for brotherly counsel and material aid, and for the transfer, under all the forms and securities of law, of an amount of property which, left to ourselves, we would not have realized in a generation."

He called attention to the publishing interests, and the need for their more active promotion. "We must become a reading people," he said, "if we would acquire influence, overcome opposition, and maintain ourselves respectably among the Churches of the land."[18]

In keeping with the Bishop's recommendation, the Conference elected three bishops: Joseph A. Beebe of North Carolina, Lucius H. Holsey of Georgia, and Isaac Lane of Tennessee. They were three wise selections. Each made outstanding contributions to the Church. Lucius Holsey was the most remarkable. Just thirty years old, "at the time of his election he was without doubt the youngest man elected to the Methodist episcopacy. More, no man ever won the office within so short a time from the beginning of his ministerial career. Licensed to preach in 1868, he was a bishop in 1873."[19] Holsey was noted for his intellectual brilliance, his preaching gifts and his organizing abilities.

At this Conference Dr. Samuel Watson, the white minister who had started the *Christian Index* in 1868 and had edited it for five years, found it necessary to give up the work. The Conference expressed its gratitude. E. B. Martin was elected his successor as editor, and also as the Book Agent. Finally, the bishops were instructed to take measures looking to the establishment of an institution of learning.

To the preachers and evangelists of the new Church no greater tribute can be paid than the rapidity with which the Church grew. In 1873 there were 67,888 members. In 1874 there were

74,769, and in 1878 more than 100,000, a gain of over 40,000 in five years. The C.M.E. Church had become one of the fastest growing of the Methodist bodies among blacks.

A good example of how this growth was achieved is given by Isaac Lane, one of the newly elected bishops. In clear, terse language he describes his own experiences, which are fairly typical of all pioneering Methodist preachers in spreading Methodism across the nation. His accounts give impressive insights into both religious and social conditions prevailing at that time.

In those early days of the freedom of the race the people were crude and had their own ideas of religion, of the ministry, and especially of the bishops. There was such curiosity attached to the coming of a bishop. This situation had to be met and in a way satisfied in order to reach the people in the interest of the Church.

After our election and consecration, Bishop Miles called us together, and then and there we allotted and assigned the work for the year. I was called upon to preside over the Northwest Texas, the East Texas, and the Louisiana Annual Conferences. At that time our entire connection was composed of mission Conferences when compared with the work as it is organized to-day, and my work was from every viewpoint missionary. The territory was exceedingly large, covering the present States of Texas, Oklahoma, and Louisiana. As all know, this territory was wholly undeveloped and sparsely settled by a wild and adventurous people, who cared very little for the Church, religion, and the ministry. Railroads were very few, and most of the traveling had to be done by stage, on horseback, by boat or on foot. To travel over this vast territory entailed many hardships, deprivations and much suffering. Pen cannot describe, tongue can never tell, nor can language express the mental anguish and the physical pain I endured on those perilous trips. I shall never forget those early experiences.

My First Annual Conference

My first Annual Conference was the West Texas Annual Conference, which convened at Waxahachie, Ellis County, Tex., in 1873. En route to the seat of the Conference my experiences were everything but pleasant. I had only a small sum of money, and while on a train a man robbed me of that. I had to go through St. Louis and Sedalia, Mo., and then via the St. Louis and Texas Central Railroad. I reached the State line of Texas and Oklahoma (then the Indian territory). It was about sundown, and I had some sixty miles yet to go before reaching Dallas, my destination. Here I found Rev. A. J. Burrows hard at work. From Dallas I went to Waxahachie, a small town about sixty miles south of Dallas.

The Conference was well attended; but the year had been a hard one for the brethren, and their reports were very poor. The preachers had not received very much in the way of support, and the general interest of the Church had suffered likewise. To indicate the nature of the support that was given, I give one item that will be quite interesting to the students of the conditions that prevailed during those days. For the support of the bishop the Conference had been asked to raise forty dollars, and they reported having raised three and one-half dollars. It was at this place that one of those unpleasant events took place—viz., the African Methodist Episcopal Church had gotten a hold among our people and greatly divided them. As a result the African Methodist Episcopal Church did not do very much and made impossible the success we would have had under favorable conditions. I lectured and preached and exhorted and helped them in every way I could and then left for my next appointment.

With the adjournment of [his third Annual] Conference my first year as a bishop came to a close. I had worked hard during the year and had but little financial help. On my salary the Church had paid me only one hundred and sixty dollars and fifteen cents during the year, and my expenses necessarily carried me far into debt. My note was about to fall due, and something must be done to enable me to meet it. My wife and children had a crop of cotton. This I sold, and with the money I paid the debt and took up the note. I then worked hard to replace this money. I cut wood and hauled it to town and sold it, making enough money thereby to buy such things as clothing and other provisions that were needed by my family. This was a hard year for me and one that I shall never forget. The labor, deprivations, and hardships I endured were enough to bring tears to my eyes. The young ministers of our Church, even those serving missions to-day, do not know our suffering during those early pioneer days of our Church.[20]

The takeover of C.M.E. Church properties by other black denominations mentioned by Lane was one of the severest problems that the C.M.E. Church had to face. The General Conference of the M.E. Church, South, gave to the C.M.E.'s the buildings and other properties formerly used by its colored congregations. However, in many cases when such congregations would be taken into the A.M.E. and A.M.E.Z. denominations, the church buildings would be taken too. When the C.M.E.'s would call for the return of the property, their appeals were either ignored or refused. In an effort to end this the C.M.E. bishops Miles and Vanderhorst, on May 1, 1872, addressed the following letter to the bishops of the A.M.E. Church:

To Your Honorable Body, Hoping God's Blessing May Attend You, and that You May Have a Pleasant Session—Greeting:

DEAR BRETHREN AND SIRS: This being the first session of your General Conference since we have effected our separate organization, we desire to live in peace with all men, and especially with Christians. So we concluded to drop your honorable body a few lines, asking you to take some steps to settle the difficulty that now exists between our Churches with regard to our church property which your congregations are now occupying without any legal right by the decision of the General Conference at Memphis, Tenn., in 1870. We assure you that we wish to live in peace with your Church, and do not wish to go to law for our churches. If it pleases your honorable body to appoint a committee to meet us, rest assured that your committee will be met with due respect on our part. We believe these little questions in law are injurious to our race, and we think that something should be done on both sides to stop the contention and bring peace between us. Some of your ministers in the past have been very hostile to us, forbidding us to preach in our own churches that were occupied by your congregations, for which we are very sorry. We only ask that which is ours under the law of the land, and we assure you that if we have any of your houses of worship we are ready and willing to give them up; and we ask your honorable body to turn over to us all of our church property throughout the South without the trouble of lawsuits. We await your answer.

W. H. MILES
R. H. VANDERHORST,

Bishops of the Colored Methodist Episcopal Church in America."[21]

Nearly a year later, April 1, 1873, the A.M.E. bishops replied: "Touching the question of property, we are willing to act strictly according to the principle of equity and right, and earnestly hope that all disputes regarding the same may be amicably adjusted."[22] The unfair occupation of property continued nevertheless for several years.

The *Christian Index* had a lively history for the last two of its first five years. Dr. Samuel Watson, white, the first editor and creator of the *Index*, had to give up the work in 1873. The Reverend E. B. Martin was appointed to succeed him in March 1873. After six months, in September 1873, he announced to the Bishops that he was called to preach and not to edit a paper. He resigned. In November, Reverend J. W. Bell was appointed editor. He was also pastor of Center Street Church in Louisville. Within two months he ran into trouble with Bishop Miles, and in January 1874 he was "removed" both from the *Index* and the Church. The Reverend Alexander Austin was chosen editor in January, but in May he was "removed." It may have been because of the many complaints that arose over the irregular way the *Index* was received by subscribers, orders for books not filled, and other business faults. In August 1874, W. P. Churchill was made Editor and Business Manager of the Book Concern, giving both enterprises a more stable existence.[23]

One of the early and major concerns of the new Church was the matter of education. Both leaders and people recognized the need for education among the three million black freedmen, and especially among the ministers.

In 1873 Bishop Miles undertook to start the first school or "university." His hope was that this would be the central institution to which secondary or "feeder" schools would send their graduates. He bought land in Louisville, and sent out letters of appeal to raise $50,000. The General Conference of 1874 approved the plan and urged the Church to support it. Bishop Miles traveled widely, North and South, seeking funds. He planned to start a school in Sardis, Mississippi. The whole plan received popular approval. Many pledged and made contributions. The gifts, however, were small and insufficient. The property in Louisville had to be sold, and the first effort failed.[24]

Bishop Miles was personally disappointed, but the Church did not lose its determination. In 1878 the Tennessee Conference started a school project. A committee was appointed, and four acres of land were purchased in Jackson, Tennessee. Bishop Lane assisted. The school began in 1882 in a two-story frame building with Miss Jennie Lane as principal. It was called Jackson High School. Later, in 1887, under the Reverend F. T. Sanders the name was changed to Lane College.[25] Lane College has grown until today it is a fully accredited college with over seven hundred students.

At the General Conference of 1882,

Bishop Holsey was sent as a fraternal delegate to the General Conference of the Methodist Episcopal Church, South, then in session in Nashville, Tenn. He was instructed by our General Conference to ask for assistance in building up our educational projects, and any conclusions reached by him and the Methodist Episcopal Church, South, would meet the endorsement of our Church.

Bishop Holsey's visit to the General Conference of the Methodist Episcopal Church, South, had seemingly so stirred that Church that they decided to do something in a tangible way to assist us in establishing schools where young men could prepare for the ministry and young women could fit themselves as teachers. Their General Conference authorized its bishops to appoint a Commissioner of Education, together with three trustees, who should work in harmony with such a number from our Church in any worthy move to found a school or schools for our denomination. Accordingly, on August 29, 1882, at the call of Bishop Pierce, all of our bishops, with distinguished men from the Church, South, met in the First Methodist Church of Atlanta, Ga., and discussed things educational. A board of trustees was formed; the school at Jackson, Tenn., already in an embryonic state, was to receive aid; and a school was located at Augusta, Ga. This school was afterwards named Paine Institute, in honor of Dr. Uriah Paine, who endowed it with $25,000.[26]

The rapid growth of the C.M.E. Church in the years since 1870 has required development of many boards and agencies to handle connectional affairs. At present these affairs are under eight departments or boards: the Department of Finance, the General Publishing Board, the General Boards of Pensions, Missions, Christian Education, Evangelism, and Lay Activities, and the Woman's Missionary Council.[27]

The Department of Finance was organized in 1922. It is located in Memphis, Tennessee, which is the headquarters of the Church. The Annual Budget of the Church in 1974 was $1,479,000. This amount is apportioned among the episcopal districts. Nearly half, 40.6 per cent, is devoted to educational institutions. The Church has five colleges and one theological seminary.[28]

One of the most important of the General Boards is the General Board of Christian Education. It has charge of the schools and colleges of the Church as well as the whole program of religious education and youth work. Some of the most distinguished leaders of the Church have headed this Department, among them the Reverends J. A. Martin, B. Julian Smith, and C. D. Coleman, all of whom later became bishops. Bishop Smith kept the Department closely related to national and international movements. He also did much to advance the training of ministers. Under his leadership Phillips School of Theology became an original member of the Interdenominational Theological Center in Atlanta.

The C.M.E. Church has a Board of Pensions and a Minimum Salary Plan. It was one of the first black churches to have such a plan, whose purpose is to lift the salaries of black ministers, which are notoriously low.

The Church has three publications: *The Christian Index,* and the *Western* and *Eastern Christian Indexes.* The first-named is connection-wide; the other two are regional.

FOREIGN MISSIONS

The C.M.E. Church did not begin work in foreign fields until late in its history. The Reverend John Wesley Gilbert, the first black teacher in Paine College, did take a long, adventurous trip into the interior of Africa in company with Bishop Lambuth of the M.E. Church, South. Gilbert wrote back thrilling accounts of his experiences, with appeals for others to follow him in African service. Nothing was done, however, for near half a century.

In 1956 Bishops B. W. Doyle and A. W. Womack visited several West African countries to explore the possibilities of work for their Church in those countries. In 1960 Dr. Joseph Wright, a Ghanaian, invited the C.M.E. Church to take over a school that he headed which was the largest secondary school in Ghana. Bishop E. P. Murchison and Dr. M. L. Breeding, General Secretary of the Board of Missions, went to Ghana and effected the change. The C.M.E. Church now has other schools and about 3,000 members in Ghana.

In 1960 Bishop Murchison and Dr. Breeding were invited to Nigeria by the Reverend E. B. Ekop to consider transferring a group of churches headed by Reverend Ekop into the C.M.E. Church. The group numbered about 12,000 members. The transfer was effected.

In 1961 Bishop Murchison, accompanied by Bishop P. R. Shy, went to Nigeria to arrange for the acceptance of the United African Church into the C.M.E. denomination. This group, of about 40,000 members and 200 preachers, had formerly been under the Church of England, but they wanted to be in a black denomination. They were received, and their leader, the Reverend J. H. U. Edidaha, was made a presiding elder. He is a respected and influential leader.

The C.M.E. Church now has about 200,000 members in Africa. Since the schools in both Ghana and Nigeria have been taken over by the governments, the Church now concentrates its work in education on providing scholarships to students in secondary schools and then in helping the graduates of those schools to come to the United States for advanced study. Six such students have received Ph.D. degrees. The Church also conducts pilot day-care centers in Ghana and schools for training in-service ministers in Nigeria.

Bishop Bunton headed the African work until 1974. It is now under Bishop John M. Exum. The Reverend Isaiah Scipio is General Secretary of the Board of Missions, and Bishop P. R. Shy serves as Consultant.

CHAPTER XIV

Methodism in Mission

THE COMING OF FREEDOM with the end of the Civil War was for all Negroes, both slave and "free," the answer to long and anxious prayers. As W. E. B. DuBois expressed it in his classic work, *The Souls of Black Folk:*

> Away back in the days of bondage they thought to see in one divine event the end of all doubt and disappointment; few men ever worshipped freedom with half such unquestioning faith as did the American Negro for two centuries. To him, so far as he thought and dreamed, slavery was indeed the sum of all villainies, the cause of all sorrows, the root of all prejudices; emancipation was the key to a promised land of sweeter beauty than ever stretched before the eyes of wearied Israelites. In song and exhortation swelled one refrain—Liberty; in his tears and curses the God he implored had freedom in his right hand. At last it came—suddenly, fearfully, like a dream.[1]
>
> For the first time in their lives, they could travel; they could see; they could talk to friends and sit at sundown and in moonlight, listening and imparting wonder tales. They could hunt in the swamps and fish in the rivers. And, above all, they could stand up and assert themselves. They need not fear the patrol; they need not cringe before a white face and touch their hats.[2]

Yet the liberated slaves soon found that the freedom for which they so long had prayed brought with it overwhelming problems and responsibilities for which they were almost totally unprepared. Several factors combined to create the difficulties. First was the personal unpreparedness of the freedman. For the first time "he felt the weight of his ignorance—not simply of letters, but of life, of business, of the humanities, the accumulated sloth and shirking and awkwardness of decades and centuries shackled his hands and feet."[3]

Secondly, "the whole economy of the South was in shambles. The destructive war had been fought for the most part on Southern soil. Cities were destroyed, homes and schools burned, and looting generally took place. Charleston, Columbia, Atlanta, Chattanooga, and Vicksburg were among the cities most severely damaged. Plantation production was reduced to a minimum."[4]

A third and most serious problem for the freedmen was the Southern racial attitude. As Brawley puts it: "their defeat in war, the freedom granted the slaves, and military occupation by the Federal Government, [created] a feeling of distrust[;] and there was fear of the Freedmen lest they and the Northern group would form a coalition to inflict reprisals upon the South."[5] This fear and resentment along with the old ideas of the Negro's biological and intellectual inferiority, which most Southerners never gave up, led to an attitude of resistance to Negro progress and the determination to keep the Negro "in his place," that is, as near to his former slavery as possible.

A personal example will illustrate the freedmen's plight. Isaac Lane writes in his autobiography:

After Lee had surrendered and the Confederacy had gone to pieces and Jefferson Davis had become a refugee, our owners called us together and told us we were free and had to take care of ourselves. There I was with a large dependent family to support. I had no money, no education, no mother, no father to whom to look for help in any form. Our former owners prophesied that half of us would starve, but not so. It must be admitted, however, that we had a hard time, and it seemed at times that the prophecy would come true; but the harder the time, the harder we worked and the more we endured. For six months we lived on nothing but bread, milk, and water. We had a time to keep alive; but by praying all the time, with faith in God, and believing that he would provide for his own, we saved enough to get the next year not only bread, milk, and water, but meat also.[6]

Isaac Lane was in Kentucky where slavery was mild and the problems of freedom were least severe. Plantation slaves in the deep South had it much worse.

Thus at the end of the war the nation was confronted with four million emancipated persons who were destitute and helpless in the midst of a hostile environment. They constituted not only a national problem, but actually a national peril. They needed help. And almost providentially the help came. It came first from the Federal Government through the Freedmen's Bureau, and it came secondly from private concern expressed mostly through the churches.

Even before the end of the war most of the major denominations in America, such as the Congregationalists, the Baptists, Presbyterians, and Methodists, were beginning to serve the freedmen in many ways. Each had a Freedmen's Aid Commission through which it worked. They set up schools, Sunday schools, and churches, and gave aid to the poor and orphans. Eventually the separate denominational commissions were joined into one National Commission to avoid duplication and for greater efficiency. It was not long, however, before each of the denominations decided to carry on its own program independently in order to make clearer its own contribution to the problem, and also as a means of winning converts for itself from among those whom it served. The Methodists decided to do this in 1866.

A convention of Methodist leaders was called to meet in Cincinnati, Ohio, on August 7, 1866, to consider "whether the times and work require the organization of a society to be controlled entirely by members of our own Church."[7] The Convention found that for the large amount the M.E. Church was expending the work could be done more effectively and the Church would receive greater benefit if it directed its own programs. Consequently it was "resolved, That the time has come for the organization of a Society for the relief and education of the Freedmen and people of color in general, to cooperate with the Missionary and Church Extension Society of the Methodist Episcopal Church."[8] A constitution for the Society was adopted, officers were elected, and the Freedmen's Aid Society of the Methodist Episcopal Church was formed. The first officers were: Bishop

Davis W. Clark, President; the Reverend J. M. Walden, Corresponding Secretary; and the Reverend R. S. Rust, General Field Superintendent. Among the three Vice-Presidents was Major General Clinton B. Fisk, for whom Fisk University was named.

The bishops of the M.E. Church almost immediately after the organization was formed, on November 8, 1866, issued an appeal to the pastors and members of the Church for support of the Society. They said:

> The emancipation of four million of slaves has opened at our very door a wide field calling alike for mission and educational work. It has developed upon the Church a fearful responsibility. Religion and education alone can make freedom a blessing to them. The school must be planted by the side of the Church; the teacher must go along with the missionary. In no other way can our work reach its highest success among the Freedmen of the south.
>
> The time may come when the States of the South will make some provision for the education of the colored children now growing up in utter ignorance in their midst. But thus far they have made none, nor perhaps can it soon be expected of them. Christian philanthropy must supply this lack. While other churches, North and South, are entering this broad field, we have our own work and our own duty to perform. We cannot turn away from the appeal that comes home to our consciences and hearts. Nor can we delay. *The emergency is upon us, and we must begin our work now.*
>
> . . . There are openings for hundreds of teachers at this moment. Hundreds of teachers are ready to go. The means to send them are only wanting.[9]

The Society was formed in 1866, incorporated in 1870, and at the General Conference of 1872 it was "recognized as a regular constituted society of the Methodist Episcopal Church."[10]

The Society plunged at once into its work. Within the first year and a half 59 schools had been established in ten Southern States. At the end of the first decade, 1876, the report to the General Conference stated that

> The influence of the Society is felt all over the South. Fifty thousand have been taught in its day, and a larger number in the Sunday Schools. Hundreds of preachers now laboring among this

people and thousands of teachers engaged in instructing the children have been taught in institutions established and sustained by this Society, which has provided in the South a school property worth more than two hundred thousand dollars.[11]

By 1916, the end of its first fifty years, the Society had established 12 colleges, 20 academies, 1 theological seminary and 1 medical school for Negroes; and 3 colleges and 19 academies for whites.

Dr. James P. Brawley, for twenty-four years President of Clark College, one of the Society's schools, has published a detailed, carefully documented account of the Society's work: *Two Centuries of Methodist Concern*.[12] He gives the history of each of the institutions. He relates how the Society began with elementary schools for both children and adults, but soon moved up to academies, preparatory schools, and colleges. In 1866, for instance, there were 7,000 pupils in the elementary schools. In 1885 there were 4,263 students of whom 4,143 were in the lower grades; only 120 were in college. In 1916, by contrast, the enrollment in the lower schools had dropped to 1,756, but the college enrollment was 3,250.

In 1866, when the Society began, it owned no property. Schools were begun in church basements or old buildings, wherever unused space could be found. By 1884 the Society had land and buildings worth $366,000, and by 1916 the value of school plants and equipment was $2,007,550.[13]

The instruction offered in the Society's schools had two main objectives. One was to teach the Freedmen and their children how to make a living; the other was to teach them how to make a life. Both of these were necessary to overcome the degrading effects of two and a half centuries of human slavery. In general there were three fields of instruction: (1) the academic; (2) the practical, or agricultural and industrial; and (3) the cultural. In the academic field the student received a good standard education in terms of the times on both the high school and the college levels. In colleges, for example, they were taught such subjects as mathematics, which included geometry, algebra, trigonometry, and calculus; English, Latin, history, philosophy, physics, chemistry, and "analytics." One intention of the academic field was to provide teachers and preachers who were much needed for spreading the work of instruction. Teacher training was given in "normal schools," that is, in schools going through the first two years of college. Graduates from these schools received teaching certificates upon graduation. These "normal" schools continued through the first half of the twentieth century.[14] Ministerial students studied first in theological departments, but later, when these departments were discontinued, they went to Gammon Theological Seminary in Atlanta, the one full-fledged seminary for Negro students in the Methodist Episcopal Church.

In the practical field the aim was to prepare students for the skilled trades, thereby enabling them to rise in the economic scale. In agriculture, for example, it is one thing to know how to chop cotton, which most slaves mainly had done. It is another to know how to operate a farm: to plan for land use, to arrange financing, to carry out the scientific cultivation of crops and animal husbandry, to understand marketing products, and the other aspects of skilled farming. In such instruction the students were given opportunities to develop independent careers and incomes as entrepreneurs. The tragedy was that agriculture had acquired such an opprobrious if not despicable regard among Negroes as a result of slavery that few students would enter it.

In industrial training students were trained for the skilled crafts and trades. For example, Claflin University around 1900 taught twenty trades and industries in its Mechanical and Industrial departments. Among the crafts taught were cabinetmaking and building construction; for girls there were nurse training, dress cutting, fitting and making, artistic painting and needlework.[15]

Cultural instruction was imparted not so much in courses as in activities and by the examples of teachers. Much was taught through the daily routines of school life, such as early rising, orderliness in personal appearance and in rooms, required attendance at devotional and inspirational exercises, and, of course, maintaining respectful and respected relationships with one's schoolmates. The aim of it all was to develop in the student a sense of self-respect and personal dignity; to lay the foundation for a pattern of life that would be self-fulfilling mentally, morally, physically, and spiritually. To a child coming out of the squalor of slave "quarters," or to a child reared under the anti-Negro preachments and violently repressive practices of the Reconstruction South, such as the Ku Klux Klan, for example, to such a black child one of the most helpful things that could be taught was to see himself as a child of God and therefore as a respectable human being worthy of the best in the American culture. The schools established by the Freedmen's Aid Society of the Methodist Episcopal Church made this kind of teaching a cardinal element in their programs.

As time passed and the Society got further and further away from the Freedmen there were many attempts to change the name to bring it more into conformity with what the Society was actually doing. This seemed especially necessary since the Society was working with whites also. In response to repeated efforts, in 1888 the name was changed to the Freedmen's Aid and Southern Education Society. In 1908 the white work (22 schools) was taken out of the Society and put under the Board of Education of the M.E. Church. The original title of Freedmen's Aid Society was restored. In 1920 the Society was changed to the Board of Education for Negroes, and in 1928 this Board was made a Department of Education for Negroes in the General Board of Education of the Methodist Episcopal Church. After unification of the three Methodist bodies in 1939 the name became the Department of Educational Institutions for Negroes.[16] Since 1968 the black colleges are under the Board of Higher Education and Ministry without separate designation.

In their first message to the Church regarding the Society the bishops of the M.E. Church said: "There are openings for hundreds of teachers . . . Hundreds of teachers are ready to go." These volunteers moved in the noblest of spirits. Theirs was not to be an easy lot and they knew it. In the words of Brawley:

> . . . the missionaries who went into the South . . . the early presidents and principals of the schools and the early teachers, faced stern and abusive opposition. They had to confine their social life for the most part to the schools where they worked and to the constituency for whom they labored. They were ostracized in the communities and were not welcomed even in the Methodist

churches of the South. Consequently, they identified themselves with the churches established by the Church Extension Society of the Methodist Episcopal Church and with the Negro Conferences which were then mixed, and also with the Negro churches. It was difficult for the workers to extend themselves into the larger community and to get the support which would have made progress much more rapid. But in the face of opposition and difficulties these devotees to this task persevered and accomplished a magnificent work.[17]

Through their years of dedicated service they wrote one of the brightest pages in the history of Christian missions.

THE WOMAN'S HOME MISSIONARY SOCIETY

From the very beginning women played a large part in the work of the M.E. Church among the freedmen of the South. Many of the missionaries who came to serve as teachers, as religious workers and as workers in programs dispensing aid were women.

However, there was a desire on the part of leading women of the Church for larger and more organized participation. The needs were great, and there was much that the Freedmen's Aid Society was not able to do. The General Conference of 1878 mentioned that while much was being done for the freed men, little was being done directly for freed women. Since women were prevented from being directors in the Freedmen's Aid Society (the constitution provided that only males could be), the answer seemed to be a society of their own.

In 1880 in Cincinnati, in the same church, Trinity, in which the Freedmen's Aid Society had been formed, a group of women leaders organized the Woman's Home Missionary Society. They were some of the leading women not only in the Church but in the nation. Mrs. Rutherford B. Hayes, wife of the President of the United States, became the first president of the Society. Mrs. D. W. Clark and Mrs. J. M. Walden, wives of bishops, and Mrs. R. S. Rust, wife of the first General Field Superintendent of the Freedmen's Society were among the first officers. These women knew well the missionary program of the Church through association with their husbands, and they were also strong Christian leaders in their own right.

The women wanted not to duplicate the existing work, but rather to supplement it. Therefore, instead of traditional schools, they set up "Homes," institutions that would provide home training and industrial training for women and girls along with some academic training. Some of the Homes were set up separately, but most were located on college campuses and their work was dovetailed into the programs of the schools. By 1900 sixteen Homes had been established, nine on school campuses and seven separately. In the educational work of the time these Homes were widely known and highly appreciated for their contribution to the intellectual and cultural development of black girls and women. A history of each institution is given by Mrs. Ruth Esther Meeker in the volume *Six Decades of Service*.[18]

As educational levels for Negroes were raised through the years, the Homes on college campuses became dormitories for women or departments of home economics. Four of the separate homes are presently in existence serving as boarding high schools for Negro youth. They are filling a much needed place in the total program of black education.

In 1926 the Woman's Home Missionary Society joined with the Board of Education to make Bennett College in Greensboro, North Carolina, formerly co-educational, a college for women. It has since become one of the most outstanding schools of its kind in the nation.

Initially responding to a crisis, and then continuing to serve through the years, the Methodist Episcopal Church, through these two agencies, the Freedmen's Aid Society and the Woman's Home Missionary Society, has not only exemplified the Christian mission at its noblest, but has helped a struggling people to make the climb from slavery to freedom in a shortness of time that is one of the marvels of human history.

It has been mentioned that by 1916 the Methodist Episcopal Church had established 12 colleges, 20 academies, 1 theological seminary, and 1 medical school for Negroes. Some of these institutions have been discontinued or have been transferred to other auspices. The schools that are extant are: Bennett, Bethune-Cookman, Claflin, Clark, Huston-Tillotson, Paine, Philander Smith, Rust and Wiley Colleges, Dillard University and Morristown (Junior) College, Gammon Theological Seminary and Meharry Medical College. Most of these schools are leading institutions. All are accredited.[19]

Much has been said about the educational work of the white Methodists who came South to work among the freedmen. But there were also many others who came and served with equal dedication and effectiveness in religious and social areas. They did much to make progress possible despite the violent, repressive, anti-Negro nature of Southern life.

A detailed description of their labors cannot be given here. One example will show the spirit, the labors, and the sufferings of these workers. The Reverend Gilbert Haven, who became a Bishop of the Methodist Church in 1870, chose Atlanta for his residence. He was especially active and courageous. Dr. Richard S. Rust, Secretary of the Freedmen's Aid Society, said of him:

> ". . . the iron of oppression had entered into his own soul, and he remembered them that are in bonds as bound with them. He identified himself with God's suffering poor, and enjoyed no privileges denied to his poor brethren.
>
> "In returning from a conference, when refused the privilege of conversing with one of the [Negro] preachers in the car in which he was seated, he retreated with the preacher to the car set apart for colored people, and remained there in conversation until forcibly ejected by the conductor."[20]

These workers organized churches, set up annual conferences of the M.E. Church (North) among the freedmen across the South, enlisted and trained leaders, and eventually built up a membership of over 300,000, the fourth in size of the black Methodist groups.[21]

THE WORK OF THE BLACK CHURCHES

In the work among the freedmen the Black Methodist bodies were quite as much interested in promoting education as was the white Northern M.E. Church. They recognized fully the place of education in the advancement of the people. Bishop Miles of the C.M.E. Church had said, "We must become a reading people." Bishop Clinton had said it was the aim of the A.M.E.Z. Church to take ignorance by the neck and choke it to death. Bishop Daniel Payne had already begun with Wilberforce University.

There was this difference, however. The black churches did not have the reservoir of educated persons from which to recruit teachers. They also were poor. Yet using such persons as they could find and utilizing the funds given by sacrificing members, the black churches were able to set up many schools throughout the South. Although they were called "academies" or "universities," in the beginning they were little more than grade schools or high schools. Through the years many were discontinued or turned over to public educational authorities. Some have continued to the present time, and some of these are now fully accredited institutions.

The present schools in the A.M.E. Church are Wilberforce, Morris Brown, and Allen Universities, Paul Quinn, Edward Waters, Daniel Payne, Kittrell and Shorter Colleges, and Payne and Turner Theological Seminaries. The last named, Turner Seminary, is a constituent member of the Interdenominational Theological Center in Atlanta.[22] The A.M.E. Zion Church has one college, Livingstone, in Salisbury, North Carolina. It is fully accredited. The Church has one theological seminary, Hood, located at Livingstone College.[23] The C.M.E. Church, the smallest of the three denominations, has five colleges, all accredited: Lane, Payne, Miles, Texas, and Mississippi Industrial Colleges. The Church has one seminary, Phillips, which is also a member of the I.T.C. in Atlanta.[24]

When taken together this group of schools, some of which are among the most distinguished in the black educational effort in America, represent a noble effort, almost a "bootstrap" effort, of a struggling people to lift themselves to the highest levels of American culture.

PART IV

Today
and Tomorrow

CHAPTER XV

Current Developments

WE HAVE SEEN HOW the black Methodist bodies grew very rapidly following the Civil War. This growth occurred, of course, among the freedmen of the South who readily joined these organizations of their own black people in large numbers. The growth continued, less rapidly, but steadily, through the first half of the twentieth century. The rate of growth can be seen from the following table.

Denomination	1856	1880	1906	1926	1972
A.M.E.	19,963	400,000	600,000	750,000	1,100,000
A.M.E.Z.	4,600	250,000	350,000	500,000	770,000
C.M.E.		120,000	250,000	350,000	466,000

The new growth was heavily rural and Southern since the members were the former plantation slaves. At one time the rural proportion was as high as 72.8 per cent.[1]

With such a large proportion of rural members, the black Methodist bodies were affected by the heavy rural to urban migrations that occurred during and following the First and Second World Wars. In addition, the rural membership is still being reduced by the contemporary migration resulting from agricultural changes in the South. The change from cotton to cattle, especially in the Southeast, the mechanization of agriculture and the growing of pine trees have caused a sharp decline in the black Southern rural population. This in turn has meant a decline in rural church membership. Because of loose and inaccurate record-keeping in rural churches and a lack of follow-up when members move, large numbers of members are lost to the denominations. It means further that the former rural masses have little religious guidance and service as they make the difficult transition from rural to urban living.[2]

Yet despite any loss of members, and despite their failure to grow as much as they might have, the three black Methodist bodies in the hundred years since freedom have grown until today together they number well over two million, the second largest component in the world Methodist movement.

Perhaps a further word should be said about the black rural Methodist church. In American Protestantism the rural portion has been a neglected portion. Rural churches are mostly small, and among blacks rural members are mostly poor. This in turn means that the rural ministry is poorly supported, and men of ability as a rule are not attracted to rural service. In fact, appointment to a rural charge is often regarded as a demotion, if not a punishment. Thus lacking in strong leadership, the Church among Negroes in the rural South has not played the leading and helpful role that it could have and should have played in the social development of its people. Had the Church done so, the present plight of vast numbers of blacks hopelessly trapped in city slums and ghettos might have been significantly different.

Early in their histories the black Methodist bodies became imbued with the noble aim to "redeem Africa," that is, to Christianize the un-Christianized or "heathen" African continent. This was, to be sure, a noble aim, but a far larger one than small churches with limited resources could possibly achieve. Bishop Daniel A. Payne of the A.M.E. Church saw the impracticality of such an aim and forcefully spoke against it.

In 1852 in an address to the New York Conference, Bishop Willis Nazrey said that it was "the duty of the A.M.E. Church to assist in sending the Gospel to the heathen, who are out of the limits of civilization and Christianity. We have as an Episcopal Church, as much right to look after perishing Africa, the West India Islands, St. Domingo and others—and all those who are not Christianized—as any other Christian Church upon the face of the globe."[3]

Bishop Payne in his *History* replied:

But in our opinion the good Bishop erred in his views of the relation of the A.M.E. Church to the cause of foreign missions. Now, the right to do a thing involves the duty to do it, but the duty also involves the ability. Now, where there is no ability to perform an act, there can be no duty to perform it; hence, to exercise a right under such circumstances would place us in a very painful and ridiculous position—even in the position of the man who commenced to build, but was not able to finish his house, and therefore became the laughing-stock of his neighbors. The zeal of the Bishop outran his knowledge of the cost and difficulties of establishing missions in foreign lands. Even the planting of one foreign mission necessitates an outlay that our Connection was not altogether prepared to meet . . .[4]

Later, regarding a similar statement made in 1856 that "We believe our Church is destined, under God, to diffuse itself into every region where immortal souls are to be found," Bishop Payne wrote: "[This] idea and belief . . . is both absurd and ridiculous."[5]

Yet though the idea was beyond practical attainment, it was a great inspiration and led to worthy achievement. Through the work of missionaries abroad supported by church workers at home the A.M.E.'s now have four episcopal districts on the continent of Africa: one district for West Africa and three districts for the southern part of the continent, the most extensive mission program of any of the black Methodist bodies. The A.M.E.Z.'s have mission work in Ghana, Nigeria, and Liberia. Much of this program is in day schools on the grade and high school levels. There are four schools in Ghana and twenty in Liberia. The schools in Nigeria have been taken over by the Government. There is a teacher training college in Ghana and a college and seminary in Angola.

The C.M.E.'s have recently begun mission work in Ghana and Nigeria. The Church cooperates with the Government of Nigeria in operating the schools.

To the end of making work more stable and intensive, the black churches now have or have had some native African bishops. Some Churches also require American bishops to reside on the African field during the period of their assignment. The foreign mission work is supported through the efforts of missionary societies at home. Under Bishop W. J. Walls of the A.M.E.Z. Church a plan of African Memorial Banks was evolved which has resulted in larger amounts being raised for the work abroad.[6]

However, when all of the efforts of the three denominations are combined, the funds, the schools, the churches, the mission stations and other projects, the total is small when compared with other church bodies, and is infinitesimal in the face of the overall need. The effort of the black churches is a long way from fulfillment of the aim to "redeem Africa." The hope is that the work will grow, and that, as many still feel, there may yet be a unique contribution that American black Christians can make to their fellow blacks in Africa.

At the present time the missionary programs of the black churches are being affected, as are the programs of the white churches, by contemporary developments in Africa, particularly the political independence of the African nations, the demand for indigenous leadership, and the demand for patterns of Christianity that conform to native life and culture. Up to now the forms of Christianity carried to the Africans by the black church are identical to those of the white church, and bear the stamp of being both Western and American. Whether the black churches can adapt to African demands sufficiently to meet the challenge of the present African situation is yet to be seen. Certainly here is a tremendous opportunity for black Methodism.[7]

THE EPISCOPACY

In the development of the black Methodist bodies one of the most unique features is the nature of the episcopacy or bishopric. While the black bodies are patterned very closely after the white, this office in the black churches has acquired an authority, an autonomy, and a dominance far in excess of that office in the white churches.

There are several reasons for this development. First, there was the lack of education and lack of experience in organizational management that obtained among Negroes both slave and free at the time the black churches were started. In general, before emancipation any kind of organized activity among blacks was suspected, socially disapproved, and legally forbidden. Education of blacks was very rare in the North and it was a criminal offense in the South.

The new black Methodist bodies had to live and grow despite these handicaps. The black Methodist churches, unable to operate at all in the South, went right ahead with their expansion in the North, and became nationwide (with the exception of the South) in their extent.

The lack of education and experience among the people placed a great burden upon the leadership of the churches. Daniel Payne as well as other leaders complained about the problem.[8] Much time had to be given to interpretation, correction, and instruction which would not have been necessary had the people simply been able to read. Methodism as a faith is comparatively simple, but in its church organization it is complex, detailed, and highly political. The necessary dependence upon the leadership for guidance and interpretation in this complicated system gave the leader an importance and authority which he otherwise might not have had. At the same time, the complexity of the Methodist system and the ignorance and inexperience of the people was an opportunity for irregularities of many kinds.

In the beginning the offices of Bishop among the A.M.E.'s and Superintendent among the A.M.E.Z.'s were not very attractive. To be head of a handful of small, struggling churches was a chore as much as an honor. In addition the whole idea was questionable to many. The assumption by Richard Allen of the title of "Bishop" was not only a pioneering act, it was almost an audacious one. The Methodist Episcopal Church had refused to ordain Negroes even to the lower orders of the Methodist ministry. Yet here was a man who assumed the highest office. It was mainly the personal prestige and position of Richard Allen that kept the act in the eyes of many people from being ridiculous. Also the work of supervising the churches was hard, dangerous, and very poorly remunerative. The early men such as Richard Allen, Christopher Rush, Morris Brown, and many who worked with them, were earnest, dedicated, self-sacrificing men who were interested mainly in the expansion of their churches and thought little about reward for themselves.

Through the labors of these early men the churches grew, and thus the office of Bishop grew in influence and importance. The black Methodist churches gradually became the instruments for the expression of black hopes and protests as well as centers for progressive black activities; and the leaders of the churches became the national spokesmen for their people.[9] The meeting of A.M.E.'s with President Andrew Jackson in 1834, and the conference that Bishop Daniel Payne had with President Lincoln in 1862 are illustrations of the rising influence of the churches and their leaders.

The growth in importance and prestige of the top officers soon attracted men of leadership aspirations. Indeed, the bishopric in the black churches prior to the Civil War came to be the highest of the few offices open to Negroes. In American Methodism the highest office, Bishop or Superintendent, is elective and for life. The growth in size gave the position power, and led to electioneering or "campaigning" for it which began to appear in the second half of the nineteenth century. Daniel A. Payne, himself a Bishop and one of the most outspoken commentators upon the character of the episcopacy, describes vividly the development of the bishopric in his church in the forty-four years from 1844 to 1888:

> When I take up the telescope and look back over the distance of forty-four years—four-tenths of a century—upon the sixty-eight men and the elements composing the General Conference of 1844, and compare it with the men and the elements which composed the General Conference of 1888, I perceive a strong and striking contrast. The men who made up the Conference of 1844 went there with singleness of heart and with but one aim. That was to improve the condition of the Connection by some simple needed

amendments to the Discipline. To our own knowledge there were but two aspirants to the episcopal office—viz.: William Paul Quinn and Richard Robinson. They had no episcopal committee to examine the characters of Bishop Morris Brown and Bishop Edward Waters. The friends of Quinn and Robinson were innocent of political combinations because they were ignorant of them, and were also innocent and ignorant of the intrigues and cunning of politicians; because they had not been trained in the caucus or in the ways of scheming politicians. In that General Conference brethren differed in regard to this or that measure, but differed peacably—without bluster. There was excitement, it is true; but a man and a body of men can be excited without bluster. In that General Conference there was great respect for moral character and great value set upon the knowledge which comes from the experience of age. No man impeached for immorality was allowed a seat in it. But the General Conference of 1888, embracing about two hundred and fifty delegates, included many who went there determined to be put into office themselves or to put their favorites in by hook or by crook. The aspirants for the episcopal office and for the position of secretaries could be counted by the scores. To effect their purpose combinations and other political measures were employed. It was even rumored that some of the delegates sold their votes; but as this is such an awful charge it should not be believed without the most convincing proof. Hence the aspirants had their particular friends operating as agents to solicit votes. There was a greater number of educated and good men in the General Conference of 1888 than in the General Conference of 1844, and so also there was a greater number of bad men—by which I mean men governed by no holy principle, but by their blind passions and still blinder ambitions. Hence there was not only excitement, but the most shameful bluster. Many paid little or no regard to moral character, so that the wisdom and superior knowledge and moral excellence and greater usefulness of the majority were set aside and crushed out by bluster and brilliant rhetoric, which made virtue appear as vice, and vice as virtue.[10]

Daniel Payne, of course, was an idealist. He held the highest standards of Christian conduct for the ministry and he followed these rules in his own life. To him just seeking high office in the Church was un-Christian.[11] Yet when full allowance is made for the severity of his criticisms, it is now clear that he was calling attention to practices and abuses which being permitted to continue have weakened the influence of the Church as a corrective force in society and may have lowered it in popular respect.

But far worse than objectionable methods of attaining the bishopric is the behavior of some successful candidates after they have attained it. In American Methodism bishops are elected for life. Given this security and with limited accountability, many bishops proceed to rule with autocratic methods and to institute programs for their personal benefit as well as for the Church's. The Reverend George A. Singleton, a general officer in the A.M.E. Church, gives this picture of episcopal autocracy:

> During the Quadrennium of 1924–28, there was a mounting crescendo of criticism against the use of the "Episcopal big Stick," and "burdensome assessments." There was a corresponding belief that certain Bishops had served too long on their respective Districts, and should be removed. One had been on a District twenty years, and another sixteen. "Little Episcopal principalities" had been built up, and the common expression was "My District." The spirit of freedom in the ministerial ranks was crushed. In some instances a brother minister was not permitted to make a motion unless he first told the Presiding Bishop in private what it was. There was the tragic picture of a minister who had for some reason gotten on the wrong side of a Bishop and rose to ask pardon. The Bishop requested him to apologize on his knees! Another said to an Annual Conference with reference to appointments: "If you can't plow that mule, bring me the bridle." Again: "I've got the biscuits!" "There is nothing beyond the Episcopacy." "You can't do anything to a Bishop. Once a Bishop, always a Bishop." "You needn't think you're too big to be removed." The Episcopacy had reached untenable heights. A challenging pamphlet came out of Tennessee under the caption: "Reformation or Revolution." It bore the signatures of the Reverends Elmer Reid, G. L. Jackson, and M. E. Jackson.[12]

Or two further statements:

> Bishop Vernon soon became involved in serious difficulties with the men of his district. There were complaints about mistreatment, tyrannical acts and mishandling of church finances on the part of the Bishop.[13]

Murmurings and protests began to arise when Bishop Sims caused to be levied an assessment of $10.00 a year upon each church member in his diocese. For example, this meant that under this plan, the members of Bethel Church, New York, would be assessed a total of $28,000 annually. Roughly speaking, for his district as a whole, the total for the quadrennium would add up to about $1,000,000. The protests became so vocal that certain ministers in the New York area appealed to the Bishops' Council in the spring of 1945, and requested that Bishop Sims be removed from presiding over the New York area.[14]

These statements have to do with the A.M.E. Church which discusses its virtues and foibles with surprising candor. But the practices are by no means limited to that Church. In greater or lesser degree they are to be found in all of the black Methodist churches.

For example, Bishop Lane of the C.M.E. Church mentions this instance:

> In 1910 the General Conference of our Church convened in Augusta, Ga. This Conference was largely attended. As usual, the greatest interest was centered in the election of the bishops and general officers. Contrary to our custom and all precedents, some ambitious men resorted to political methods to promote their friends and measures. I do not mean to say that all of the previous General Conferences had been free from political trickery. Such could not be successfully maintained. But I do assert that never before was there so much boldness and effrontery as was displayed at this Conference in such methods and actions. As a natural result, some of the brethren became distrustful of the others and at every point showed their distrust by being ready to impugn their motives and call into question their integrity and honor. This was very unfortunate and greatly embarrassed the Church and its work during the quadrennium.[15]

However, while the A.M.E.'s are most vocal in acknowledging offenses, they are also most vigorous in trying and punishing offenders. In the case of Bishop Vernon mentioned above, he was suspended and was never reinstated. On the following day Bishop Joshua H. Jones was tried and suspended for mishandling funds. After his death, however, it was found that he was not guilty as charged, the suspension was removed against his name, and his estate was reimbursed for any losses.[16]

Bishop Ransom states that from time to time the Church "is swept by a tide of righteousness, and woe be to the man who happens to be standing in the path of the periodical sweep of that tide." A mighty sweep of this tide occurred in 1946 when in a special session of the General Conference the Church expelled Bishop David H. Sims, mentioned above, and Bishop G. E. Curry. Bishop M. H. Davis was also suspended, but later restored.[17]

The tide of righteousness returns and continues to sweep, and there are always persons in its path. But not all persons are drowned. Many survive and are often able to continue their former practices. Some are able to visit punishments on their accusers. But again, much episcopal misconduct is possible mainly through the ignorance or indifference of the members. Professor Charles V. Hamilton, who has written lucidly and accurately about *The Black Preacher in America*, makes this informative explanation after discussing two cases:

> The black preachers at the top of their hierarchical structures are given substantial legal leeway in which to operate. They are able to enter into contractual arrangements which are not illegal, and because of the deference paid to them and their positions, they frequently are not questioned in their various financial operations. When conflicts do develop, it is usually legally too late to do anything about them. They have secured their legal positions and are usually strong enough politically within the hierarchy to withstand any attempts at reprisals from within the denomination. The instances of property being held in their own names, property purchased with church funds, while clearly not illegal, are surely practices that would be frowned upon in most other business arrangements. Therein lies a great part of the answer. While many of these men are definitely hard-headed businessmen, at the same time they are perceived by the church people as "men of God." Such men are "above" mere mundane, material matters. This attitude has caused no small amount of anguish at times. It is probably the case that more internal accountability should be enforced initially and continuously, and more scrutiny given to the legal operations of

the clergy. Some ministers would undoubtedly interpret this as offensive and insulting to their integrity, but that would have to be the risk or price incurred.[18]

There is another distinctive feature about the black Methodist bodies, and that is the nature of the General Conferences. These meetings called quadrennially for the transaction of important church business have evolved into boisterous, often brawling political conventions in which the serious consideration of religious and social concerns is often sublimated to getting candidates elected to general offices. In 1947 Bishop Ransom wrote:

Those who have followed me through these pages may have noted that, in referring to the different General Conferences, no reference has been made to noteworthy legislation, or original programs to meet the changed conditions following two World Wars through which we have passed in recent years. The reason for this is plain. The chief concern of the delegates is not about enlightening and forward looking legislation, but with the election of Bishops and general officers. Having done this, we are ready to adjourn and go home as soon as we can get all the increase of money we can for salaries and for the different departments of the general church.[19]

The setting of the Conferences have all the air of political conventions. Hallways and corridors are filled with booths, tables, and stands covered with signs, placards, and posters, and littered with handbills, cards, and pamphlets all proclaiming the virtues of some candidate who is announced to be "worthy" or "deserving of support," many of whom, so the literature says, were left "at the gate" or "in the door" at the last election, and deserve now to be pushed in. There is much buttonholing, promising, and trading, some of it in cash. Because of the intense interest in elections, little serious business is done until after the elections, and if the election is protracted, not much time is left for business.

On the floor of some Conferences when issues arise that are emotionally tinged, there are scrambles for the microphones, fist fights erupt, and epithets fly. At one Conference an effort was made to move all bishops to break up episcopal control. The resolution was read by the Reverend Joseph Gomez, later a Bishop. In Dr. Singleton's words again:

The effect was electrical. The scene cannot be described. Hundreds of delegates were on their feet at once. The platform was astir. The status quo Bishops were caught completely off guard. Bishop Johnson: "The Chair recognizes Dr. J. W. Walker of North Carolina." He was a portly man, slightly round-shouldered, dark-brown-skinned, clean shaven, with a shrill, keen voice. It rang out: "Mr. Chairman, I second the motion." Then pandemonium did break loose for fair. There was a lot of moving about, talking in little groups and gesticulating. An attempt was made to intimidate the Presiding Officer from the platform, but he stood like Athanasius at Nicea—"a rock amidst a stormy sea." The Chairman called for unreadiness. Several persons were on the floor with hands directed toward him. He said: "The Chair recognizes Dr. H. Y. Tookes of Chicago." He came forward to the stand and said: "Mr. Chairman, I move that the resolution be tabled by a secret ballot." There was so much noise that many did not hear the "by ballot." The platform contended that he did not say ballot. Bishop Johnson said: "Mr. Tookes is of age, let him come forward and repeat what he said! Tookes, did you not say, 'by secret ballot'?" He replied: "Yes." More noise, and milling about. Someone on the platform attempted to intimidate the Presiding Officer. He said: "You can't scare me. There is nothing before the house but vote on tabling the resolution. If you want it, vote 'No'; if you do not want it vote 'Yes.' Prepare your Ballots." The vote was taken: 569 "No" and 263 "Yes." The resolution was then before the house for disposition. At this point Bishop Flipper unconsciously helped the passage when he remarked: "We have submitted the assignment of the Bishops to the Episcopal Committee as a matter of convenience, and the Conference has no right to instruct the Episcopal Committee, in reference to the assignment of Bishops. If you do, I tell you, the Bishops will assign themselves at this General Conference." The original motion was put and was carried 641 to remove, against 263.[20]

There is a story that was common in black Methodist circles some years ago. There was a fine, deserving man who had run for Bishop several times and always failed. A group of friends who wanted to see him elected went to him before the Conference and asked him who was his campaign manager and where were his headquarters. He replied that his campaign manager was Jesus and his headquarters were in heaven. He ran in the election and failed again. His friends went back to him and quietly advised that he change his campaign manager and move his headquarters closer to earth. Next time, so the story goes, he won.

As already indicated these conditions and practices do not go unopposed. Efforts have been made to curb the power of bishops by requiring periodic changes of assignments, by outlawing extra assessments and special funds, and by closer and more accurate methods of accounting. In 1944 Dr. Charles Leander Hill, a preacher in the A.M.E. Church, wrote a scholarly, widely distributed pamphlet entitled "The Episcopacy—Its Functions, Its Authority, Its Limitations."[21] He maintained that among A.M.E.'s the episcopacy is not diocesan and sacerdotal, but itinerant and presbyterial; that bishops are consecrated to an office, not ordained to an order higher than the eldership; that by definition bishops are simply first among equals; that all absolutism, monarchism, fascism, totalitarianism are negated by both the doctrines and polity of African Methodism, and hence the statement that that is not a democratic form of government is false and unfounded in the realm of fact, and that sovereignty is vested solely in the General Conference, to which the Bishops are amenable.

Shortly after the pamphlet appeared Dr. Hill gave up his work as Dean of Turner Theological Seminary and accepted a small rural church in South Carolina. It was generally felt that he feared being punished. Yet such a powerful preacher was he that great crowds came out to his little church to hear him.

There are a number of factors that give promise of bringing about a softening of episcopal dominance. The increasing number of trained ministers, the increase of educated members, the present revolt of younger people against all forms of rigid authority and discipline—these may help to restore the spirit of self-sacrificial brotherhood in which the Methodist ministry began and in which it ought to move.

Also it is not to be assumed that all bishops are the same and that church meetings are always worldly and unruly. The episcopate in each of the three black Methodist bodies has been graced with men of high Christian character who have rendered great service to their churches and noble social leadership to their people. Men such as Richard Allen, Henry McNeal Turner, and Daniel Payne; James Varick, Christopher Rush, and J. J. Clinton; William H. Miles, Lucius Holsey, and Isaac Lane stand as symbols of what the black episcopacy has been and must be.

Neither are all general conferences the same. Some are less stormy than others, and some churches are more orderly in their activities than others. But at a time like this when humanity is facing the possibility of self-extinction, and when the average black man needs the leadership and help of his Church as much as if not more than ever in his history, it is worse than ridiculous to spend so much time, money, and effort on trivialities, that is, on who gets what job, when the Church should be trying to see what it can do to help the black masses in America to attain a more abundant life.

UNION AND ECUMENICITY

From their very beginning the desirability of union between the two black Methodist bodies was seen and considered. Both were offspring of the same parent body, the Methodist Episcopal Church; both held the same faith, and with minor exceptions were governed by the same polity. If the two could unite it would eliminate needless competition and duplication and make a larger, stronger Church. Yet for over a hundred and fifty years union has not been achieved between the two, and, after 1870, between the three black bodies.[22]

In 1820 when the members of Zion Church in New York faced the question of joining with the Bethelites or A.M.E.'s, the answer was "No." In 1864 and 1868 attempts were made again. Much was at the initiative of the A.M.E.Z. Church. But each time there were points that could not be reconciled by the negotiating committees or that were unacceptable to the general and annual conferences of the respective denominations. An attempt was made again in 1884, and although the plan devised was acceptable to the Zion Bishops and conferences, the A.M.E. Bishops were divided and the attempt fell through.

In 1908 a Tri-Federation Council of the Bishops of the A.M.E., A.M.E.Z. and C.M.E. Churches was formed. It was hoped that from this group would come such common productions as a catechism, hymnal, and form of service that could be used in the three bodies. It was also hoped that this would lead directly to union. A plan of union again was approved by all three General Conferences, but when the plan was submitted to the Annual Conferences, the A.M.E. and A.M.E.Z Conferences accepted, but the C.M.E.'s rejected it, and thus the idea failed again. The Tri-Council idea remained dormant for many years, but in 1965 it was revived. Meetings were held in 1967 and 1969. All were marked by enthusiastic calls for union, but so far it has not occurred. Bishop W. J. Walls, one of the most active and influential members, wrote in 1974:

> Each church is on record with the majority strongly favoring organic union. On one word this entire subject hinges: *Readiness*. Are we ready to give and take, to sink ambitions, and to become Christian in spirit enough to bring these churches together so that they shall stay together? Is it our intention to try for the advantages of each other or to use each other to obain advantages of and from each other? The historic answer to these questions has always proven the latter. We have differed only at points, when one felt that he had the advantage of the other by some point of superiority, or was suspicious each of the other on the insincerity of leadership.
>
> Can we treat with each other fairly enough to bring to pass the happy outcome of three connections which have gone their different ways; two for more than a century and three quarters, and one for more than a century?[23]

The black churches will not join with each other, but they do belong to and share prominently in interchurch, federated, and ecumenical organizations. They are members of the World Methodist Council, the World Federation of Methodist Women, the Federal and National Councils of Churches of Christ in the U.S.A., the World Council of Churches, and the Consultation on Church Union. They of course belong to the National Fraternal Council of Churches, an organization composed of twelve leading black denominations.

In all of these organizations the representatives of the three
bodies hold important posts and play prominent parts in the activities. In 1881 at the first Ecumenical Conference, or World
Methodist Council as it is now called, held in London, Dr. J. C.
Price of the A.M.E.Z. Church won international fame as an orator. In 1971 at its twelfth session of the same Council, Bishop
Herbert Bell Shaw was made a member of the eight-member
presidium.[24] Bishop B. Julian Smith has served as a member of
the Central Committee of the World Council of Churches and as
a Vice-president of the International Council of Christian Education.

There is at least one way in which two of the black Methodist
Churches are working together. The A.M.E. and the C.M.E.
churches are both constituent members of the Interdenominational Theological Center in Atlanta. This institution is a
federation of the seminaries of seven denominations. It has a central administration and a single faculty. It is fully accredited, and
therefore each participating seminary is accredited. Thus two of
the black Methodist churches now have accredited schools for
the training of their ministers. The A.M.E.Z.'s have not yet
joined the Center.

Black Methodist churches, like those of other denominations,
are rendering vital public service by serving as sponsors for
government-financed projects that aid the elderly and poor.
Low-cost housing projects, low-cost housing for elderly citizens,
day-care centers for children of working mothers, programs of
meals and transportation for the elderly and needy, are conducted by churches across the nation. As a rule, these projects
are in the larger cities and are conducted by the larger churches.
These are crucially needed services in the black community at a
time when unemployment is high and incomes are uncertain and
low.

CHAPTER XVI

The Black Man in United Methodism

In 1844 THE METHODIST Episcopal Church suffered the most serious split in its history. The issue that caused the split was, of course, Negro slavery. Many Northern Methodists were opposed to slavery. Some were even abolitionists. They felt that slavery should be abolished and that slaveholders should not hold office in the Church, especially the clergy. In contrast, the Methodists living in the South, where slavery had become entrenched and where the slave system had become the way of life, not only accepted slavery but defended it and tried to justify it on Scriptural grounds. They contended that slavery was not a moral issue but a political one, and that the Church had nothing to do with it. Therefore, in the General Conference of 1844 when the differences between the two sides could not be reconciled, the Southern Methodists withdrew and a year later, 1845, formed the Methodist Episcopal Church, South.[1]

At the time of the split the great majority of black Methodists were in the Southern Church. In 1848 they numbered 127,248, and in 1860 there were 207,766.[2] They were the slaves in the plantation missions or segregated members of white congregations in Southern towns. In some cases the black members had their own separate churches under white leadership.

In the North it was just the opposite. The black membership of the Methodist Episcopal Church, North, had remained smaller than in the South. In 1856 there were about 100,000, or less than half the number in the Southern Church.[3] This small size was due in part to the black Methodist bodies, the A.M.E. and the A.M.E.Z., which took some members from the white M.E. Church. It was mainly due, however, to the fact that black Methodists in the North were largely free Negroes and their number was small. Thus down to 1860 the great majority of black Methodists had long been in the Southern Church.

In 1870, however, the Southern Church helped to set up its black membership in a separate body or denomination, the Colored Methodist Episcopal Church (see Chapter XIII). In this way the Southern Church divested itself completely of its Negro members, and thus became an all-white church. With the exception of financial aid to the educational program of the black (C.M.E.) Church and a few missionary projects, the Southern Church had no association with Negroes. The Southern Church also became strongly racist or anti-Negro in attitude. The Church became one of the main bastions of the idea of Negro inferiority and of resistance to "social equality." Such ideas were proclaimed both in writings and in sermons. To be sure, there were some Southern Methodists who courageously maintained a Christian, brotherly attitude toward Negroes. A great example is Bishop A. G. Haygood, author of *Our Brother in Black*.[4] But such persons spoke and acted as individuals, and they sometimes paid a dear price for their Christian liberalism. The great majority of Southern Methodists became and remained openly if not avidly anti-black.

Thus down to the Civil War the Southern Church had most of the Negroes, but after the War the situation was reversed. As a result of its mission work among the freedmen, black membership in the Northern Church grew by leaps and bounds. In 1860 there were one hundred thousand blacks in the M.E. Church. About ten years later there were 174,000, almost a 70 per cent increase. And the number kept growing. In 1939 there were over 300,000, the third or fourth largest group of black Methodists in the nation. After 1870 it was the Northern Church that had the blacks; the Southern Church had none. It was strictly all-white.

The Negroes who joined the M.E. Church after the Civil War did so for several reasons: first, because of the educational and other services rendered to the freedmen; secondly, because they wanted to be part of the main body of Methodism, rather than in the separate all-black churches which in reality were segregated Methodist churches. A further reason is well stated by Bishop Willis J. King, one of the Negro Bishops of the M.E. Church:

> More important [to the Negro members], however, than rights and prerogatives was the instinctive conviction, evident from their earliest connection with the people called "Methodists," that this fellowship represented a communion that was seriously seeking to build a brotherhood among all men. They believed that their membership in such a fellowship would help in the achievement of world brotherhood.[5]

Their membership, however, was not entirely happy or free from problems. These came both from outside and inside the Church. From outside came taunts from the black churches that M.E. Negroes were members of a "Jim Crow" church; that they did not and would not have full participation in the life and work of their church. Bishop Daniel A. Payne of the A.M.E. Church had predicted that because of his minority status, "the existence of the colored man in the M.E. Church, always was, still is, and ever must be a mere cipher." He further charged that M.E. blacks lacked independence and a sense of self support.[6]

Inside the Church the Negro members were faced with the fact of segregation. They felt subordinated and pocketed. For example, the 300,000 black members were organized into 19 black annual conferences. Until 1920 these were presided over by white Bishops. There was little fellowship at the local church level. In the twentieth century, especially after the First World War, this separation or segregation was increasingly disturbing. Yet there had been some progressive steps in the Negro's situation. The annual conferences did give the blacks representation in the General Conference of the Church. Also in 1920 two black

Bishops were elected for service in America, Matthew W. Clair, Sr., and Robert E. Jones. They were elected, however, on separate or segregated ballots and they presided over all-black areas.

But the most serious problem for the black members in the early twentieth century grew out of the movement toward unification of the three major white Methodist bodies, the Methodist Episcopal, the Methodist Episcopal, South, and the Methodist Protestant Churches.

The main problem for blacks centered around the union of the two major bodies, the Churches North and South. The problem was not only for blacks, but blacks themselves were the problem. As one student expressed it: "Despite all the manifold problems and complexities involved in the unification of the two Methodisms, the principal issue separating them, and the one on which unification would either succeed or fail, was the Negro in the Methodist Episcopal Church."[7] The Northern Church had a long established interest in the Negro and was determined to maintain it. The Southern Church objected to any plan of union that would include Negroes. "It was the desire of this branch of Methodism to have the Negro in the northern branch set aside in a separate unit outside of the new united Church to be."[8] Or as Bishop Willis J. King expressed it:

> From the standpoint of the Southern Church, with its history and social background since the division in 1844, and its definite action of 1870, in which it set up its Negro membership into an independent denomination, the logical status of the Negro in any plan for the reorganized church, seemed to be the establishment of the Negro group into a separate denomination, either alone, or with other Negro groups, with no organic relation to the white membership of the church, and leaders argued for that position for many years during the period of negotiations.[9]

But despite fixed attitudes and emotional blocks, the reasons for uniting the Churches were becoming more and more clear and impelling. For example, in the border states such as Maryland, Delaware, Kentucky, and Missouri, where both the Northern and Southern denominations maintained congregations that were almost identical in character, the separation was irrational and irritating.[10] The two Churches were already cooperating in various ways. They had produced a common hymnal and had adjusted rivalries on the mission field. The spirit of ecumenism and cooperation was rising in Protestant thought. Both of the Churches and their leaders were active in the Federal Council of Churches. In 1934 all Methodists celebrated the sesquicentennial anniversary of the founding of the Methodist Episcopal Church and in 1938 they celebrated the two hundredth anniversary of Wesley's Aldersgate experience. The forces for union were strong and getting stronger.

One author has pointed out that unification is a process and not an event. In 1925 a Plan of Union was worked out, but it failed to be approved by a sufficient number of the annual conferences of the Churches. A Joint Commission was again appointed to produce a Plan of Union that would be acceptable to the North and South. It met in 1935. "As had been the case in every other meeting of the commission, the critical question focused on the Negro . . . Was it possible to devise a plan for union which would not offend Southern sensibilities and yet adhere to the North's historic mission to the Negro?"

The Commission felt that it had devised such a plan when it reported in August 1935. The plan provided for the nation "to be divided into six administrative areas, five of which were geographical, while one, the Central, was to be a non-geographical grouping of the bulk of the Negroes in the Methodist Episcopal Church."[11] It was based on race.

The plan met with approval by both the Southern and Northern Churches. For the Southern Church the Plan had two distinct advantages. First, it effectively isolated it from nearly all contact with the Negro membership. Secondly, it permitted that Church to retain a large measure of control over its affairs. The Plan gave similar control to the Northern Church.[12]

But the Plan met with immediate and vigorous opposition from Negroes. Their position was simple: putting all Negroes into one separate Jurisdiction based on race was outright segregation, and this they did not want. To be sure, *de facto* segregation had always existed in the Methodist Episcopal Church, but this Plan would make segregation legal and would write it into the Constitution of the Church. This was not only un-Christian, but it would be a bad example for the Church to set before the nation.

The debate that followed in the years between 1935 and 1939, the time of unification, was earnest, deeply felt, and sometimes bitter. In the debate the Negro churchmen bore themselves with dignity, conviction, and credit. In general, Negroes were not opposed to unification, but they were opposed to the Plan. They wanted union without segregation. Dr. James P. Brawley, a delegate to the General and Uniting Conferences, says:

> It was the hope of the Negro membership of the Methodist Episcopal Church that his status would be improved in the new United Church and that no structural organization would set him apart and give him less dignity and recognition than he already had . . . He, therefore, rejected the plan of union . . . This was a stigma too humiliating to accept."[13]

Among the Negro Leaders in the struggle were Bishop Robert E. Jones, elected in 1920, and one of the two first black Methodist Episcopal Bishops elected for service in America (although over all-black conferences); Dr. Willis J. King, President of Gammon Theological Seminary in Atlanta; Dr. Alexander P. Shaw, editor of the *Southwestern Christian Advocate;* and Dr. John W. Haywood, Dean of Morgan State College. These men all pushed the side of their people with vigor and courage. Bishop Jones and Dr. King were members of the Joint Commission. For a while these two were unfairly criticized for not preventing the passage of the Plan, but, as a matter of fact, both had opposed the Central Jurisdiction idea.

As time for the General Conference of 1936 approached and it was seen that the plan of union would be adopted anyway, some black leaders began to feel that it might be unrealistic to hope for the elimination of all segregation all at once, and that it might be wise to accept unification with the Central Jurisdiction, looking forward to eventual improvement. This was forcefully said by Dr. Haywood:

> The proposed plan is clearly and admittedly an accommodation to racial and sectional differences . . . I am not now, and never have been, under any illusions about the amount and quality of the religion possessed by the people in the churches now proposing to

unite . . . and so I have always expected a normal, perfectly human plan of union, characterized by many of the faults that characterize the churches proposing to enter the union. We have, I frankly confess, such a plan in this proposal. We must never forget that human brotherhood is a goal. And goals, we must ever remember, are at the end, not at the beginning of the journey.[14]

But despite moderating considerations, Negroes unitedly rejected the Plan. Of the 47 black delegates to the Conference, 36 voted against the Plan, and 11 abstained. The whites voted for the plan, 470 for and 83 against. When the plan was later presented to the 19 black annual conferences, they voted 7 against, 2 for, and 9 abstaining since the Central Jurisdiction was already a *fait accompli*.

According to Brawley, "It is reported that when the General Conference delegates arose, after the voting, to sing 'We Are Marching Upward to Zion,' the Negro delegates remained seated and some of them wept."[15]

The Southern Church voted overwhelmingly for the Plan at its General Conference in 1938. Thus with the three bodies voting favorably (the Methodist Protestant had previously approved), the union was consummated in Kansas City, Missouri, on Wednesday, April 26, 1939. The feelings of Negro members of the Methodist Episcopal Church are well described by two black participants in the Uniting Conference, one a delegate and the other a speaker.

"As a member of that delegation," said Dr. James P. Brawley,

I shared the emotions of 47 other Negro delegates in the assemblage—the emotions of pride, regret and fear, and the emotion of hope.

There was pride because we were identified with a great church that had brought to that significant moment of history a great heritage. We, as Negroes, were not merely beneficiaries of that heritage, but had helped to enrich the heritage from the beginning; for as the venerable Dr. M. S. Davage so aptly said in his eloquent address to that conference, "In the beginning of Methodism was the Negro."

We had pride because, numbered among the Methodist Episcopal bishops were three of our group, who had been elected to his high office by two previous General Conferences—Bishops M. W.

Clair, Sr. then in retired relation, and Robert E. Jones, both elected in 1920; and Bishop Alexander P. Shaw, elected in 1936.

There were emotions of regret and fear—regret that The Methodist Church in the making had seen fit to write legal segregation into its constitution, which was a far step backward and a retreat from the high ground this great church had taken on the moral issue of race in years past. *There was fear* because we faced an unknown way and an uncharted sea in the church where racial misunderstanding was rampant, and we feared that it would take much more time than the church could afford, to correct its mistake and come to a relationship of true brotherhood.

We shared hope, because we were Negroes, who in all the crucial hours and experiences of hundreds of years had learned never to lose hope and to lean with faith upon the God of human justice.[16]

Dr. Matthew S. Davage, then Secretary of the Department of Negro Work in the M.E. Church, who was the speaker for the Negroes on the Conference program, delivered a memorable address. He said in part:

In the beginning of Methodism was the Negro . . .

When the plan of union was proposed and adopted, two questions immediately arose. First, what will be the attitude of the united Church toward its Negro membership? and second, what course should Negro members follow in the best interest of all concerned? The answer to the first question is that *every right of the Negro has been conserved and guaranteed by the letter of the law*. It is in the constitution. That is something! But our experience before and especially during this conference assures us that above and in addition to the law and permeating it is a spirit of genuine Christian brotherhood which makes the law potent and vital. In this conference, we have received every consideration and have been shown every courtesy.

Our answer to the second question is that it is our deliberate judgment that the advancement of the Kingdom and the interests of all races can best be served by *cooperation*, founded on faith and good will, rather than by separation, motivated by fear and ill will. We have no criticism for those of our people who in an earlier day withdrew and established a church of their own. Perhaps that was the only solution possible at that time. We have only admiration for the way in which they have maintained and carried on the work of their several denominations. We feel we would have their prayers and blessings and best wishes, as we attempt a more difficult and delicate task. But it is a task freighted with far greater potentialities for the future of the people. People who think at all must realize that without regard to denomination and success or failure of our venture in this co-operative Christian enterprise will surely affect for good or ill the destiny of every Negro in America.

This is a new day and a new Church with a new vision and new courage. This world is shrinking and constantly growing smaller. The retreat method (running from difficulties) is outmoded because there is scarcely any place left to go. We, therefore, think it better to say, "Come and let us reason together," than to say, "Let us walk in separate and divergent paths." If civilization is to endure, nations and races must learn to live and work together in peace. If eventually and inevitably this must be done, then why not now?

No, we do not choose to establish another weak denomination whose supreme effort would of necessity be exerted in a selfish struggle to save itself. There are too many of that sort now whose only word is a wail of want and whose only message is a piteous appeal for funds. What manner of service could such an organization hope to render to a people so greatly in need of help and guidance? As Negroes, we want to be done with littleness and narrowness. We want wider horizons! We need to be identified with something large. Too often, the Negro is circumscribed and limited in his contacts and cut off from so many agencies and influences which are uplifting and ennobling. We are restricted and forced to think too much about ourselves. Our souls feel the blighting effects of frustration, and as a result, strange, weird religious cults are developing among us. We are in danger of becoming religious introverts. We want to feel the challenge and the thrill of greatness. We want to lift up our cast-down eyes from the insignificant clods to the hills and even to the great stars of God. We want room in which to expand and grow and to develop to the utmost whatever talents God has given us. We are, therefore, glad to be an organic part of a great Christian fellowship—a Church whose parish is the world and whose plans and program are as broad as humanity's need. In short, we do not want to be a church whose *appeal is merely racial.* We want to be in a church which embraces all mankind, and *is big enough for God.*[17]

Negroes were not the only ones displeased with the Plan of Union. Some Southerners did not like the whole idea of cooperation with other Churches. Among them were Bishops Warren A. Candler and Collins Denny.[18]

There were Northerners who favored union, but did not like the segregation it imposed on the Negro members. Dean Lynn Harold Hough of Drew Theological Seminary said: "In the face of this unanimous opposition by the Negro brethren and against what we so loudly profess as a church, makes this a day of unutterable ignominy for the Methodist Episcopal Church."[19] Dr. Mark A. Dawber, Executive Secretary of the Home Missions Council, introduced the following resolution at the meeting of the Wyoming Conference at its meeting in April 1937, which was adopted:

> Be it resolved: That we regret that some more acceptable way was not provided to deal with the Negro situation. We are not satisfied with that section of the plan that calls for a separate jurisdiction for our Negro members, and we desire that our Negro brethren shall know our attitude and our conviction in regard to this matter.
>
> But, desiring in every way to achieve the larger objectives of unification, and if the plan is approved, we cast our vote for the plan in the hope that in the course of time those adjustments will be made that will modify the plan to the satisfaction of our Negro brethren who are not satisfied, and to all those who share with them this feeling.[20]

But like it or not, the Central Jurisdiction was a fact with which the new Methodist Church would have to live for the next twenty-five years or more.

TOWARD AN INCLUSIVE CHURCH

The first General Conference of the new Central Jurisdiction met in St. Louis, Missouri, June 18 to 23, 1940. It consisted of nineteen annual conferences and 320,000 members.

Bishop Robert E. Jones presided. In his episcopal address he pointed out that the Central Jurisdiction was a segregated, racial arrangement, set up in concession to strong racial prejudices. Negroes at first had opposed the plan, but in the interest of Methodist unification had finally come to accept it in the hope that a better arrangement would eventually be achieved.

However, he said, in accepting the plan all had not been lost. There were actually some gains.

In the first place, the Central Jurisdiction has all the privileges and powers and identically the same status that the other five jurisdictions have. We have the same proportionate representation of the annual conferences in the General Conference. Our delegates are accorded in the General Conference every right and privilege belonging to every other delegate. The Central Jurisdiction is represented upon every board in the Church. This is not racial representation; it is jurisdictional representation, and in this, particularly, there is a gain, for there were boards in the former Methodist Episcopal Church on which there were no Negroes.

In accepting the jurisdictional conference we lose nothing in our constitutional rights and privileges. We still have our right to initiate constitutional changes and to vote upon constitutional changes wherever originated, and upon whatever subject involved. In a close constitutional vote the vote of the Central Jurisdictional might be vital.

We gain the privilege of electing our own bishops who at once become full members of the Council of Bishops with the same status of bishops similarly elected . . .

Why, then, did those of us who constitute the Central Jurisdiction accept this restriction constituting a jurisdiction on racial lines? Answer: Morally we refuse to desert an effort to work out an ideal. The ideal is alluring . . . The undertaking of interracial Christian brotherhood which is now being made by the Methodist Church is in some respects the most notable experiment that has been essayed in the history of the Christian church . . . We of the Central Jurisdiction of the Methodist Church have an advantage for the promotion of interracial Christian brotherhood which is not held by any other religious group of people . . .

It therefore behooves us at the very beginning of our career as a separate jurisdiction to recognize the gravity of our responsibility as well as the favorableness of our opportunity. It is a responsibility we should by no means shirk; and it is an opportunity of which we should hasten to take every advantage.[21]

Yet despite the good will with which the Negroes were at least formally accepting the Central Jurisdiction, it was still unsatisfactory to many Methodists. This was especially true for some Northern whites, such as Bishop Francis McConnell; Dr. Ernest Fremont Tittle, distinguished pastor of Evanston, Illinois; and Dean Lynn Harold Hough of Drew Theological Seminary. They resented the segregated nature of the Jurisdiction plan. The plan, of course, was unsatisfactory to most Negroes.

To intensify the issue, there was a strong liberalizing tendency in human relations in America and in the world following the Second World War. America had emerged from the war as the world's leading nation and as the champion of smaller and minority groups. There were the declarations on human rights by America and the United Nations in 1948, and later by the World Council of Churches. In 1954 the United States Supreme Court outlawed segregation in public education. Shortly after, in the 1960s, there began the great push for civil rights in America which broke down segregation barriers in many areas. All of this made it difficult for the the Church to retain any segregated arrangement.

In response to trends and pressures the Methodist Church in 1948, 1952, and 1960 appointed commissions to study the situation of minorities in the Church and also to study the whole jurisdictional system, especially the Central Jurisdiction. In 1956 the General Conference adopted Amendment IX to its Constitution which gave annual conferences the right to change from one Jurisdiction to another, and a local church the right to change from one Annual Conference to another if the change were acceptable to all parties involved. This later came to be known as "voluntarism."[22]

Meanwhile, the Central Jurisdiction felt that it should make its own position clear. In 1956 a study commission was appointed which recommended that a Jurisdiction-wide study be made. A Committee of Five was appointed of which Dr. James S. Thomas, later Bishop, was Chairman. A conference of leaders of the Jurisdiction was held in Cincinnati in 1962. On the basis of the conference and their studies the commission reported to the Jurisdictional Conference in 1964. It recommended that the Central Jurisdiction be eliminated as soon as possible, but that efforts be made to see that transfers would not work to the disadvantage of Central Jurisdiction conferences or churches.

In 1964 the Commission on Inter-Jurisdictional Relations which had been appointed previously by the General Conference reported:

> Your commission believes that the continuation of the Central Jurisdiction is unsound. It is a handicap to the Methodist Church in promoting work among Negroes. It is both a fact and a symbol of racism within the Methodist Church and is incompatible with the basic principles of equality.[23]

The Commission was continued by the General Conference to consummate the dissolution of the Central Jurisdiction by 1968. Meanwhile, five Annual Conferences had voluntarily transferred out of the Central Jurisdiction by 1966. A special session of the Jurisdiction was held in 1967 to conclude its existence. Bishop L. Scott Allen was elected in that session to replace Bishop M. L. Harris, who died in 1966. All of the Conferences of the Central Jurisdiction had been merged into white Conferences by 1972.

The process of merging the white and black Jurisdictions had been marked by fears on both sides. Blacks feared that since they constituted only one-thirtieth of Methodist members, they would lose many offices if merged into the main body. Under the jurisdictional system the number of blacks on boards and agencies had increased from 40 to 101. They especially feared that no black bishops would be elected by predominantly white Jurisdictions. Whites in turn feared black participation and black take-over. An article in the *Christian Advocate* by Grover C. Bagby proved that this fear was wholly unreal. He showed that in the Annual Conferences of the Southeastern and South Central Jurisdictions, where Negro membership was largest, that, after merger, in only one Conference would Negro membership be as much as 20 per cent. In all others it would range down to about 3 per cent, in most cases being about 5.[24]

Time has tended to dissipate both fears. Blacks have been elected or appointed to administrative offices and have served as District Superintendents and other conference officers in Southern Jurisdictions. Three black bishops have been elected by predominantly white bodies, making seven black bishops now serving in America. Blacks continue to hold prominent offices in national boards and agencies. At present there is not much integration in local churches, but this can be expected to grow.

In the fellowship and participation of its black members, the Methodist Church, as Bishop Jones said in 1940, is the leading Church in the world.

PROTEST MOVEMENTS

The civil rights push of the 1960s in the social and economic orders had its counterpart in religion. In the predominantly white denominations the push was expressed through "black caucuses," groups of black members who organized to protest against segregation and discrimination in church life and work. Two main complaints were against the failure to appoint blacks to major positions and to include them at decision making points in the denominations.

Persons from the black denominations, where the caucus movement was not possible, joined with the caucus members to protest discriminations in the interdenominational and ecumenical activities of the Christian Church, such as the National and World Councils of Churches. They protested not only against overt acts of discrimination, but also against ideological and theological discriminations, such as the exclusively white imagery of Christianity, that is, Christ, the Madonna, and even God Himself conceived in Caucasian forms without regard to the concepts of other ethnic groups in the Christian fold. Resistance to this kind of discrimination led to the "Black Theology" movement.

In 1967 persons from the black denominations joined with the various caucuses to form the National Conference of Black Churchmen. The activities of this group are described by Professor Gayraud C. Wilmore in *Black Religion and Black Radicalism*.[25] The black Methodist bodies did not officially endorse the organization, but members of these bodies, bishops and other leaders, did take part in its activities and held prominent offices.

At the present time the N.C.B.C. is not very active, due to lack of official sponsorship, and especially to lack of funds. The organization has pointed up, however, some serious needs in human relations in the larger Christian family in America.

In United Methodism the black caucus movement took the form of Black Methodists for Church Renewal, organized in 1968. Like similar groups it called attention to racial faults both in the structure and in the activities of the Church. But since the United Methodist Church, as mentioned, was and is working to improve the situation of minorities in its membership, the B.M.C.R. is able now to change its role from mainly one of protest to the role of promoting cooperation and true Christian fellowship throughout the Church. According to its Chairman, Clayton E. Hammond, in an address delivered at the Eighth Annual Meeting in Chicago in 1975, B.M.C.R. needs now to turn its attention to revival of the spirits of the black members. "The radical challenge facing us," he said, "is the turning from renewal to survival—the revival and survival of the black minority in United Methodism."[26]

CHAPTER XVII

Summary and Prospect

SUMMARY

IN THE PRECEDING CHAPTERS we saw something of the birth and growth of a great religious movement. From this cursory review we can learn much about religion and religions, and about the parts they play in the development of mankind.

We saw the Methodist movement begin in the religious experience of one man or small group of men. Yet that individual experience was contagious, and when proclaimed with determination and conviction it caught fire in other breasts. Beginning in England as a drive for piety in the Anglican Church, it brought hope, self-respect, and moral integrity to vast numbers of poor, depressed, hopeless people, victims of the industrial revolution, and to members of the upper classes as well.

Through Irish converts the new faith came to America. The first bearers of Methodism were two men and a woman, Philip Embury, Robert Strawbridge, and Barbara Heck. Among the first respondents were a number of Negroes. Betty, a black woman, was at Embury's first service in New York City, and Aunt Annie Switzer, another black woman, was a member of the first society organized by Strawbridge in Maryland. Among contributors to the construction of the first meeting house in New York were several Negro slaves. Thus Negroes were part of American Methodism from its inception.

The Methodist movement arrived in America at a most propitious time. There was little religion in the colonies prior to the Revolutionary War. There were, to be sure, the great revivals and Whitefield's preaching, but these were occasional activities. On the whole there was little regular church life in the colonies, and little religious interest. Moral standards were low, and life was rough and brutal. Many people were hungry for spiritual leadership and development.

Methodism seemed providentially suited to the colonial situation. It involved little theology and less ritual. It consisted primarily of a vivid personal experience based on a simple, direct faith. It was well suited to the unlettered colonial masses, and especially suited to the slaves. It was taken to the people, both slave and free, by courageous, zealous preachers, who permitted nothing to stop them in their mission of preaching the word.

But despite its suitability, proclaiming the Methodist message was difficult and often dangerous. To begin with, many colonists did not like Methodists or Methodism, and resented the preachers' interference with their ways of life, even their corrupt ways. This led, of course, to the physical persecution of the preachers. The determination of the preachers to continue in the face of vicious opposition is a high example of prophetic courage.

It was, however, in the fight against slavery that the Church had its hardest and most baffling struggle. Beginning with Wesley, Methodism held that slavery was wrong. The early preachers were imbued with this conviction. They started out with a forthright attack, a clear call for abolition. But slavery was more than personal sins. It was an entrenched economic, social, and political system involving vast vested interests moved by the passion for profit no matter how inhumane the process. Such evil does not yield easily.

It was in the struggle with slavery that American Methodism learned what was a sad fact for itself and, indeed, for mankind: the Church like everything else in life, is affected by and adjusts itself to prevailing conditions of its day. Very early in its history the Church had to decide whether to continue to preach and practice the brotherhood that Jesus proclaimed, fight the slaveocracy and possibly die or remain a small extremist sect; or whether to soften its voice on slavery, accept segregation and subjection of black members, which was the prevailing social practice, and thus live and grow in numbers and influence. Officially the Church chose the latter course.

One reason for the choice is the fact that the Church was not a separate body of saints living in a purist world passing judgment on its fallible fellows outside. In its evangelizing efforts the Church had taken in many who were mild on slavery or were slaveholders themselves. Some of these, like William Winans, James O. Andrew, and William Capers, believed that Negro slavery was right and good, that it was not an immoral institution, and that it had some beneficent effects on the slaves. At any rate, they reasoned, slavery was a political issue, and therefore not a proper province for the Church. Thus in its very composition the Church became compromised, and could only speak with a divided voice. The Church was in the world, but also the world was in the Church.

Here then in early Methodism is seen one of the fateful facts of religion made clear by modern psychology: in the quest for standards of righteousness man has only the human mind, and the mind is an undependable instrument. It yields to selfish, unrighteous pressures, and if we are not careful it will build theologies and moral and ethical systems to justify and support its capitulations, and then with great ecclesiological pomposity hold that these systems are sacred and divine. It is this that makes every preachment questionable and every standard unsure.

This is the plight of the human heart in its quest for righteous standards. Therefore, man's righteous thoughts, frail as they are, are all that humanity has to hold to. In Christian culture the Church is the keeper of those thoughts.

The softening stand on slavery led, of course, to the separation and segregation of blacks in the life of the Church. It again was a result of the social system. Even the Quakers who were loud in their call for abolition were reluctant to accept blacks as members of the Societies. The black pew in the back of the Church or in the balcony, and in the South the slave gallery or separate meetinghouse, were regular features of ante-bellum worship.

This segregation led to separation, especially in the North where free blacks had some opportunity to express themselves. They formed congregations where they could worship by themselves without the humiliating ostracisms imposed by whites. They also wanted services that would express their hopes and sufferings, and epecially the passion for freedom.

Thus two great separate black Methodist bodies were born, the A.M.E.'s in 1816, and the A.M.E.Z.'s in 1822. They were small in the beginning, but they grew in spite of difficulties until today they are the largest separate components in American Methodism.

Yet though the Church accepted compromise in its ideals of righteousness, the ideal did not die. It continued to live in the hearts of some who kept up the call for abolition. Some became active in the national abolition movement. A few examples were James O'Kelly, Freeborn Garrettson, Orange Scott, and George Storrs. They refused to be silenced and they won an increasing hearing.

Moreover, there were some blacks who felt that withdrawal and separation were not the only approach to better human relations. Another way, they felt, was to stay in the main body and to work there for brotherhood and an inclusive Church. They did this in spite of calumny, ridicule, and rejection both from black separatists and white segregationists.

Also, in the South where the slave system prevented any thought of abolition, the sense of guilt over slavery and concern for the slave resulted in setting up the Mission to the Slaves. Some Southern Methodists wanted at least to save the slave's soul, a real value at the time. Though the motives for the Mission were vitiated if not ignoble, they did express a degree of genuine concern for the slave in a region where this kind of concern could be expressed without too much penalty.

In the struggle with slavery it is clearly seen that human affairs sometimes move to desired ends in ways above and beyond the conscious plans of men. In 1816 it was hard to believe that slavery would end through a bitter, bloody civil war. But this was the way of history, and in this history Methodism played a heroic part. Freedom finally came in 1865.

We have seen how prior to the Civil War the independent black Methodist denominations were confined almost exclusively to the North. The one large A.M.E. church of about two thousand members in Charleston, South Carolina, under Morris Brown was closed in 1822, and he was forced to flee. It was not until the end of the war that the black churches could live and work in the South. But as the war was ending, while the guns were still sounding, the black churches moved in to begin their work of evangelism among the freedmen. Their growth was phenomenal. The A.M.E. Church grew from 15,000 in 1860 to 450,000 in 1880, and 600,000 in 1906. The A.M.E.Z. Church grew from 4,600 in 1860 to 400,000 in 1880, and 500,000 in 1906. The third black Methodist denomination, the Christian Methodist Episcopal, founded in 1870, started with 67,000 members. They became one of the fastest growing, reaching 350,000 in 1906.

But the black Churches were not only out to gain new members. They sought to render services, too. They set up schools, and conducted cultural and charitable programs, all aimed at lifting the lot of the destitute, bewildered, and beleaguered freedmen. The black Churches were preceded in this work by the white Methodist Episcopal Church (North), which had already begun work among the former slaves. Because of its greater resources in people and finances the white Church could do much more than the black, but both white and black working together gave to the world one of the brightest examples of Christian mission in the history of the Church. They brought education, vocational training, and cultural development to thousands of black people, young and old, who otherwise would not have had it. Some of the schools they established have become today leading educational institutions.

After the Emancipation the black denominations were free to develop their organizational structures. They experienced the thrill, the pride, the power of large organization, but they incurred the problems and troubles common to large organizations. Lucrative, powerful positions developed as the bodies grew, and struggles for such positions was the inevitable result. Ambitious men and women, who wanted power for power's sake as much as for Christ's, rose to dominant positions in the church hierarchies. The ministry of self-sacrificing service began to lose its appeal as the desired goal of a preacher's life. The episcopacy loomed as the highest and therefore the most desirable end to a ministry, and if this were not to be attained, then a lucrative general office in the national bodies was an attractive point of promotion and possibly a step toward the bishopric. Complex systems of political scheming and maneuvering permeated the life of the Church, bringing corrupt practices and taking attention away from the primary purpose of Methodism, which was to save souls, not to elect candidates.

Perpetuating offices became as much a motive in church development as fashioning a structure for more efficient evangelizing and Christian service. Thus it is the fear of losing lucrative general offices that is the main barrier to cooperation or union among the black Methodist denominations. Large sums are wasted in maintaining superfluous positions.

Problems such as these are at least partly responsible for the lack of growth of the churches in recent decades and for reduced effectiveness as a corrective influence in society. There is some evidence that the churches are becoming aware of these problems, and perhaps this awareness may lead to constructive reforms.

PROSPECT

Today there are three major black Methodist bodies in America. Will they always be separate, doing in small ways what could better be done in a large, united way? At present there is little indication of any early change. Yet cooperation, if not organic union, would be most helpful.

First, there could be cooperation in publications, particularly in Christian education materials, hymnals, disciplines (or rule books), and some church journals. Combined resources would make possible the employment of more highly trained personnel, would improve the quality of teaching materials, and doubtless would still reduce costs.

A second point of cooperation could well be in foreign missions. Combined resources would mean more efficient staffing, more lasting or permanent projects, better financing, and, above all, mission programs adequately suited to today's conditions in Africa. Emphasis could be placed on developing indigenous leadership in education and in the church for self-sustaining African institutions.

As to union with white Methodists, the black bodies will likely maintain a fraternal, interdenominational relationship in an inclusive Methodist fellowship, rather than to enter into an organic union. There is, however, a growing consciousness in the white Church that black Methodists are part of the same movement, branches of the same tree. Cooperation in joint programs will doubtless result.

There is one area in which joint action by the black bodies is critically needed, and that is in spiritual service to the black masses in American urban communities. The hopeless, helpless condition of these black people is a serious threat to the progress, if not the survival, of the race. The same conditions that faced free Negroes in 1830 confront blacks today, our great recent progress in civil rights to the contrary notwithstanding. When people are idle and unable to support themselves, it is then that frustration, despair, and surrender take over and vice and crime run rampant. The Church helped our fathers to survive slavery. It must help black people today to outwit stagnation, to keep their sense of respect for other black people and their respect for themselves; it can help blacks to turn idleness into efforts at self-development; it can turn blacks from exploitation of blacks to a sense of communal, interdependent, cooperative living achieved by pooling energies and resources in activities for the good of all.

This can be done, but it will take people who know human psychology well enough to penetrate resistant minds. It will also be costly, far more than one congregation or denomination can afford. But three denominations embracing two million members can together amass the skills, the resources, the leadership necessary for an intensive program of spiritual service. They can develop pilot projects that can be adopted by governmental and other agencies.

The Church at work in these ways is the only hope of overcoming the emasculatory effects of generations of relief and welfare. It is the only hope of reclaiming present youth from disillusionment and loss of faith in life.

Black Methodism has served as a source of salvation to many millions in its history. It is needed as much as ever, now.

Notes

CHAPTER I

1. John never used his middle name. See L. Tyerman, *The Life and Times of the Rev. John Wesley, M.A.* (London: Hodder Stoughton, 1878), p. 15. Also John Telford, *The Life of John Wesley* (New York: Eaton and Mains, 1898), p. 11.

2. Wade Crawford Barclay, *History of Methodist Missions* (New York: The Board of Missions and Church Extension of the Methodist Church, 1949), p. xix.

3. Robert Southey, *The Life of Wesley*, J. A. Atkinson, ed. (London: Frederick Warne and Co., 1889), pp. 27 f. See also L. Tyerman, op. cit., pp. 66 f.; and John Telford, op. cit., pp. 58 ff.

4. *George Whitefield's Journals*, new edition (Guilford and London, 1960), p. 58.

5. Robert Southey, op. cit., pp. 54–56. Also L. Tyerman, op. cit., pp. 146 ff.

6. *The Journal of John Wesley*, Nehemiah Curnock, ed. (London: Epworth Press, 1938), I, entry for December 2, 1737, p. 400.

7. *The Letters of the Rev. John Wesley*, John Telford, ed., standard edition (London: Epworth Press, 1931).

8. *The Journal of John Wesley*, I, p. 407.

9. John Wesley, *Thoughts Upon Slavery*, 1774, a pamphlet, printed in *The Works of the Rev. John Wesley, A.M.*, John Emory, ed. (New York: John T. Waugh, 1835), VI, pp. 278–93.

10. Joseph Tracy, *The Great Awakening* (Boston: Tappan and Bennett, 1842), pp. 95 ff.

11. Benjamin Brawley, *Early Negro American Writers* (Chapel Hill, N.C.: University of North Carolina Press, 1935, reprinted 1968), pp. 21–30 and 37–39. Phillis Wheatley's first printed poem was "On the Death of Rev. Mr. George Whitefield."

12. *George Whitefield's Journals*, p. 422.

13. *Works of the Rev. George Whitefield, M.A.,* 6 vols. (London, 1772), II, p. 209.

14. *Three Letters of the Rev. Mr. George Whitefield* (Philadelphia, 1740), Letter III, p. 13.

15. *The Journal of John Wesley,* II, p. 439.

16. Ibid., I, pp. 475–76.

17. Wade C. Barclay, op. cit., p. xvi.

18. *The Letters of the Rev. John Wesley,* III, p. 195.

19. Wade C. Barclay, op. cit., I, p. xviii.

20. Holland N. McTyeire, *A History of Methodism* (Nashville, Tenn.: Publishing House of the M.E. Church, South, 1884), pp. 211 f.

CHAPTER II

1. Gayraud S. Wilmore, *Black Religion and Black Radicalism* (Garden City, N.Y.: Doubleday & Company, Inc., 1972), p. 22. Some of the leading African scholars are John S. M'biti, C. C. Baeta, and E. Bolaja Idowu.

2. Roger Bastide, *African Civilizations in the New World* (New York: Harper and Row, 1971), pp. 3 f.

3. See the article "Lourdes" in the *New Catholic Encyclopedia,* 1967 ed., VIII, pp. 103 ff. for Our Lady of Lourdes's shrine.

4. John S. Mbiti, *Concepts of God in Africa* (New York: Frederick A. Praeger, Inc., 1970), pp. 327–36.

5. John S. M'biti, op. cit., p. 175.

6. John S. M'biti, *African Religions and Philosophy* (New York: Frederick A. Praeger, Inc., 1969), pp. 15–16, 29–57.

7. The Gospel According to St. Luke 7:19–23.

8. John Wesley, *Primitive Physick* (London, 1747).

9. Leslie D. Weatherhead, *Psychology, Religion and Healing* (New York: Abingdon Press, 1952).

10. John S. M'biti, *African Religions and Philosophy,* p. 207.

11. John S. M'biti, ibid., p. 268.

12. John S. M'biti, ibid., pp. 209 f.

13. J. G. Frazer, *The Golden Bough* (New York: The Macmillan Co., 1922) abridged ed., pp. 677 f.

14. U. B. Phillips, *American Negro Slavery* (New York: D. Appleton-Century, 1933), p. 39. This figure of ten million evidently does not include those who were killed in raids on villages or who died in the march to the sea. The total loss of life in the slave trade was much higher.

15. John Wesley, *Thoughts Upon Slavery,* 1774, a pamphlet, printed in *The Works of the Rev. John Wesley, A.M.,* John Emory, ed. (New York: John T. Waugh, 1835), VI, pp. 278–93.

16. *The Works of the Rev. John Wesley, A.M.,* VII, p. 237. Also John Hope Franklin, *From Slavery to Freedom,* 3rd ed. (New York: Alfred A. Knopf, 1967), pp. 53–59.

17. John S. Bassett, *A Short History of the United States* (New York: The Macmillan Co., 1923), p. 138.

18. For the development of the American slave system, see John S. Bassett, op. cit., pp. 138–40; John Hope Franklin, *From Slavery to Freedom*

(New York: Alfred A. Knopf, 1967); for the economic aspect of slavery see U. B. Phillips, *American Negro Slavery.*

19. J. S. Bassett, op. cit., pp. 346–52, 428–30; J. H. Franklin, op. cit., chs. XI–XIV.

20. Harry V. Richardson, *Dark Glory* (New York: Friendship Press, 1945), p. 4.

21. For an example of a "good" plantation with milder conditions than are here depicted, see Frederick L. Olmsted, *A Journey in the Seaboard Slave States* (New York: Dix and Edwards, 1856), pp. 418–48.

22. Roger Bastide, op. cit., pp. 23 f.

23. Marcus W. Jernigan, "Slavery and Conversion in the American Colonies," *American Historical Review,* Vol. XXI, No. 3, April 1916, pp. 504–27.

24. For example, the Negro members of John Street Church in New York City petitioned Bishop Asbury in 1780 for the right to meet by themselves.

25. J. F. Hurst, *The History of American Methodism* (New York: Eaton and Mains, 1903), IV, pp. 151 ff.

26. This was true in the North, but separate, independent black churches among Methodists were not permitted in the South.

27. Donald G. Mathews, *Slavery and Methodism* (Princeton, N.J.: Princeton University Press, 1965), p. 70.

28. See Chapter IX.

29. Charles Colcock Jones, *The Religious Instruction of the Negroes in the United States* (Savannah, Ga.: 1842; New York: Kraus Reprint Co., 1969), pp. 125–27. Jones, like missionaries of his time, had only a contemptuous disregard for the Negro's native beliefs and practices. He does, however, give an accurate picture of the beliefs and practices.

30. William Jay, *Miscellaneous Writings on Slavery* (Boston: John P. Jewett and Company, 1953), p. 471.

31. For a discussion of Voodoo and other non-Christian religions see Gayraud S. Wilmore, *Black Religion and Black Radicalism* (Garden City, N.Y.: Doubleday & Co., Inc., 1972), pp. 26–35.

32. The Reverend Thomas Bacon, *Two Sermons Preached to a Congregation of Black Slaves, at the Parish Church of S. P. in the Province of Maryland* (London, 1782). Quoted in H. Shelton Smith, *In His Image, But—*, pp. 11–12.

33. A copy of the Sermon is in the New York Public Library, rare book section.

CHAPTER III

1. Abel Stevens, *History of the Methodist Episcopal Church in the United States of America* (New York: Carlton and Porter, 1866), 4 vols., I, pp. 53–57. Also, W. J. Walls, *The African Methodist Episcopal Zion Church* (Charlotte, N.C.: A.M.E. Zion Publishing House, 1974), p. 39.

2. *The Journal of the Rev. John Wesley,* V, p. 330 n. Also Wesley's *Minutes of Conference* (1769), I, p. 86.

3. Robert Strawbridge came to America between 1760 and 1765 and began conducting services in Maryland. Exact dates of his early activities,

however, are not known. One of the members of the first society organized by Strawbridge was a Negro woman called Aunt Annie Sweitzer. Unfortunately in her case, as in the case of "Betty," about all that we know of her is her name. But again she proves that wherever or however Methodism started in America, Negroes were part of it from its inception. See Charles H. Wesley, *Richard Allen*, p. 40.

4. Letters of John Wesley, III, p. 192.

5. Abel Stevens, *History of the Methodist Episcopal Church* (New York: Eaton and Mains, 1866), I, pp. 120, 129.

6. H. N. McTyeire, *A History of Methodism* (Nashville, Tenn.: Publishing House of the M.E. Church, South, 1884), p. 254.

7. Matthieu Lelievre, *John Wesley, Sa Vie et Son Oeuvre* (Paris: Librairie Évangélique, 1891).

8. Abel Stevens, op. cit., p. 267.

9. The Hon. John M'Lean, *Sketch of Rev. Philip Gatch* (Cincinnati: Swormstedt and Poe, 1854), pp. 8–18. Also, Abel Stevens, op. cit., I, pp. 191–92.

10. *Experience and Gospel Labors of the Rev. Benjamin Abott. To which is annexed a Narrative of His Life and Death* (New York: John Firth, 1854), pp. 55 f. Also, Abel Stevens, op. cit., I, pp. 195–201.

11. *Experience and Gospel Labors of the Rev. Benjamin Abbott*, pp. 56 f. Also, Abel Stevens, *History of the Religious Movement of the 18th Century*, I, p. 142, and Abel Stevens, *History of Methodism*, I, pp. 260–61.

12. Letter to Mr. Wesley by Garrettson, written from Halifax, Nova Scotia, April 20, 1785. Quoted in Nathan Bangs, *The Life of Rev. Mr. Freeborn Garrettson* (New York: J. Emory and B. Waugh, 1832), pp. 168 ff.

13. John Wesley, *A Calm Address to Our American Colonies*, a pamphlet (London, 1775).

14. Abel Stevens, *History of Methodism*, I, pp. 118 f.

15. Asbury's *Journal*, November 12, 1771.

16. Abel Stevens, *History of the Methodist Episcopal Church*, I, p. 212.

17. Abel Stevens, op. cit., I, pp. 241 f.

18. Ibid., pp. 236 f.

19. Letter to Wesley, quoted in Abel Stevens, op. cit., I, p. 103.

20. Letter to Wesley, April 1771, quoted in Abel Stevens, op. cit., I, p. 106.

21. *The Experience and Travels of Mr. Freeborn Garrettson* (Philadelphia: Parry Hall, 1791), pp. 76 f.

22. Nathan Bangs, *History of the Methodist Episcopal Church*, I, pp. 111 f.

23. Andrew Bryan, a Negro Baptist preacher, would not permit Negroes to attend church who did not have permission from their masters.

CHAPTER IV

1. For a description of slave status and the laws governing slavery, see John C. Hurd, *The Law of Freedom and Bondage in the United States*, 2 vols. (Boston, 1856), I, pp. 249 ff.

2. An example of Negroes in commerce is Peter Williams, slave of a "Mr. Aymar," a tobacconist in New York City. Williams learned the business from his master. Later when Aymar, who was a loyalist, had to flee New York after the Revolutionary War, Peter, with the help of the Trustees of John Street Church, bought his freedom, went into the tobacco business and became quite successful.

3. Quoted in H. Shelton Smith, *In His Image, But—* (Durham, N.C.: Duke University Press, 1972), p. 18.

4. For a thorough and competent review of antislavery efforts in colonial times, see H. Shelton Smith, op. cit., Chapter I.

5. General Rules of the United Societies, written by Wesley in 1739.

6. John Wesley, *Thoughts Upon Slavery* (London, 1774).

7. Anthony Benezet, *Some Historical Account of Guinea* (Philadelphia, 1771). George S. Brookes, *Friend Anthony Benezet* (Philadelphia, 1957), pp. 84–85.

8. Letters of John Wesley, John Telford, ed., 8 vols. (London, 1931), VIII, p. 265.

9. *Journal and Letters of Rev. Francis Asbury*, Clark, Potts and Payton, eds., 3 vols. (Nashville, 1958), I, pp. 273–74.

10. Nathan Bangs, *The Life of the Rev. Mr. Freeborn Garrettson*, p. 41.

11. Journals of Conferences, 1780 to 1784, in Donald Mathews, *Slavery and Methodism*, pp. 295–98.

12. Ibid., pp. 297–98.

13. In 1784 John Wesley, after finding ecclesiastical precedent both in Scripture and in early church history, consecrated Dr. Thomas Coke, who was a priest in the Church of England, a Superintendent (later called "Bishop") in Methodism and sent him to America to ordain Francis Asbury and to consecrate him a Superintendent so that the two of them could supervise and promote the rapidly growing work in America. In keeping with these directions, Dr. Coke arrived in Philadelphia in December 1784 and immediately called a conference which met during Christmas week, and thus became known as the Christmas Conference.

The reasons for Wesley's action are clear. First, America was now a separate, independent nation, no longer under British government and resentful of British influence. Methodism could not any longer be well directed from England. Secondly, Methodism in America was without the sacraments of Baptism and the Lord's Supper. Methodist preachers were unordained, there were no Anglican bishops in America, and there were few Anglican priests since many of them had returned to England during the Revolution. A ministry was needed for a separate American Church. This Dr. Coke was sent to provide.

14. W. W. Sweet, *Virginia Methodism* (Richmond, Va.: Whittet & Shepperson, 1950), pp. 105–8.

15. H. Shelton Smith, op. cit., p. 39.

16. *Extracts of the Journals of Rev. Dr. Coke's Five Visits to America* (London: G. Paramore, 1793), pp. 35 f. Also, Samuel Drew, *The Life of Rev. Thomas Coke, D.D.* (London, 1817), pp. 133 ff. Also, Warren T. Smith, "Thomas Coke's War on American Slavery" in *Journal of the Interdenominational Theological Center*, II, Fall 1974, No. 1, pp. 1–11.

17. Asbury's Journal, I, p. 488. Also Mathews, op. cit., p. 12.

18. Quoted in H. Shelton Smith, op. cit., pp. 41 f.

19. Donald G. Mathews, op. cit., pp. 15 f.

20. For Methodist Conference actions on slavery from 1789 to 1844, see Donald G. Mathews, op. cit., pp. 293–303.

21. Minutes of the Georgia Annual Conference, 1837.

22. Wade C. Barclay, op. cit., p. 55.

23. Donald G. Mathews, *Slavery and Methodism*, Chapter II, "Compromise Confirmed," pp. 30–61. Also, Barclay, op. cit., II, p. 104.

24. Donald G. Mathews, op. cit., pp. 120 f.

25. Wade C. Barclay, op. cit., I, p. 101.

26. Ibid.

27. In a convention in Utica, New York, which opened on May 31, 1843, 152 delegates from 94 towns and nine states organized the Wesleyan Methodist Church. Besides being opposed to slavery they eliminated the episcopal form of government and gave laymen equal representation in conferences.

28. Wade C. Barclay, op. cit., p. 107. Also, Donald G. Mathews, op. cit., pp. 251 ff.

29. *Journal of the General Conference*, Methodist Episcopal Church, 1884, p. 73.

30. *Journal of the General Conference*, Methodist Episcopal Church, 1844, p. 84.

31. *Journal of the General Conference*, Methodist Episcopal Church, 1844, pp. 109–11.

32. Donald G. Mathews, op. cit., p. 279. For a vivid, moving account of the 1844 General Conference, see Donald G. Mathews, *Slavery and Methodism*, Chapter IX.

CHAPTER V

1. Richard Allen, *The Life, Experience and Gospel Labors of the Rt. Rev. Richard Allen*, George A. Singleton, ed. (New York: Abingdon Press, 1960), p. 30.
The autobiography of Richard Allen is the basic and most important document extant relating not only to his own life, but also to the development of Methodism among blacks in the period from 1776 to 1816. It was discovered by chance among old papers in an attic by Daniel A. Payne in 1852. It is a brief document filling only thirty-five printed pages. Allen wrote it from memory in 1826 near the end of his life long after the events had occurred. His son was his amanuensis. Unfortunately the story ends at the founding of the A.M.E. Church in 1816 and tells nothing of his part in the subsequent development of this Church. (Preface to Daniel A. Payne's *History of the A.M.E. Church*, pp. iv and v.)

2. Chapter III, supra.

3. John Firth, *Experience and Gospel Labors of the Rev. Benjamin Abbott* (New York: Hunt & Eaton, 1801), p. 120.

4. Richard Allen, *Life, Experience and Gospel Labors*, p. 27.

5. Charles H. Wesley, *Richard Allen, Apostle of Freedom* (Washington, D.C.: Associated Publishers, 1935), p. 130.

6. Charles H. Wesley, op. cit., p. 130.

7. Richard Allen, op. cit., p. 15.

8. Richard Allen, op. cit., p. 16.
9. Ibid.
10. Ibid., p. 15.
11. Ibid., pp. 20–21.
12. Ibid., p. 21.
13. Charles Wesley, op. cit., pp. 111–17.
14. Richard Allen, op. cit., p. 22.
15. Ibid., pp. 22–23.
16. Ibid., p. 24.
17. Ibid., p. 25.
18. Ibid.
19. Ibid., pp. 27–28.
20. Ibid., p. 29.
21. "A Narrative of the Proceedings of the Colored People During the Awful Calamity in Philadelphia in 1793." In the *Life, Experience and Gospel Labors of the Rt. Rev. Richard Allen*, pp. 48 ff.
22. Richard Allen, op. cit., p. 61. In his Journal entry for October 25, 1795, Bishop Asbury wrote: "The Africans of this town desire a church which, in temporals, shall be altogether under their direction, and ask greater privileges than the white stewards and trustees ever had a right to claim."
23. Richard Allen, op. cit., p. 26.
24. Ibid., p. 35.

CHAPTER VI

1. Charles Wesley, *Richard Allen*, pp. 124–28, for origin of the churches in Baltimore, Wilmington, New York, and elsewhere.
2. Richard Allen, *Life, Experience and Gospel Labors*, p. 25.
3. David Smith, *Biography of Reverend David Smith*. Also, Charles Wesley, op. cit., p. 130.
4. Josephus R. Coan, "Daniel Coker: 19th Century Black Church Organizer, Educator and Missionary," *Journal of the Interdenominational Theological Center*, III, No. I, Fall 1975, pp. 17–31.
5. Charles Wesley, op. cit., pp. 141–42.
6. Peter Spencer, History of Union American Methodist Church printed in *Proceedings of the Quarto-centennial Conference of the African M.E. Church of South Carolina, May 15–17, 1889* (Charleston, S.C., 1890), pp. 229–34, B. W. Arnett, ed. Also, Charles Wesley, op. cit. pp. 133–34.
7. Charles Wesley, op. cit., p. 134.
8. David Smith, op. cit., p. 24.
9. David Smith, op. cit., p. 24.
10. Daniel A. Payne, *Recollections of Seventy Years* (New York: Arno Press and The New York Times, 1968), pp. 100–1.
11. B. W. Arnett, *Proceedings of the Quarto-centennial Conference of the African M.E. Church of South Carolina, May 15–17, 1889* (Charleston, S.C., 1890), p. 384.
12. Preface to the Discipline of the A.M.E. Church.

13. A careful and scholarly biography of Richard Allen is Charles H. Wesley's *Richard Allen, Apostle of Freedom* (Washington, D.C.: Associated Publishers, 1935).

14. Daniel A. Payne, *History of the A.M.E. Church*, Chapter III, "Results of Separation from the M.E. Church."

15. Ibid., p. 28.

16. Ibid., pp. 22, 32.

17. Ibid., p. 23.

18. David H. Bradley, *A History of the A.M.E. Zion Church*, 2 vols. (Nashville, Tenn.: Parthenon Press, 1956), 1, pp. 71–72.

19. Daniel A. Payne, op. cit., p. 53.

20. Charles H. Wesley, *Richard Allen*, p. 96. Incidentally, when the spurious slave catcher was jailed for falsely seizing Allen, it was Allen who had him released from jail.

21. Charles Wesley, op. cit., pp. 185–88.

22. Daniel A. Payne, op. cit., p. 47.

23. Ibid., p. 65. Santo Domingo is the eastern and Spanish part of the island Haiti.

24. Ibid., pp. 66 f.

25. Ibid., p 106.

26. Charles Wesley, op. cit., pp. 163–64.

27. *Minute and Trial Book,* Bethel A.M.E. Church, Philadelphia, 1822–35, p. 82.

28. Ibid., pp. 108 f.

29. Ibid., p. 110.

30. Carol V. R. George, *Segregated Sabbaths: Richard Allen and the Emergence of Separate Black Churches, 1760–1840* (New York: Oxford University Press, 1973), pp. 93–97.

31. Charles Wesley, op. cit., p. 219. The management of businesses and care for his family in addition to the tasks and responsibilities of his episcopal and ministerial offices all bear witness to the energy, the drive and the determination of this remakable man.

32. Richard Allen, *Life, Experience and Gospel Labors,* "Acts of Faith," p. 43.

33. Charles Wesley, op. cit., pp. 253–54.

34. R. R. Wright, *Bishops of the A.M.E. Church* (Philadelphia: A.M.E. Sunday School Union, 1963), pp. 72 ff.

35. Daniel A. Payne, *History of the A.M.E. Church*, p. 95.

36. Ibid., p. 95.

37. Ibid., p. 96.

38. Ibid., p. 96.

39. Ibid., p. 97.

40. Ibid., p. 107.

41. Ibid., p. 112.

42. Ibid., p. 117.

43. Ibid., p. 148.

44. Ibid., pp. 152–53.

45. Penelope Bullock, *The Negro Periodical Press in the United States, 1838–1909* (Unpublished Ph.D. thesis, University of Michigan, 1971), pp. 24–25.

46. Daniel A. Payne, *History of the A.M.E. Church*, p. 98.

47. Ibid., p. 98.
48. Ibid., p. 100.
49. Ibid., p. 142.
50. Ibid., pp. 133–34.
51. Ibid., p. 115.
52. Ibid., p. 121.
53. Daniel A. Payne, *Recollections of Seventy Years*, pp. 11–17.
54. Ibid., pp. 27 f.
55. Ibid., pp. 64–65.
56. Ibid., pp. 75–76.
57. Daniel A. Payne, *History of the A.M.E. Church*, pp. 141–42.
58. Ibid., pp. 168–69.
59. John B. McMaster, *A History of the People of the United States*, VI, p. 231. (Quoted by Wade C. Barclay, *History of Methodist Missions*, II, p. 59.)
60. The Methodist "Articles of Faith" were Wesley's adaptation of the Thirty-nine Articles of the Church of England.
61. "The General Rules," A.M.E. Discipline, Rule 4.
62. Daniel A. Payne, *History of the A.M.E. Church*, p. 101.
63. Daniel A. Payne, *Recollections of Seventy Years*, p. 255. Also, J. R. Coan, *Daniel A. Payne, Christian Educator*, p. 130.
64. Daniel A. Payne, *History of the A.M.E. Church*, pp. 412–18.
65. Ibid., pp. 112 f.
66. Ibid., p. 99.
67. Ibid.
68. Daniel A. Payne, *Recollections of Seventy Years*, p. 140.
69. The A.M.E. Church had representation at the Evangelical Alliance in London in 1846 in the person of the Reverend M. M. Clarke. Daniel Payne was also to have gone but was turned back by a storm at sea.

CHAPTER VII

1. See Chapter III.
2. *Annals of the New York Conference, Methodist Episcopal Church*, p. 209. Also, D. H. Bradley, *History of the A.M.E. Zion Church*, Part I, 1796–1872 (Nashville, Tenn.: Parthenon Press, 1950), pp. 46 ff.
3. The white person was probably needed to see that the meetings stayed in the theological and ritualistic tradition of Methodism, as well as to be a monitor against rebellious activity.
4. Christopher Rush, *A Short Account of the Rise and Progress of the African Methodist Episcopal [Zion] Church in America* (New York: Privately published, 1843), p. 10. Also, Seaman, *Annals of New York Methodism*, says these were the only Negro Methodist preachers at this time. (Bradley, op. cit., p. 45).
5. The Episcopal Church waived the requirement of Greek and Hebrew and ordained Jones a deacon in 1795 and a priest in 1804.
6. Christopher Rush, op. cit., pp. 9–10. Also D. H. Bradley, op. cit., p. 45.
7. Christopher Rush, op. cit., pp. 9–10. John J. Moore, *History of the A.M.E.Z. Church;* Bradley, op. cit., p. 48. Negro projects at that time were commonly labeled "African."

8. Christopher Rush, op. cit., pp. 10–11.

9. Ibid., p. 13. Also, Bradley, op. cit., p. 49.

10. Bradley, op. cit., pp. 50–54.

11. Ibid., p. 51.

12. Bradley, op. cit., pp. 50–54.

13. Christopher Rush, op. cit., pp. 25–26.

14. Ibid., p. 11.

15. Ibid., p. 30.

16. Ibid., pp 32–51.

17. Minutes of the Common Council of the City of New York, 1784–1831. Also quoted in Bradley, op. cit., pp. 65–68.

18. Christopher Rush, op. cit., pp. 56 f.

19. Bradley, op. cit., pp. 83–84.

20. Christopher Rush, op. cit., pp. 38–39. Also Bradley, op. cit., p. 78; Moore, op. cit., p. 43.

21. Rush op. cit., pp. 56–58. Also Bradley, op. cit., pp. 92–93.

22. Rush, op. cit., pp. 72 f.; Bradley, op. cit., p. 90.

23. David H. Bradley, op. cit., p. 95. Also, Christopher Rush, op. cit., p. 78 (1886 ed.).

24. Christopher Rush, op. cit., p. 81; David H. Bradley, op. cit., pp. 97–98.

25. David H. Bradley, op. cit., pp. 96–97.; Christopher Rush, op. cit., p. 74 (1866 ed.).

26. Christopher Rush, op. cit., p. 81; J. J. Moore, *History of the A.M.E. Zion Church in America* (York, Pa., 1884), p. 99.

27. Christopher Rush, op. cit., p. 78 (1866 ed.); David H. Bradley, op. cit., p. 95.

28. David H. Bradley, op. cit., p. 96.

29. Ibid., p. 100; B. F. Wheeler, *The Varick Family* Mobile, Ala. (1906; reprint, 1966), p. 8.

30. David H. Bradley, op. cit., I, p. 91. Christopher Rush, op. cit., p. 70.

31. J. J. Moore, op. cit., pp. 348 f.; J. W. Hood, *One Hundred Years of the African Methodist Episcopal Zion Church* (New York: A.M.E.Z. Book Concern, 1895), pp. 162 ff.

32. David N. Bradley, op. cit., p. 99.

33. J. J. Moore, op. cit., pp. 349 ff.

34. Ibid., p. 350.

35. "He was possessed of extraordinary legislative ability . . . and his opinion generally controlled church legislation." Moore, op. cit., p. 352.

36. David N. Bradley, op. cit., p. 102.

37. David N. Bradley, op. cit., p. 98. Also, Christopher Rush, op. cit., p. 81 (1866 ed.).

38. J. J. Moore, op. cit., pp. 87–91, 103.

39. Ibid., pp. 54 f.

40. J. W. Hood, op. cit, p. 133.

41. Ibid., p. 143.

42. J. J. Moore, op. cit., pp. 54 ff.

43. Ibid., pp. 370 f.

44. David N. Bradley, op. cit., p. 104. J. Harvey Anderson, ed., The Official Directory of the A.M.E.Z. Church in America (New York, 1895).

Also, W. J. Walls, *The African Methodist Episcopal Zion Church* (Charlotte, N.C.: A.M.E. Zion Publishing House, 1974), pp. 129–32. This volume by Bishop Walls is a detailed, carefully researched compendium of historical information on the Zion Church.

45. Prior to 1864 the presiding officers of the A.M.E.Z. denomination were called Superintendents. The title "Bishop" was adopted in the General Conference of 1864. Both James Varick and Christopher Rush were called General Superintendents, but in 1852 the word "General" was dropped.

46. J. J. Moore, op. cit., pp. 221–31.

47. For the clearest statement on the controversy, see Hood, op. cit., pp. 71–80.

48. J. J. Moore, op. cit., pp. 219 ff.

49. David H. Bradley, op. cit., pp. 107–23.

50. Quoted by Bradley from the Jamestown, New York *Sun*, September 3, 1950. Bradley, op. cit., pp. 109–10.

51. David H. Bradley, op. cit., pp. 110 f.

52. J. W. Hood, op. cit., p. 15.

53. For the life of Frederick Douglass, see: *Narrative of the Life of Frederick Douglass an American Slave* (Written by Himself) (Boston: Anti-Slavery Office, 1845), *My Bondage and My Freedom* (New York: Miller and Onlor, 1855), *Life and Times of Frederick Douglass* (Cleveland, O.: Hamilton, Rowell & Co., 1883).

54. W. J. Walls, op. cit., pp. 153–55.

55. Jermain W. Loguen, *The Rev. J. W. Loguen as a Slave and as a Freeman* (Syracuse, N.Y., J.G.K. Truair and Co., 1859), pp. 339–40.

56. J. W. Hood, op. cit., p. 180.

57. Earl Conrad, *Harriet Tubman* (Washington, D.C.: Associated Publishers, 1943), p. 61. Also quoted in David H. Bradley.

For another biography of Harriet Tubman, see: Sarah H. Bradford, *Harriet the Moses of Her People* (New York: Lockwood & Son, 1886).

58. David H. Bradley, op. cit., pp. 51–54. Also, Christopher Rush, op. cit., pp 21–22.

CHAPTER VIII

1. *Journal*, General Conference, Methodist Episcopal Church, 1856, p. 199.

2. Daniel A. Payne, *History of the A.M.E. Church*, pp. 20 f.

3. Ibid., p. 14.

4. Christopher Rush, *History of the A.M.E.Z. Church*, p. 32. Also, David H. Bradley, *History of the A.M.E.Z. Church*, I, p. 72.

5. Daniel A. Payne, *History of the A.M.E. Church*, p. 20.

6. Ibid., p. 95.

7. Ibid., p. 20.

8. For a discussion of the Quaker attitude on Negroes, see H. Shelton Smith, *In His Image, But—*, pp. 24–36.

9. Quoted in L. M. Hagood, *The Colored Man in the Methodist Church* (Cincinnati: Cranston and Stowe, 1890), p. 46.

10. Donald G. Mathews, *Slavery and Methodism*, Chapter V.

11. Daniel A. Payne, *History of the A.M.E. Church*, p. 10.
12. L. M. Hagood, op. cit., p. 88; also pp. 72–82 for reasons for the Church's refusals.
13. L. M. Hagood, op. cit., pp. 92 f.
14. *Journal*, General Conference, Methodist Episcopal Church, 1864.
15. J. R. Coan, *Daniel A. Payne, Christian Educator*, p. 98.
16. Ibid., p. 99.
17. Quoted in L. M. Hagood, op. cit., pp. 136–37.
18. See Chapter XIV.
19. L. M. Hagood, op. cit., p. 124.

CHAPTER IX

1. Nathan Bangs, *A History of the Methodist Episcopal* Church (New York: Carlton and Porter, 1860), II, p. 119.
2. Richard Allen, op. cit., pp. 25–27.
3. Wade C. Barclay, *History of Methodist Missions*, I, p. 56.
4. Donald G. Mathews, *Slavery and Methodism* (Princeton, N.J.: Princeton University Press, 1965), pp. 113–47.
5. Wade C. Barclay, op. cit., I, 164–66.
6. Ibid., p. 166.
7. Donald G. Mathews, op. cit., p. 67.
8. Ibid., p. 68.
9. Ibid., p. 68.
10. Ibid., p. 68.
11. Ibid.
12. Ibid., p. 69.
13. Ibid., p. 69.
14. *Southern Christian Advocate*, February 8, 1838, p. 134.
15. Ibid., July 23, 1841, p. 21.
16. Charles C. Pinckney, "An Address delivered in Charleston before the Agricultural Society of South Carolina at Its Anniversary Meeting," Charleston, 1829, pp. 4–5, 10–14, 16–18.
17. In 1836 the South Carolina Conference said that the Scriptures authorized the positions of master and salve, South Carolina Conference Minutes, 1836, p. 30; also 1839, p. 14.
18. South Carolina Conference Minutes, 1833, p. 16; 1834, p. 21; 1838, p. 17; 1839, p. 18; 1841, p. 18; 1843, p. 13.
19. Donald G. Mathews, op. cit., p. 74.
20. Donald G. Mathews, op. cit., pp. 75–76.
21. From a letter of William Capers to Wilbur Fisk, September 12, 1833, quoted in Mathews, op. cit., p. 75.
22. Donald G. Mathews, op. cit., pp. 75–76.
23. Charles Colcock Jones, *The Religious Instruction of the Negroes in the United States* (Savannah, Georgia, 1842; New York: Kraus Reprint Co., 1969), pp. 125–27.
24. Donald G. Mathews, op. cit., pp. 77–78. The passages in Paul's letters to the Ephesians, 6:5–6, and to Timothy, 6:1–2, were stressed to impress the obligation of the slave to be faithful to masters.
25. Capers' catechism was not the only one. Presbyterians, Episcopalians,

and Baptists each had one or more catechisms for the instruction of slaves and children in the rudiments of the Christian faith.

26. Charles Colcock Jones, op. cit., pp. 94–99.

27. Report of the Missionary Society, South Carolina Conference, 1841, pp. 12–17. Charles Colcock Jones, op. cit., p. 86.

28. Donald G. Mathews, op. cit., p. 85; Anti-Slavery Lecture, February 1839, p. 1; Anti-Slavery Reporter, November 1840, p. 70.

29. Ibid., p. 87.

CHAPTER X

1. *The Life, Experience and Gospel Labors of the Rt. Rev. Richard Allen (autobiography)*, p. 29.

2. J. B. Wakeley, *Heroes of Methodism*, pp. 29 ff. Also in Abel Stevens, *History of the Methodist Episcopal Church*, (New York: Carlton & Porter, 1867), III, pp. 360 f.

3. W. P. Harrison, *The Gospel Among the Slaves*, pp. 247–48.

4. H. N. McTyeire, *A History of Methodism* (Nashville, Tenn.: Publishing House of the M.E. Church, South, 1889), p. 589.

5. H. V. Richardson, *Dark Glory* (New York: Friendship Press, 1945), pp. 7–8.

6. Charles H. Wesley, *Richard Allen*, pp. 59 f.

7. "A Dialogue Between a Virginian and an African Minister," a pamphlet by Daniel Coker, Dorothy Porter, ed., in *Negro Protest Pamphlets* (New York: Arno Press, 1965), pp. 15 ff.

8. *The New York Packet* (a newspaper), September 11, 1786.

9. Stevens, *History of the Methodist Episcopal Church* (New York: Carlton and Porter, 1868), 4 vols., II, pp. 174 f.

10. Thomas Coke, *Journal*, Also Stevens, op. cit., p. 176.

11. Abel Stevens, op. cit., pp. 174–57.

12. Francis Asbury, *Journal*, entries for June 29, 1780, and October 27, 1781.

13. Freeborn Garrettson, *The Experience and Travel of Mr. Freeborn Garrettson* (Philadelphia: Parry Hall, 1791), p. 225.

14. Abel Stevens, *History of the M.E. Church*, II, pp. 448–49. Also Freeborn Garrettson, op. cit., p. 224.

15. Asbury's *Journal*, entry for May 21, 1781. Also Freeborn Garrettson, op. cit., p. 220.

16. Abel Stevens, op. cit., p. 175. Note: The correct year of Hosier's death is 1806.

17. W. P. Harrison, *The Gospel Among the Slaves* (Nashville, Tenn.: Publishing House of the M.E. Church, South, 1893), pp. 341–60.

18. Abel Stevens, *History of the Methodist Episcopal Church*, IV, p. 225.

19. William M. Wightman, *William Capers, Including an Autobiography* (Nashville, Tenn.: Southern Methodist Publishing House, 1858), pp. 124–29.

20. William C. Barclay, *History of Methodist Missions*, I, pp. 205 f. Also James B. Finley, *History of the Wyandott Mission* (Cincinnati, Ohio,

1840), p. 76; and W. W. Sweet, *Methodism in American History* (New York: Methodist Book Concern, 1933), pp. 190 ff.

21. Two poetic attempts to recover the quality of early black preaching will be found in James Weldon Johnson's *God's Trombones* and Paul Lawrence Dunbar's poem "An Antebellum Sermon."

22. J. R. Coan, *Daniel Alexander Payne, Christian Educator* (Philadelphia, Pa.: A.M.E. Book Concern, 1935), p. 60.

23. J. R. Coan, op. cit., p. 64.

24. Benjamin Abbott, *Experiences and Gospel Labors of the Reverend Benjamin Abbott* (New York: Hunt and Eaton, 1854), pp. 167–68.

25. Benjamin Abbot, op. cit., p. 114.

26. W. H. Wightman, *William Capers*, p. 54.

27. Winthrop D. Jordan, *White Over Black* (Chapel Hill, N.C.: University of North Carolina Press, 1968), p. 328.

28. Daniel A. Payne, *History of the A.M.E. Church*, pp. 348–51.

CHAPTER XI

1. Daniel A. Payne, *History of the A.M.E. Church*, p. 468.

2. For an example of early white missionary efforts among black freedmen, see C. S. Smith, *History of the A.M.E. Church*, II, p. 54.

3. Daniel A. Payne, op. cit., p. 468.

4. Daniel A. Payne, op. cit., p. 468.

5. Ibid., p. 469.

6. See Chapter XIII.

7. Daniel A. Payne, op. cit., p. 470.

8. Ibid., p. 471.

9. Daniel A. Payne, op. cit., pp. 470 f.

10. Ibid., p. 472.

11. Wesley J. Gaines, *African Methodism in the South* (Atlanta: Franklin Publishing Co., 1890), pp. 18 f.

12. Ibid., p. 13.

13. Statement of the Reverend Andrew Brown, quoted in the Reverend Wesley J. Gaines, *African Methodism in the South or Twenty-Five Years of Freedom* (Atlanta: Franklin Publishing House, 1890), pp. 18–19.

14. W. J. Walls, *The African Methodist Episcopal Zion Church*, pp. 188–90.

15. Charles S. Smith, *History of the African Methodist Episcopal Church*, (Philadelphia: Book Concern of the A.M.E. Church, 1922), pp. 99–100.

16. Ibid., p. 71.

17. Ibid., p. 68.

18. *Discipline of the A.M.E. Church*, 1972, pp. 248 ff. Also, E. A. Adams, Sr., *Yearbook and Historical Guide to the African Methodist Episcopal Church* (Columbia, S.C.: Bureau of Research and History, 1955), pp. 55 ff.

19. *A.M.E. Discipline*, 1972, pp. 250 f.

20. C. S. Smith, *History of the A.M.E. Church*, II, pp. 174 ff.

21. Ibid., pp. 175 ff.

CHAPTER XII

1. W. J. Walls, op. cit., p. 186.
2. J. W. Hood, *One Hundred Years of A.M.E. Zion History*, p. 245.
3. Ibid., pp. 290–91.
4. W. J. Walls, op. cit., pp. 187–88.
5. Ibid., p. 188.
6. J. W. Hood, op. cit., pp. 289–97.
7. W. J. Walls, op. cit., pp. 188 f.
8. Ibid., pp. 189 f.
9. J. W. Hood, op. cit., pp. 285–87.
10. Ibid., p. 367.
11. Ibid.
12. Quoted in Walls, op. cit., p. 192.
13. J. W. Hood, op. cit., pp. 312 f.
14. J. W. Hood, *One Hundred Years of A.M.E. Zion History*, pp. 353–54; W. J. Walls, op. cit., p. 194.
15. Ibid., pp. 332–36.
16. Ibid., pp. 577–80. Also, W. J. Walls, op. cit., p. 196.
17. W. J. Walls, op. cit., pp. 196 f.
18 *The Weekly Anglo-African*, New York, December 16, 1865.
19. Op. cit., 373 f. pp. 373–74.
20. W. J. Walls, op. cit., p. 198.
21. J. W. Hood, *One Hundred Years of A.M.E. Zion. History*, pp. 328–29; W. J. Walls, op. cit., p. 195.
22. W. J. Walls, op. cit., p. 196.
23. W. J. Walls, op. cit., pp. 220–21. Also, the *A.M.E. Zion Quarterly Review*, April 1892, pp. 299–301.
24. W. J. Walls, op. cit., pp. 221 ff.
25. Ibid., p. 199.
26. J. W. Hood, *One Hundred Years of A.M.E. Zion History*, pp. 369–70.
27. W. J. Walls, op. cit., p. 199.
28. J. W. Hood, op. cit., p. 380.
29. W. J. Walls, op. cit., pp. 200–1.
30. For a description of Southern tenancy, see Arthur F. Raper and Ira De A. Reid, *Sharecroppers All* (Chapel Hill, N.C.: University of North Carolina Press, 1941). Also for the black church in the rural South, see H. V. Richardson *Dark Glory*.
31. W. J. Walls, op. cit., p. 244.
32. Ibid., p. 228.
33. Ibid., p. 229.
34. *The Star of Zion*, November 12, 1896.
35. W. J. Walls, op. cit., p. 230.
36. Ibid.
37. Ibid., pp. 232 f.
38. Ibid., p. 233.
39. *Minutes*, Twenty-Seventh Quadrennial Session, p. 259. Also, Walls, op. cit., p. 240.

40. W. J. Walls, op. cit., p. 240.

41. W. J. Walls, op. cit., p. 24.

42. Ibid. p. 242.

43. Ibid., pp. 244 f.

44. Ibid., p. 246.

45. Quadrennial Report, Department of Foreign Missions, 1972. pp. 18–21.

46. W. J. Walls, op. cit., p. 249.

47. *Minutes*, Thirty-Eighth Quadrennial Session, p. 167.

48. Quadrennial Report, Department of Foreign Missions 1972, pp. 15–16; also, W. J. Walls, op. cit., p. 250; Quadrennial Report, Second Episcopal District, 1972, pp. 4–5.

49. W. J. Walls, op. cit., p. 268.

50. Ibid.

51. Ibid., p. 282.

52. Ibid.

53. Ibid., p. 285.

54. Ibid., p. 294.

55. Ibid. p. 289.

56. Ibid., pp. 289 f.

57. Ibid., pp. 294 ff.

58. *Minutes*, Genesee Annual Conference, 1858, p. 15. Also, W. J. Walls, op. cit., p. 284.

59. J. W. Hood, *One Hundred Years of A.M.E. Zion History*, pp. 82–84.

60. See Chapters XIV and XV.

CHAPTER XIII

1. At the time of its founding in 1870 this Church was named "The Colored Methodist Episcopal Church in America." In 1956 the name was officially changed to "The Christian Methodist Episcopal Church."

2. H. N. McTyeire, op. cit., pp. 670 ff.

3. Donald G. Mathews, pp. 81–83.

4. C. H. Phillips, *History of the Colored Methodist Episcopal Church in America* (Jackson, Tenn.: C.M.E. Publishing House, 1898,) pp. 24 ff.

5. C. H. Phillips, op. cit., p. 27.

6. Quoted by C. H. Phillips, op. cit., p. 31.

7. C. H. Phillips, op. cit., p. 35.

8. Daniel A. Payne, *History of the A.M.E. Church*, p. 469.

9. C. H. Phillips, op. cit., pp. 204–8.

10. Daniel A. Payne, loc. cit.

11. C. H. Phillips, op. cit., pp. 50 f.

12. Isaac Lane, *Autobiography of Bishop Isaac Lane, D.D.* (Nashville, Tenn.: Publishing House of the M.E. Church, South, 1916), p. 148.

13. C. H. Phillips, op. cit., pp. 196–204.

14. Ibid., pp. 71 ff.

15. *The Christian Index*, January 1873.

16. *The Christian Index*, June 12, 1873.

17. Quoted in C. H. Phillips, op. cit., p. 58.

18. Ibid., pp. 58 f.

19. Ibid., pp. 213–18.

20. Isaac Lane, op. cit., pp. 70–79.

21. C. H. Phillips, op. cit., pp. 78 f.

22. Ibid., pp. 78–83.

23. C. H. Phillips, op. cit., p. 83.

24. C. H. Phillips, op. cit., p. 106.

25. C. H. Phillips, op. cit., pp. 121 f. Under the twenty-year presidency of Dr. C. A. Kirkendall (now Bishop), 1950–70, the College underwent extensive academic development. It is now a fully accredited college of over eight hundred students.

26. C. H. Phillips, op. cit., p. 129. Since its founding in 1882, Paine College has become one of the leading black private colleges, fully accredited, with 725 students, a physical plant of $5,267,000 value, and an endowment of $427,000. It has had a black President since 1970.

27. Joseph A. Johnson, *Our Faith, Heritage and Church* (privately published, 1975), pp. 112 ff. This book by Bishop Johnson provides a much needed manual on the structure and work of the Church.

28. Ibid., p. 111.

CHAPTER XIV

1. W. E. B. DuBois, *The Souls of Black Folk*, p. 18.

2. W. E. B. DuBois, *Black Reconstruction, 1860–1880*, p. 122.

3. W. E. B. DuBois, *The Souls of Black Folk*, p. 20.

4. James P. Brawley, *Two Centuries of Methodist Concern* (New York: Vantage Press, 1974), pp. 43 f.

5. James P. Brawley, op. cit., p. 45.

6. Isaac Lane, *Autobiography of Bishop Isaac Lane, D.D.* (Nashville, Tenn.: Publishing House of the M.E. Church, South, 1916), pp. 56 f.

7. Report of the *Freedmen's Aid Society, 1866–1875*, p. 3.

8. Ibid., p. 10.

9. *Freedmen's Aid Society Report, 1866*, p. 1.

10. *Sixth Annual Report, Freedmen's Aid Society of the Methodist Episcopal Church, 1873*, pp. 36 f. Also quoted in Brawley, op. cit., pp. 63–64.

11. *Journal of the General Conference of the Methodist Episcopal Church*, 1876, pp. 623 ff.

12. James P. Brawley, op. cit., Parts II and III, pp. 55–154.

13. *General Conference Journal, 1916*, p. 1419. Also quoted in Brawley, op. cit., p. 87.

14. J. P. Brawley, op. cit., p. 211.

15. Ibid., p. 211.

16. Ibid., pp. 67 f.

17. Ibid., p. 81.

18. Ruth Esther Meeker, *Six Decades of Service, 1880 to 1940* (New York: Woman's Home Missionary Society, Methodist Episcopal Church, 1969).

19. James P. Brawley, *Two Centuries of Methodist Concern*, Part IV, "Historical Account of Individual Institutions," pp. 155 ff.

20. Address by Richard S. Rust in *Memorials of Gilbert Haven*, W. H. Daniel, ed. (Boston: B. B. Russell and Co., 1880), pp. 202 ff.

21. A brief but inclusive statement about these workers is in J. B. F. Shaw's *The Negro in the History of Methodism*, pp. 150 ff.; also in J. P. Brawley's *Two Centuries of Methodist Concern* and Ruth Meeker's *Six Decades of Service*. There were also some white Southerners who served among the freedmen, resigning their connection with the M.E. Church, South, and joining Negro annual conferences. One such person was the Reverend O. R. Franklin of Alabama.

22. A.M.E. Discipline, 1972, pp. 250 f.

23. W. J. Walls, *The A.M.E. Zion Church*, pp. 310 ff.

24. Joseph A. Johnson, *Our Faith, Heritage and Church* (privately published, 1975), p. 111.

CHAPTER XV

1. *U. S. Census of Religious Bodies, 1936*, I, p. 79.

2. H. V. Richardson, op. cit., pp. 54–67: "Migration."

3. Daniel A. Payne, *History of the A.M.E. Church*, p. 292.

4. Ibid., pp. 293 f.

5. Ibid., pp. 407 f.

6. W. J. Walls, *The A.M.E. Zion Church*, pp. 242 f.

7. J. R. Coan, "The Redemption of Africa," an article in the *Journal* of the Interdenominational Theological Center, I, No. 2, Spring 1974, pp. 27–37.

8. See Daniel A. Payne, *History of the A.M.E. Church*, pp. 52ff.

9. For example, the service celebrating the outlawing of the American slave trade in 1807 was held in Zion Chapel in New York City with Peter Williams, Jr., preaching the sermon. See Chapter VII.

10. Daniel A. Payne, *Recollections*, pp. 329 f.

11. J. R. Coan, *Daniel A. Payne, Christian Educator*, pp. 128 f.

12. George A. Singleton, *Romance of African Methodism* (New York: Exposition Press, 1952), pp. 162 ff.

13. Reverdy C. Ransom, *The Pilgrimage of Harriett Ransom's Son* (Nashville, Tenn.: A.M.E. Sunday School Union, 1950), p. 272.

14. Ibid., p. 307.

15. Isaac Lane, op. cit., p. 127.

16. Reverdy C. Ransom, *The Pilgrimage of Harriett Ransom's Son*, pp. 273 ff.

17. Ibid., pp. 303 ff.

18. Charles V. Hamilton, *The Black Preacher in America* (New York: William Morrow & Company, Inc., 1972), pp. 158–59.

19. Reverdy C. Ransom, op. cit., p. 272.

20. George A. Singleton, op. cit., pp. 166 ff.

21. An address delivered before the Connectional Council of the A.M.E. Church in 1944, and later published as a pamphlet. Quoted in its entirety in E. A. Adams, Sr., *Yearbook and Historical Guide to the A.M.E. Church*, 1959, pp. 31–42.

22. For a brief account of the efforts at union see J. B. Shaw, *The Negro in the History of Methodism* (Nashville, Tenn.: Parthenon Press, 1954), pp. 125 ff. Also, W. J. Walls, *The A.M.E. Zion Church*, pp. 459–77.

23. W. J. Walls, op. cit., pp. 476 f.

24. W. J. Walls, op cit., pp. 481 f.

CHAPTER XVI

1. See Chapter IV.

2. H. N. McTyeire, op. cit., p. 670.

3. *General Conference Journal, Methodist Episcopal Church, 1856*, "The Bishop's Address," p. 199.

4. A. G. Haygood, *Our Brother in Black* (Nashville, Tenn.: M.E. Church, South, Publishing House, 1881).

5. Willis J. King, "The Negro in Methodism to 1939," in the *Central Christian Advocate*, October 1, 1967, p. 7.

6. Daniel A. Payne, *History of the A.M.E. Church*, p. 10; see also Chapter VIII.

7. Lawrence O. Kline, "The Negro in the Unification of American Methodism," *The Drew Gateway*, Drew University, Madison, N.J., Vol. 34, No. 3, Spring 1964, pp. 128–49.

8. James P. Brawley, "Methodist Church from 1939," *Central Christian Advocate*, October 15, 1967, p. 3.

9. Willis J. King, op. cit., p. 8.

10. Lawrence O. Kline stresses this point in his article "The Negro in the Unification of American Methodism," *The Drew Gateway*, Spring 1964, p. 130.

11. Lawrence O. Kline, op. cit., p. 136.

12. Ibid.

13. James P. Brawley, op. cit., p. 4.

14. John W. Haywood, "This Damnable Unification Plan," *Southwestern Christian Advocate*, Vol. 57, No. 18, April 23, 1936, p. 261.

15. J. P. Brawley, op. cit., p. 4.

16. Ibid., p. 4.

17. J. Beverly F. Shaw, *The Negro in the History of Methodism* (Nashville, Tenn.: Parthenon Press, 1954), pp. 170–72.

18. Lawrence O. Kline, op. cit., p. 144.

19. *Central Christian Advocate*, Vol. 142, No. 2, January 15, 1967, p. 6.

20. Lawrence O. Kline, op. cit., p. 145.

21. J. B. F. Shaw, *The Negro in the History of Methodism* (Nashville, Tenn.: Parthenon Press, 1954), pp. 189 ff.

22. James P. Brawley, *Central Christian Advocate*, October 16, 1967, p. 7.

23. James P. Brawley, op. cit., p. 8.

24. Grover C. Bagby, *Christian Advocate*, November 8, 1966.

25. Gayraud C. Wilmore, *Black Religion and Black Radicalism*, pp. 271 ff.

26. From an address delivered by Clayton E. Hammond, March 18, 1975, printed in proceedings of the Eighth Annual Meeting of B.M.C.R., in its publication entitled *NOW*.

Index

Abbott, Benjamin, 37, 40–41, 64, 69, 121, 182
Abolitionism(ists), 51, 52, 55, 58, 72, 105–6, 151, 159, 185–86, 286, 287; leaders, 140–42
Adams, Lewis, 214
Addison, Joseph, 18
Africa, 7, 8, 14–15, 19, 217–18, 290; A.M.E. Church, 203; C.M.E., 238–39; culture/history, 14–15; emigration, 94, 115, 215 (see American Colonization Society); "the Fatherland," 214; independence, 218, 256; languages, 15; missions to, 202–3, 238–39, 255–56; "redeeming," 215, 254–55, 256; religion, 14–15; scholars, 15, 17, 293 n 1; South, 202, 203, 218; tribes, 16ff. (see also under country); West, 14, 202, 217, 238–39, 255; Zion Church, 214ff.
"African," use of term, 129
African Chapel. See under John Street Church
African Christians, 202
"African Church," term, 125–26
African Conference, 128
African Memorial Banks, 217, 256
African Methodist Episcopal Church. See A.M.E. Church
African Methodist Episcopal Church Magazine, 100–1, 106

African Methodist Episcopal Zion Church, 117–47. See A.M.E.Z. Church
Afro-Americans, use of term, xv
Aggrey, James E. K., 216
Agriculture, 213, 245, 253–54
Alabama, 194, 198, 209–10
Allegheny Conference, 137
Allen, L. Scott, 281
Allen, Richard, 37, 65, 67–75, 77–79, 88, 95, 120, 122, 126–27, 129, 133, 170, 176, 266, 299 n 20; achievements, 186; A.M.E., 80ff., 85–87, 91, 92–97, 112, 114; biography, 94; bishop, 170, 174, 257–58; characteristics, 82, 96, 134, 136, 258; Christian Endeavor Fellowship, 201; death, 92–97, 112, 114; education, 121; family, 95, 97; "Father Allen," 83, 96; influence, 94, 184; ordination, 148, 149; prestige, 82, 97; slavery, 185; successors, 97
Allen, Richard, Jr., 81, 84, 95
Allen, Sarah (Mrs. Richard), 97
Allen, Yorke S., Jr., 13
Allenites, 126, 127, 134, 135–36, 149
Allen University, 250
Alleyne, Cameron C., 217, 218
Alstork, John W., 209–10
A.M.E. Church, 65, 76–116, 126, 156, 288, 300 n 69; budget, 200;

C.M.E., 235–36; Conferences,
84ff., 93, 98, 149, 186; Discipline,
99, 104, 107; "Dollar Money
Plan," 200; education, 103–4,
106–8, 112, 200ff., 203, 250;
Episcopacy, 113–16, 202, 257ff.,
260–62, 265; ethical/cultural
standards, 108–11; evangelists, 99;
first/second decades, 84–92;
founders(founding), 75, 77, 82, 83,
99, 108–9, 117, 158, 174, 287, 297 *n*
1; growth, 97–99, 111–12, 149ff.,
202–3, 288, rate, 253–54; historians,
87, 149, 199; independence, 224;
leaders, 84ff., 90, 113, 114, 116, 149,
271; literature/publications,
99–104, 201, 202, 203; membership,
85–86, 87, 97, 98, 112, 114, 146, 225,
228, 234, 270; ministry, 81–88, 112,
170, 174, 196; missionaries, 113,
202–3, 255; music, 111;
organization, 112, 147, 200; origin,
149; Philadelphia Convention,
80–84, 99; Reconstruction/
expansion, 191–203, 205ff.; *Review*,
202; "Rules," 110–11; salaries, 112;
separation, 126, 146–47; setbacks,
89; slavery, 90–92, 115–16; Sunday
Schools, 200ff.; union, 266, 268;
Young People's Program, 200–2.
See Africa; Allen, Richard, *and*
Payne, Daniel A.
America, 5–6, 8, 15, 17; Methodism,
13, 35–49; church membership, 30;
slave trade, 19, 20. *See* American
Colonies
American Board of Commissioners
for Foreign Missions, 159
American Colonies, 42, 63; "Great
Awakening," 8; religion, 8, 37, 39,
285; slavery, 21–23
American Colonization Society, 94,
115, 153, 202; objectives, 159
American Revolution, 24, 25, 37, 51,
57, 69, 285; ideology, 119
American Wesleyan Observer, The,
58
A.M.E.Z. Church, 87, 114, 117–47,
156; -A.M.E., 98, 200, 204ff., 212,
213, 218; assessments, 220; budget,
220; Conferences, 135, 137–38, 139;
dissidents, 137–39, 210 (*see under*
name); education, 214, 216,
221–22, 250; Episcopacy, 257ff.,
268; founders(founding), 117,
121, 143–46, 158, 174, 287; growth,
135–37, 213, 288, rate, 253–54;
historians, 121, 175; independence,
224; leaders, 132–35, 136, 140–42,
205ff., 210–12, 222; membership,
137, 146, 148, 225, 230, 270;
ministry, 185, 208, 209, 222–23;
missions, 137, foreign, 214–18, 255,
to South, 204ff.; Mother Church,
206; name, 123; organization, 138,
147, 219–21, 300 *n* 45;
Reconstruction/expansion,
204–23; rural areas, 213–14;
separation, 126–31, 146–47;
slavery, 139–43, 185; Sunday
School, 221–22; trustees, 123, 124,
125; union, 266ff.; West Indies,
218–19; women's organizations,
220–21; writings on, 141. *See* John
Street Church
Ancestor worship, 16
Anderson, James, 131
Anderson, William, 79, 80
Andrew, James O., 26, 59–61, 159,
161, 286
Anglican Church, 3, 12, 49, 284. *See*
Church of England (C of E)
Angola, 7, 8, 14
Animism, 16
Apostles, 37
Arabs, 14
Arago, 192, 193
Arizona, 212
Arkansas, 198, 211
Arminianism, 223
Asbury, Francis, 12, 37, 38, 43–45,
48, 56, 70ff., 74, 78, 79, 120, 121,
132, 155; characteristics, 134, 168;
Hosier, H., 171–73; *Journal*, 52,
84, 171, 172; ordination, 296 *n* 13;
position, 53, 70; slavery, 52, 54
Asbury Church, 125, 126, 127, 128,
129–30, 131–32, 134, 137, 144, 146
Atlanta, Ga., 237, 249, 268, 274;

Gammon Theological Seminary, 245; I.T.C., *vi*, 250, 268
Attleboro, Pa., 80, 85; separation, 66, 74, 80
Augusta, Ga., 195, 210
Austin, Alexander, 236

Bacon, Thomas, 30, 31
Baeta, C. C., 293 *n* 1
Bagby, Grover C., 281
Bahama Islands Conference, 218–19
Baltimore, 37, 44, 59, 76, 78, 79, 80; Conferences, 53, 137, 150, 192, A.M.E., 84–85, 86, 90, 91, 103, 113–15; separation, 66, 74
Bambuti tribe, 16–17
Bangs, Nathan, 151, 159
Baptism, 12, 49
Baptists, 25ff., 159, 165, 169–70, 181, 242; Convention for Foreign Missions, 159
Barbados, 216
Barclay, Wade, 109
Bastide, Roger, 15–16
Baumfree, Isabella, 141. *See* Truth, Sojourner
Baxter, Amos, 175
Beanes, Scipio, 91, 92
Beard, James A., 226
Beaufort, N.C., 206
Beebe, Joseph A., 232
Bell, J. W., 231, 236
Benezet, Anthony, 51, 52
Bennett College, 248
Bethelites, 122, 136, 149, 266. *See* A.M.E. Church
Bethel Society, 78
Bethune-Cookman College, 248–49
Bias, David, 124, 186
Bible, 26, 28, 181
Bishop, William, 138
Bishopric. *See* Episcopacy
Black, Jonah, 93
"Black caucuses," 282, 283
Black churches, 131, 263–65, 288; current developments, 253–68; ecumenicity, 266–68; Episcopacy, 256–66; growth, 253ff.; influence, 258; leaders, 257–58, 266;

membership, 290; problems, 288–89; prospects, 289–91; public service, 268; union, 266–68, 289, 290. *See also under* name
Black Code laws, 98, 115
Black history, 179
Black Methodism, 84. *See* A.M.E. Church *and* Separation
Black Methodists for Church Renewal (B.M.C.R.), 77, 283. *See* Separation
Black preaching, 180-83
Blacks, use of term, *xi*
"Black theology" movement, 282
Blackwell, George L., 212
Blair, Montgomery, 204–5
Boardman, Richard, 36, 37, 45, 48–49
Boyer, President (Haiti), 90
Bradwell, Charles, 193
Brawley, Dr. James P., 241, 244, 246, 274, 275; *Two Centuries of Methodist Concern*, 244
Brazil, 218
Breeding, Dr. M. L., 239
Bridgeport, Conn., 85
British Guiana, 218
British Honduras, 218
Broadie, George W., 194
Brooklyn, 87
Brown, Andrew, 196–97
Brown, John M., 194, 198
Brown, Morris, 85, 86, 89–90, 97, 106, 111, 174, 258, 259, 288; Allen, 90; A.M.E., 89–90; bishop, 114; death, 112, 114; slavery, 185
Brown, William, 121, 124
Brunswick, Maine, 85
Bryan, Andrew, 170, 295 *n* 23
Bryant, Dr. Ira T., 201
Buffalo, N.Y., 139
Bull, Harry, 175
Bunch, Anthony, 211
Bunker Hill, 42
Bunton, Bishop, 239
Burns, Francis, 153
Burrows, A. J., 234
Butler, William F., 205, 210

Cain, R. H., 193, 194
California, 200, 212

Calvinism, 9, 223
Cameroom: Duala, religion, 16
Campbell, J. P., 198
Camp meetings, 99, 179, 182–83
Canada, 94, 137, 140, 141–42;
    A.M.E., 112; Zion Church, 214ff.
Candler, Warren A., 278
Candler School of Theology, *vi*
Capers, William, 160, 161, 162–63,
    164, 176, 182–83, 286; Mission to
    the Slaves, 175
Caribbean Islands, cults, 29
Carman, William, 131, 174
Carr, Augustus T., 194
Cartwright, Andrew, 215–16
Catholicism, 16, 29
Central Jurisdiction plan, 128
Champion, James, 75, 77, 80, 85;
    A.M.E., 99
Charisma, 180–81, 182, 183
Charleston, S.C., 104, 288; A.M.E.,
    85, loss, 87, 89–90, 97; postwar,
    192–93
Chavis, John, 170
Christian Advocate, 281
Christian Endeavor Movement, 222
Christian Index, 232, 236, 238
Christianity, 24, 27–28, 47, 67;
    -slavery, incompatibility, 47
Christian Methodist Episcopal
    Church, 224–39. *See* C.M.E.
    Church
Christian Recorder, 202
Christmas Conference (1784), 53,
    70, 81, 296 *n* 13
Christology, 180
Churchill, W. P., 236
Church of England (C of E), 3, 5,
    24, 239, 296 *n* 13; American
    church independence, 70;
    Methodism, 12, 49; Thirty-nine
    Articles, 300 *n* 60. *See* Anglican
    Church
Cincinnati, Ohio, 247, 280
Civil rights, 280, 282, 290
Civil War, 114, 151, 154, 205, 206,
    211, 240, 241, 287, 288; aftermath,
    240ff.; end, 191–92, 207; Northern
    Church, 154–55
Claflin University, 245, 249

Clair, Matthew W., Sr., 272, 275–76
Clark, Davis W., 242–43
Clark, Mrs. D. W., 247
Clark College, 244, 249
Clement, George C., 217
Clinton, I. C., 208
Clinton, J. J., 204off., 212, 250;
    characteristics, 204, 208, 266
C.M.E. Church, 198, 224–39; Africa,
    238–39; A.M.E., 235–36; budget,
    238; education, 236–38, 250;
    Episcopacy, 228, 232, 261; foreign
    missions, 256; founding, 210, 224,
    226–27, 288, 307 *n* 1; growth, 288,
    rate, 253; leadership, 230, 238, 261;
    M.E. South, 270; name, 307 *n* 1;
    organization, 193, 237–38;
    publications, 238; Reconstruction/
    expansion, 224–39; union, 267ff.
Coan, Dr. J. R., *vi*, 203
Coke, Dr. Thomas, 37, 53, 54, 70,
    155, 296 *n* 13; Hosier, 171, 172;
    Journal, 171
Coker, Daniel, 75, 77, 78–79, 170,
    202; A.M.E., 80–82, 85, 99;
    characteristics, 81, 174;
    *A Dialogue Between a Virginian
    and an African Minister*, 79;
    education, 121, 171
Coker, Edward, 78
Coleman, C. D., 238
Colleges, 202. *See under* name
Collins, George, 124, 129
Colorado, 200
Colored, use of term, *xi*
Colored Methodist Episcopal
    Church, name change, 307 *n* 1.
    See C.M.E.
Communion, 12
Confederacy, postwar, 241
Conference in Leeds, 36
Conferences, 263–65. *See under*
    Church *and* city
Congo, 8
Congregationalists, 159, 205, 242
Consultation on Church Union, 267
Converts (conversion), 8, 11, 13,
    24ff., 35ff., 48, 49, 52, 62, 63, 70,
    163, 179; Freedmen, 242; slaves,
    161; typical, 68

Cook, Phineas, 125
Cook, Thomas, 124
Cooper, Ezekiel, 55, 128, 145
Corinthians, I, 178
Cornish, Tillman, 131
Corr, Joseph M., 84, 100
Cosmology, 180
Cotton, 22, 23, 213; economy, 57;
    gin, 50
Council of Bishops (A.M.E.), 201
Covel, Dr. James, 131
Croger, Benjamin, 87
Croger, Peter, 87
Cuff, Reuben, 80
Cults, African-oriented, 29
Curry, E. H., 210–11
Curry, G. E., 262

Daniel Payne College, 250
Davage, Dr. M. S., 275, 276–77
Davenport, Honor J., vi
Davis, Jefferson, 241
Davis, M. H., 262
Dawber, Dr. Mark A., 278
Day, William Howard, 220
Delaware, 36, 53, 63, 98, 137, 272;
    Conference, 153; separation, 76;
    slavery, 21, 98
Demerara, 218
Denmark Vesey plot, 89, 185
Denny, Collins, 278
Derry, Solomon, 209
Dillard University, 249
Discrimination,
    ideological/theological, 282. See
    Racial discrimination
District of Columbia, 137
"Doctrines and Discipline of the
    African Methodist Episcopal
    Church in America," 129
Douglass, Frederick, 58, 140, 141,
    185; fame, 140
Doyle, B. W., 238
Drew University, vi; Theological
    Seminary, 278, 280
Dublin, Morris, 93
DuBois, W. E. B.: Souls of Black
    Folk, 240
Dunston, Alfred G., 218
Durham, Clayton, 80

Duval, Nace, 175
Dwane, James M., 203

Ecumenism, 115–16, 267–68; first
    Conference, 268; spirit, 273
Edidaha, J. H. U., 239
Editors, abolitionist, 58
Education, 88, 89, 90, 92, 101, 108,
    154, 163, 181, 197, 209, 220, 242,
    243, 255, 288; A.M.E., 101–3;
    200–2, 250; A.M.E.Z., 250; Black
    churches, 223, 249–50; C.M.E.,
    250; desire for, 161; M. E.
    colleges, 248–49; of ministry,
    103–4, 106–8, 120–21 (see under
    Preachers); postwar, 214; prewar,
    222; prohibitions, 103; public, 186,
    206; segregation, 280. See
    Freedmen's Aid Society; Women's
    Home Missionary Society and
    under denomination
Edwards, John, 124, 132
Edward Waters College, 250
Eichelberger, Dr. James W., 221,
    222
Ekop, E. B., 239
Elizabethtown, N.J., 135
Emancipation, 142, 199, 215, 240,
    288; law (1829), 141; number of
    slaves, 243; Proclamation, 192
Embury, Philip, 35–37, 42, 43, 117,
    284
Emigrationists, 202
Emory University, vi
England, 3, 8, 13, 15, 42; Church of,
    3 (see Church of England and
    Anglican Church); colonists, 15,
    42–43, 219; healers, 17;
    Methodism, 12; slavery, 21;
    Society for the Propagation of
    the Gospel, 24; Zion Church, 219
Episcopacy (or Bishopric), 256–66,
    289; autocracy, 260–61, 265;
    "Functions, Authority,
    Limitations," 265; leadership, 266;
    misconduct, 262; nature/power,
    223
Episcopal Church (Episcopalians),
    27, 159; ministry, 300 n 5;
    missionaries, 165; Negroes, 73, 74

Europe, 14, 57, 95

Evangelical Alliance (London), 300
n 69

Evangelism, 159, 181, 288;
movements, 169–70

Evangelists, 24, 25, 41–42, 49, 62, 69,
70, 136, 173; A.M.E., 99; noted, 68.
See also Preachers

Evans, Henry, 37, 170, 176–79, 198;
death, 176, 178–79; faith, 180;
influence, 185; reputation, 176

Evans, James E., 225

Evil, 18–19

Exum, John M., 239

Faith, 180

Fayetteville, N.C., 176–79, 198, 206

Federal Council of Churches, 273

Federal Councils of Churches of
Christ, 267

First National Negro Convention,
94–95

Fisk, Clinton B., 243

Fisk University, 243

Flemister, Wilson, *vi*

Fletcher, Melvina, 204–5

Florida, 194, 205, 207, 211

Flushing, N.Y., 135

Foreign missions, 254–55, 290;
C.M.E., 238–39; Zion Church,
214–18

France, 8, 15; slavery, 21

Frazier, J. G.: *The Golden Bough,*
19

Frederick, J. R., 202

Free African Society, 71–72, 186

Freedmen, 201, 208, 247–49, 253; Aid
Society, 242–47, 249; churches,
242, 249–50; education, 242–49;
problems, 240ff.

Freedmen's Bureau, 242

Freedom, Negro, 240–41

Freedom Journal, 94

Free Labor Society, 186

Freeney, Charles, *vi*

Fugitive slave (s), 136, 139, 141–42,
212; laws, 98, 113, 185

Gaff, Henry, 71

Gaines, Wesley J., 195–96

Galbreath, George, 138

Gammon Theological Seminary,
245, 249, 274

Garnett, Henry H., *xi*

Garrettson, Freeborn, 37, 42, 46, 49,
68, 130, 151, 287; Hosier, 171,
172–73; slaves, 52–53; writings, 171

Garrison, William Lloyd, 58, 141;
The Liberator, 58

Gatch, Philip, 37, 39–40, 53

Genesee Conference, 137, 223

George, Bishop, 128, 130, 179

George, Carol V., 94

George, David, 169–70

Georgia, 5–6, 8, 9, 56, 170, 193, 194,
196, 210; A.M.E.Z., 210; Black
church membership, 159;
Conferences, 56–57, 210

Germany, 35

Ghana, 14, 15, 239, 255, 256

Ghettos (urban), 184

Gilbert, John Wesley, 238

Gillard, Nicholas, 80

God, 16; -man, relationship, 16–17;
slaves belief in, 27–28

Gold Coast (Ghana), 216

Golden Bough, The, 19

Gold Rush, 200

Gomez, Joseph, 264

Gospel message, 62–63

Gough, Henry D., 45, 47

"Great Awakening," 8

Greece, Ancient, 19

Greene, Dr. Sherman L., Jr., 202

Greensboro, N.C., 248

'Gregg, J. A., 203

Haiti, 90–91, 92; Zion Church, 218

Hall, Don Carlos, 85, 100

Hall, James D. S., 192

Halloway, Richard, 175

Hamilton, Charles V., 263: *Black
Preacher in America,* 262–63

Hamilton, James A., 90

Hammond, Clayton E., 283

Hammond, Jupiter, 8

Hampton Institute, 214

Harden, Henry, 80, 86, 87

Harding, Francis A., 59

Harlem, 135

Harlston, Alex, 175
Harris, Catherine, 140
Harris, M. L., 281
Haven, Gilbert, 249
Hayes, Rutherford B., 247
Haygood, A. G.: *Our Brother in Black*, 270
Haynes, Lemuel, 170
Haywood, Dr. John W., 274
Healers, 17
Hebrews, 16
Heck, Barbara, 35, 284
Henry, Patrick, 50
Herskovitz, Melville, 15
Hill, Dr. Charles L., 265
Hill, David, 205
Hill, Stephen, 80, 81, 84
Historians, 45
Hobart, Bishop, 129
Hogarth, George, 100, 106
Holsey, Lucius H., 231, 232, 237, 266
Holy Communion, 49
Home Missions Council, 278
Hood, J. W., 133, 136, 205–6, 208, 223; on ministry, 209; *One Hundred Years of A.M.E. Zion History*, 207
Hood Theological Seminary, 250
Hopkey, Sophia, 5–6, 10
Hosier, Harry (Black Harry), 37, 120, 170, 182; characteristics, 171–73; death, 176; reputation, 176
Hough, Dean Lynn Harold, 278, 280
Huston-Tillotson College, 249
Hutchinson, Sylvester, 131
Hymns, 18

Idowu, E. Bolaja, 293 *n* 1
Indentured servants, 21
Indiana, 112, 137
Indians, 7, 24, 41, 136, 160, 179; Choctaws, 7; Wesley, 5, 6–7; Wyandot, 179
Industrial Revolution, 12, 284
Interdenominational Theological Center (I.T.C.), *vi*, 250, 268
International Council of Christian Education, 268

Ireland, 13, 35
Ivory Coast, 16

Jackson, Andrew, 258
Jackson, Edward, 80
Jackson, G. L., 260
Jackson, M. E., 260
Jackson, Tenn., 226, 228, 237
Jacobs, Francis, 121, 124
Jamaica, 218, 219
James, Thomas, 140, 185
Jamestown, N.Y., 139, 140
Jarratt, Devereaux, 54
Jefferson, Thomas, 22, 50
Jehovah, 16
Jeschke, Dr. Channing, *vi*
Jesus: as healer, 17; slaves identity with, 47
"Jim Crow," 271; railroad cars, 140
Jinnings, Darius, 71, 72
Johnson, Edward, 131
Johnson, Hamilton, 215
Johnson, James B., 211
John Street Church, 36, 63, 118ff., 121, 123, 127, 143; African Chapel, 118, 121–22, 132, 137, 143; agreement with Methodist Church, 123–24; congregation, 118; preachers, 120; trustees, 123, 124
Jonathan, Edith, *vi*
Jones, Absalom, 71, 72, 73–74, 77–78, 82, 120, 170; achievements, 186; death, 74; education, 121; influence, 184; slavery, 185
Jones, Charles C., 27, 29
Jones, Joshua H., 261–62
Jones, Robert E., 272, 274, 276, 278–79
Jones, S. T., 210
Journalists, 84
Judaeo-Christian tradition, 16; -African parallels, 16–17, 18

Kansas, 199–200
Keener, John C., 225
Kentucky, 205, 210–11, 242, 272
Kenya: Akamba, religion, 16
Key West, Fla., 207
King, C. A., 208

King, John, 37
King, Willis J., 271, 272, 274
Kirkendall, Dr. C. A., 308 *n* 25
Kittrell College, 250
Ku Klux Klan, 199, 209, 246

Lacy, J. W., 218
Lake Erie, 139
Lambert, William, 86–87
Lambuth, Bishop, 238
Lancaster, Pa., riots, 57
Lane, Isaac, 232, 233–34, 241–42, 261, 266
Lane College, 237, 250
"Lay preachers," 11
Leaders(ship), 257–58, 290; volunteer, 169; women, 247–48. *See* Leaders *under* name *and under* organization
Leigh, C. C., 192
Lewis, A. D., 108
Liberator, The, 58
Liberia, 153, 174, 202, 255; Conference, 216; Zion Church, 215, 216
Liele, George, 170
Lincoln, Abraham, 115, 154, 191, 258
Literacy, 26. *See* Education
Little Rock, Ark., 211
Livingstone College, 216, 250
Loguen, Jermain W., 140–42, 185–86
London, England, 268; Birmingham Conference, 219
Long Island, 36, 48, 140, 174; separation, 66, 130
Longworth, Nicholas, 186
Louisiana, 169, 198, 207–8
Louisville, Ky., 61, 112
Luke, St., 17
Luther, Martin, preface to *Epistle to the Romans,* 10
Lutheran Church, 27, 106
Lynch, James, 192

McClaskey, John, 74, 122–23
McConnell, Francis, 280
Mack, Emanuel, 175
McKendree, Bishop, 37, 130
McTyeire, Holland N., 225, 228
Magic, 17, 18, 29

Manumission, 22, 47, 50, 150, 229
March, Jacob, 80
Marriage, slaves, 23
Martin, E. B., 232, 236
Martin, J. A., 238
Maryland, 30, 36, 53, 63, 137, 272, 284; discrimination, 115; restrictions, 98; separation, 76; slavery, 21
Mathews, Donald G., 160, 162
Matthews, Jacob, 86, 113–14, 135
Matthews, W. W., 217
M'biti, John S., 18, 293 *n* 1
M.E. Church, 25, 53, 131, 146, 288; "Articles of Faith," 300 *n* 60; Connection, 134 (*see* separates); elders, 122; failings, 117; founding, 37, 70; Freedmen's Aid Society, 242–49; Negroes, 149–52, 153, 155, 161, 167, 271, membership, 148–49, 157, 159; North, 205, 270–72, 288; offshoots, 146, 266, 269 (*see* A.M.E. Church *and* A.M.E.Z. Church); preachers, 31, 99, Black, 170ff.; separates, 123, 286ff.: first, 76–116 (*see* A.M.E. Church), second, 117–47 (*see* A.M.E.Z. Church); sesquicentennial, 273; South, 56–57, 192ff., 201, 224–31, 235, 232, 238, characteristics, 270, 272, C.M.E., 270, formation, 61, 269, membership, 271; Women's Home Missionary Society, 247–49. *See also* Methodism(ists)
Medicine men, 17, 29
Meeker, Ruth Esther: *Six Decades of Service,* 248
"Meeting Houses," 13, 38, 64
Meharry Medical College, 249
Methodism(ists), 12, 13, 25, 41, 44, 84, 127, 128; aims, 214, 215, 284; beginnings, 35–49, 284ff., holiness movement, 49, leaders, 35 (*see under* name); characteristics, 11, 36, 39, 41, 49, 62–63, 70, 113, 285, 286ff., 288–89 (*see* Episcopacy); British, 42; Discipline, 109–10, 129, 130; "experiential" form, 39–40; founder, 3; growth, 12–13; membership, 54; mission(aries),

26, 27, 240–50, 288: Black
churches, 249–50, Women's Home
Missionary Society, 247–49;
Mother Church, 36; Negroes,
43–49, 117, 284; North/South
attitudes, 158–59; opposition, 12
(*see* Wesley, John B.);
organization, 11–12, 49, 66, 257,
258; pre-Civil War, 33–187:
beginnings, 35–49, continuing,
148–56, mission to slaves, 157–66,
preachers, early Black, 167–87,
separation, 62–75, 117–47 (*see
under* name), slavery, 50–61;
racial problems, 67; segregation in
worship, 64–65; slavery, 25, 26, 27,
43, 285ff., reasons for church
moderation, 56–58; "Societies," 11,
12, 49, 117, 157, 286ff.; united,
272–83; Wesleyan, 13 (*see*
Wesley, John B.). *See* M.E.
Church
Methodist Book Concern, 55
Methodist Episcopal Church. *See*
M.E. Church *and*
Methodism(ists)
"Middle Passage," 20
Miles, William H., 210, 228ff.,
235–36, 250; characteristics, 231,
266
Miles Industrial College, 250
Militants, *xi*
Miller, Isaac, 91
Miller, Thomas, 120, 174
Miller, William, 120, 121, 125, 132,
137, 174
Minority survival, 24
Missionaries, 6, 15, 28, 29, 36, 64, 86,
153, 233–34, 240–50, 255, 256;
A.M.E., 202ff.; "assistants," 184;
characteristics, 294 *n* 29; foreign
(example), 92; to Freedmen,
192ff., 197; number, 161; postwar,
240–50; problems, 162; salaries,
234; to slaves, 26; Zion, 137;
Missions: emphasis on, 159ff.;
foreign, 214–18; Methodism and,
240–50. *See* Missionaries *and*
Mission to the Slaves
Mission to the Slaves, 60, 64, 151,

159–66, 184, 195; assistants, 175;
catechism, 164; failures, 165;
founder, 175; motives, 287;
problems, 161–62; volunteers, 169
Mississippi, 198, 211
Mississippi Industrial College, 250
Missouri, 112, 211, 212, 272
Mohammedanism, 27
Montgomery, Ala., 209
Moore, A. M., 208
Moore, George E., 124
Moore, John J., 133, 135, 136, 200,
212
Moore, William J., 207
Moravian Brethren, 10, 24
Morgan State College, 274
Morris, Robert R., 221
Morris Brown University, 250
Morristown (Junior) College, 249
Mt. Sinai, 16
Murchison, E. P., 239
Murphy, N., 193
Myths, 16, 19

Nashville, Tenn., 194–95
National Conference of Black
Churchmen (N.C.B.C.), 282–83
National Councils of Churches of
Christ, 267, 282
National Fraternal Council of
Churches, 267
National Freedmen's Aid
Association, 192. *See under*
Freedmen
National Historic Landmarks, 143
Nature appreciation (worship),
17–18
Nazrey, Willis, 112, 114, 254–55
Nebraska, 200
Negroes, 24, 118, 141, 213; in
commerce, 296 *n* 2; Conventions,
94–95, 112; discrimination, 63–65,
119ff.; education, 244 (*see*
Education *and* Freedmen's Aid
Society); emigration, 112, 215;
"firsts," 83; free, 94, 95, 147, 183,
184 (*see* Freedmen); leaders, 83
(*see* Richard Allen *and under*
Leadership); Methodism, 35ff.,
43–49, 62–63, 117ff.; North, 57,

147; origin, 14; postwar, 240ff.;
prewar, 213; restrictions on, 94,
95, 98, 131, 257; social status, 158;
urban, 290; use of term, *xi;*
Wesleys, 6–8
Newark, N.J., 135, 174
New Bedford, Mass., 87, 140
New Bern, N.C., 205–6
New England, 8, 58, 137, 151, 193
New England Christian Advocate,
58
New Haven, Conn., 130, 134, 174
New Hope, 85
New Jersey, 36, 53, 63, 76, 137
New Orleans, La., 111–12, 207
New York City, 35–36, 57, 146;
A.M.E., 86–87, 89; Asbury
Church, 86, 87, 89, 174; Bethel
Church, 103, 261; Conferences,
120ff., 129, 137, 143–44, 192, 193;
"meeting house," 43; *Packet,* 171;
separation, 80, 126; Zion Church,
66, 86, 87, 89, 174, 221. *See* John
Street Church
New York (state), 63, 76, 214, 215;
emancipation law (1829), 141
Nigeria, 10, 217, 218, 239, 255, 256
Norfolk, Va., 195
North Carolina, 46, 56, 193, 194, 196,
205–7

Obeah worship, 29
Oberlin College, 220
Ohio, 95, 102, 110, 112, 137, 154, 179
O'Kelly, James, 37, 55, 151, 287
"Old Punch," 168–69
Oregon, 212
Owen, Richard, 37
Oxford University, 3, 4–5

Paine, Robert, 226, 228
Paine, Thomas, 51
Paine, Dr. Uriah, 237
Paine College, 249, 308 *n* 26
Paine Institute, 237, 238
Pamphleteers, 51, 52
Parrinder, Geoffrey, 15
Paul (apostle) 29, 231, 303 *n* 24
Paul Quinn College, 250
Payne, Daniel A., 80, 81, 86, 87,

99–100, 101ff., 108, 149, 150, 154,
174, 181, 192ff., 228, 250, 254, 257,
271, 297 *n* 1; achievements, 186;
A.M.E. ministry, 106–8, 112, 114,
182; on bishopric, 258–60;
characteristics, 111, 259–60, 266;
education, 105–6, 108; *History of
A.M.E. Church,* 152, 255;
influence, 199, 200, 201;
leadership, 116; Lincoln, 115, 258;
Recollections of Seventy Years,
81
Payne Industrial College, 250
Payne Theological Seminary, 250
Penn, William, 50
Pennsylvania, 36, 53, 63, 76, 137
Perigan, Nathan, 39
Pettey, C., 212
Philadelphia, 8–9, 37, 57, 103, 130–31,
170, 186; A.M.E., 8off., 99, 100ff.,
106, 113–14, 117, 129, 143, 146;
Bethel Church, 66, 74, 78, 79, 82,
83, 122, pastor, 85, 90ff. (*see*
Allen, Richard); Conference, 128, 130,
137, 193, 212; St. George's, 36, 65,
71ff., 79; separation, 117, 122, 126
(*see* Bethel Church); Wesleyan
Churches, 130, 145, 146; yellow
fever epidemic, 74
"Philadelphia Movement," 126
Phillips, C. H., 225, 229, 230
Phillips Seminary, 250
Phoebus, William, 128, 130, 145
Pianko, Kobino (Frank Arthur),
216, 217
Pierce, Charles H., 194
Pierce, George F., 225, 231
Pilmoor, Joseph, 36, 37, 64
Pinckney, Charles C., 160, 161
Pittsburgh, Pa., 86, 107
Plantations, 158, 213; "good," 294 *n*
21; missionaries, 160, 169; postwar,
241; religion, 30; slaves, 22–23, 26,
184, 242
Population shifts, 253–54
Power, 288–89. *See* Episcopacy
Prayer, 29; meetings, 41
Preachers, 8, 39, 41–43, 113, 121, 155,
180, 289; *Black Preacher in
America,* 262; characteristics,

38–39, 43, 49, 289; early, 36–43, 47–49, 285: pastoral activity, 183–84, slavery, 52–53, 59 (*see* itinerant); exhorters, 66, 69 (*see* Allen, Richard); itinerant, 12, 37–38, 41–42, 53, 56, 136, 140, 172, 212; "lay," 12, 42; Negroes, 62, 66, 69, 80, 120, 167–87: early, 167–87, education, 120–21, 170–71, 199, evaluation, 179–87, famous, 171ff., 176, 179, leadership, 185, ordination, 124, 128ff., 133, 145, 152–53, 158, 170, 257, slavery 63, 185–86, training, 268; ordination, 66, 70; reactions to, 182; salaries, 38, 238. *See also under* Church *and* Denomination *and* Episcopacy
Predestination, doctrine, 9
Presbyterians, 24, 25, 26, 27, 159, 165, 170, 242
Priest-healer duality, 17
Princeton, N.J., 85, 103
Protestant Episcopal Church, 73, 121, 129
Protest movements, 282–83

Quakers, 24, 51, 52, 72, 151, 172, 286
Quinn, William P., 86, 90, 112, 114, 174, 259

Racial discrimination, 67, 77, 95, 109, 151, 241
Ralston, Robert, 72–73
Rankin, Thomas, 25, 37, 44, 48, 82
Reconstruction, 202, 213, 246; Constitutional Convention, 206; and expansion, 191–250: A.M.E., 191–203, A.M.E.Z., 204–23, C.M.E., 224–39, Methodism in Mission, 240–50
Religion, *ix*, 18, 187, 286; Africa, 15–19: Judaeo-Christian parallels, 16–17, 18 (*see under* Africa *and* country); Black, 179; -human behavior, 18; slave, 24–32
Religious persecution, 35
Revivals, 49, 285
Rice, 21, 22, 23
Roberts, Joseph J., 153
Roberts, Oral, 17

Robinson, Richard, 92, 259
Rochester, N.Y., 57, 139, 140, 142
Rome, ancient, 19, 21
Rush, Dr. Benjamin, 72, 172
Rush, Christopher, 12, 122, 131, 132, 134–35, 137, 138, 142, 149, 170, 174, 175; background, 134; characteristics, 136, 258, 266; influence, 184; leadership, 133–34; 136; ordination, 134; reputation, 206
Rust, Dr. Richard S., 154, 243, 249
Rust College, 249

Sacraments, 12, 49
Salem, N.J., 74, 80, 85
San Francisco, 212
Santo Domingo, 218, 255, 299 *n* 23
Savannah, Ga., 170, 193
"Save the world for Christ," 214
Scipio, Isaiah, 239
Scott, June, 120, 121, 124–25, 132, 133, 174
Scott, Orange, 58, 151, 159, 166, 287
Secession, 191
Segregation, 64ff., 75, 113, 136, 140, 151, 157ff., 195, 270ff., 280, 286–87; "black caucuses," 282
Senegal (Dakar), 14
Separation (separates), 65–75, 76, 286, 287. *See under* M.E. Church
"Shad-belly" coats, 186
"Sharecroppers," 213, 306 *n* 30
Shaw, Alexander P., 274, 276
Shaw, Herbert B., 219, 268
Shorter College, 250
Sierra Leone, 174, 202
Simpson, Peter, 175
Sims, Daniel H., 261, 262
Singleton, George A., 260, 264
Sipkins, Thomas, 124, 125
Slaveholders, 119, 154, 286
"Slave in religion" stereotype, 30
Slave labor, 56
"Slaveocracy," 56
Slavery, 9, 21–23, 119, 183, 191, 285ff.; A.M.E., 115–16; A.M.E.Z., 139–43; -Christianity, incompatibility, 47; disposition,

21; economic system, 50, 56; family separations, 67; "free" status, 6, 22, 68–69; Methodism, 43, 50–61, 77, 159–66, 269, 285ff.; Negro preachers, 184–85; opposition to, 7–8, 22, 24, 51, 63, 68, 140 (*see* Abolitionists); patterns, 21, 22–23, 50; postwar, 76–77; Wesley on, 20; Whitefield, 9

Slaves, 9, 23, 29, 30–32, 64; culture, 29; endurance spirit, 47; freedom, 47, 51, 52–53; literacy, 23, 26, 27; marriage, 51, 162; Methodism, 39, 43ff., 49, 157–66, 285; missions to, 26, 157ff.; number in U.S., 22; "preacher" stereotype, 180; raiders, 14, 113; religion, 24–32, 225; restrictions, 48, 162; runaway, 6, 214; spokesman, 160 (*see* Capers, William)

Slave ships, 20, 50
Slave states, 101
Slave system, 287
Slave trade(ers), 14, 15, 19–20, 50–51, 126; centers, 14; loss of life, 293 *n* 14; "Middle Passage," 20; outlawing, 309 *n* 9; statistics, 20; Wesley on, 20, 51–52

Small, John B., 216, 217, 218
Smith, B. Julian, 238, 268
Smith, Charles S., 198, 199, 201
Smith, Leven, 131, 133, 174
Smith, W. Thomas, *vi*, 175
Societies, 51, 53, 63, 64, 75. *See under* Methodism
Sorcery, 18
Soteriology, 180
Soule, Joshua, 128, 130
South, 205ff., 241, 253–54; -slavery, 22, 151
South America, 218
South Carolina, 56, 90, 159, 160, 161, 169–70, 192–94, 196; A.M.E., loss, 87, 89–90, 111; slavery, 21
Southern Christian Advocate, 160
Southwestern Christian Advocate, 274
Spain, 21
Speaks, Ruben L., 218

Spencer, Peter, 79, 80, 84
Spottswood, Stephen G., 218
Stanford, Anthony S., 193
Stevens, Abel, 38, 45, 173
Stilwell, William, 127–28, 129, 130, 131, 145; secession, 127, 133, 144
Stitt, Richard H., 222
Storrs, George, 58, 151, 159, 287
Strawbridge, Robert, 36–37, 38, 284, 294–95 *n* 3
Strong, Wilbur G., 205, 207–8, 209, 210
Suffrage movement (women's), 142
Sugar plantations, 21, 22, 23, 169
Sunday Schools, 200ff., 221, 243
Sunderland, LaRoy, 58, 159
Superstitions, 27, 29
Sweden, 18
Switzer, Aunt Annie, 284, 295
Syracuse, N.Y., 139, 142

Talbot, Samson D., 210
Tanzania: Suknma-Nyamwesi, religion, 16
Tapsico, Jacob, 80, 85, 99
Taylor, Jeremy, 3
Taylor, Robert, 193
Television, 17
Ten Commandments, 164
Tennessee, 141, 198, 210, 211
Technology, *xi*
Texas, 198
Texas Industrial College, 250
Thomas, Dr. James S., 280
Thomas à Kempis: *Imitation of Christ,* 3
Thompson, Abraham, 37, 120, 121, 124, 129, 131, 132, 133, 145, 170, 174, 175
Tittle, Dr. Ernest F., 280
Tobacco, 21, 22, 111
Travel, 88, 98, 113, 136, 240; restrictions, 137, 170
Trenton, N.J., 57, 85, 103
Tri-Federation Council, 267
Truth, Sojourner, 140, 141
Tubman, Harriet, 140, 142–43
Turner, Henry M. 193–94, 202–3, 266

Turner Theological Seminary, 250, 265

Tuskegee, Ala., 214

Tuskegee Institute, 209

Two Centuries of Methodist Concern, 244

Uganda: Amkore, religion, 16

Underground Railroad, 112, 139, 140, 142; preachers, 185; northern terminus, 214

Union American Methodist Episcopal Church, 79, 84

Union Society, 124, 132

United African Church, 239

United Brethern, 10. *See* Moravian Brethren

United Methodism, 272–83; protest movements, 282–83

United Nations Declaration on Human Rights, 280

U. S. Supreme Court, 280

Unity of life, 17

Universalism, 223

Urbanization, 253, 290

Utica, N.Y., 139

Vanderhorst, Richard H., 193, 228–29, 231, 235

Varick, James, 37, 118, 120, 129, 131, 149, 170, 174–75, 266; education, 121; leadership, 132ff., 146; ordination, 133

Varick Christian Endeavor Society, 222

Varick Memorial Institute, 216

Vernon, Bishop, 260, 261

Virginia, 36, 94, 179, 194, 208; Negro conversion, 25; slavery, 21, 53–55

Virgin Islands, 218

Voice of Missions, 202, 203

Volunteer leadership, 169

Volunteer religious workers, 183–84

Voodoo, 29

Walden, J. M., 243

Walden, Mrs. J. M., 247

Walker, D. I., 208

Walls, W. J., 141, 204, 206, 211, 212, 217, 219, 256, 267; accomplishments, 221–23

Walters, Alexander, 212, 216–17

Ward, T. M., 200

War of 1812, 82

Washington (state), 212

Washington, Booker T., 209, 214

Washington, D.C., 86, 98, 115, 200

Washington, George, 22, 50

Washington, Jeremiah M., 211

Waters, Edward, 112, 114, 259

Watson, Dr. Samuel, 226–27, 229, 232, 236

Webb, Thomas, 36, 37, 47–48

Webster, Samuel, 51

Webster, Thomas, 80

Wesley, Charles, 3, 4, 5, 13, 97; characteristics, 299 *n* 31; "conversion," 11

Wesley, John B., 3–13, 35, 37, 38, 39, 42, 43, 45, 64, 70, 81, 99; aim, 11, 49; Aldersgate, 273; American ministry, 296 *n* 13; "Articles of Faith," 109, 300 *n* 60; beliefs, 9–10; Church of England, 12, 49; "conversion," 11; followers, 147; "Holy Club," 4; influences on, 3–4; life style, 4, 5; Methodism, 10; Negroes, 7–8; opposition, 12–13, 182; slavery, 20, 51–52, 225, 285; spiritual progeny, 187; -Whitefield split, 9–10; writings, 42, 52: *Diary,* 4, *Journal,* 12, 20, *Primitive Physick,* 17, *Thoughts Upon Slavery,* 7–8, 52

Wesley, Samuel, 3, 4

Wesley, Susanna, 3

Wesleyan Journal, The, 58

Wesleyan Methodism, *ix,* 13, 50, 51, 58–59, 138, 297 *n* 27

Western culture: sacred-secular distinction, 17

Western Hemisphere: slave dispersion, 21, 23

West Gold Coast Conference, 216, 217

West Indies, 21, 29, 215, 255; Zion Church, 214ff., 218–19

Whatcoat, Richard, 70–71, 171

Wheatley, Phillis, 8

Wheeler, B. F., 132
White, Andrew, 201
White, George, 124, 135–36
White, William, 71, 72, 73, 77–78, 121
Whitefield, George, 4–5, 8–9, 10, 51, 285; *Journal*, 8–9; Wesley, 9–10
White Plains, 87
Whitney, Eli, 22
Wilberforce, William, 20, 52
Wilberforce University, 108, 154, 250
Wiley College, 249
Wilkerson, John M., 199
Williams, Carl H., 218
Williams, Edward, 80
Williams, Peter, 118, 121, 124, 196 *n* 2
Williams, Peter, Jr., 309 *n* 9
Williams, Richard, 80
Williams, Robert, 37
Williams, Samuel B., 194
Wilmington, Del., 66, 74, 79–80
Wilmington, N.C., 206
Wilmore, Gayraud C., 15; *Black Religion and Black Radicalism*, 282
Wilson, Aaron, 98
Winans, William, 286
Witchcraft, 18

Womack, A. W., 238
Woman's Missionary Recorder, 202
Women, 247, 284
Women's Home Missionary Society, 247–49
World Council of Churches, 267, 268, 280, 282
World Federation of Methodist Women, 267
World Methodist Council, 267, 268
World War I, 217, 253, 263, 271
World War II, 253, 263, 280
Worship, segregation in, 64ff., 75
Wright, Dr. Joseph, 239
Wright, Richard R., 97, 203

Yellow fever epidemic (1793), 82
Young, Henry J., *vi*
Youth, rebellion of, 265

Zamani, 18
Zion Church, 123–26, 128, 129–30, 132, 134, 149, 150, 266; Discipline, 129, 131; elders, 127, 129, 133; leadership, 132–33. *See* A.M.E.Z. Church
Zionites, 120, 122, 136, 143
Zion's Watchman, 58